Jews and Race

THE TAUBER INSTITUTE SERIES FOR THE STUDY OF EUROPEAN JEWRY

Jehuda Reinharz, General Editor

Sylvia Fuks Fried, Associate Editor

THE BRANDEIS LIBRARY OF MODERN JEWISH THOUGHT

Eugene R. Sheppard and Samuel Moyn, Editors

This library aims to redefine the canon of modern Jewish thought by publishing primary source readings from individual Jewish thinkers or groups of thinkers in reliable English translations. Designed for courses in modern Jewish philosophy, thought, and intellectual history, each volume features a general introduction and annotations to each source with the instructor and student in mind.

*Moses Mendelssohn: Writings on Judaism, Christianity, and the Bible*
  Michah Gottlieb, editor

*Jews and Race: Writings on Identity and Difference, 1880–1940*
  Mitchell B. Hart, editor

FOR THE COMPLETE LIST OF BOOKS THAT ARE AVAILABLE IN THIS SERIES, PLEASE SEE BRANDEIS.EDU/TAUBER/PUBLICATIONS/BLMJT.HTML

# Jews & Race

Edited by
Mitchell B. Hart

## WRITINGS ON IDENTITY & DIFFERENCE, 1880–1940

Brandeis University Press
Waltham, Massachusetts

BRANDEIS UNIVERSITY PRESS
brandeisuniversitypress.com


Manufactured in the United States of America
Designed by Eric M. Brooks
Typeset in Albertina and Verlag
by Passumpsic Publishing



LIBRARY OF CONGRESS CATALOGING-IN-PUBLICATION DATA

Jews and race: writings on identity and difference, 1880–1940 /
Mitchell B. Hart, editor
p. cm. — (The Tauber Institute series for the study of European
Jewry) (The Brandeis library of modern Jewish thought)
Includes bibliographical references and index.

ISBN 978-1-58465-716-3 (cloth: alk. paper) —
ISBN 978-1-58465-717-0 (pbk.: alk. paper) —
ISBN 978-1-61168-030-0 (ebook)

I. Jews—Identity. 2. Jews—Identity—History—19th century.
3. Jews—Identity—History—20th century. 4. Jews—Social
conditions—19th century. 5. Jews—Social conditions—20th
century. 6. Race—Social aspects. 7. Ethnic groups. 8. Physical
anthropology. I. Hart, Mitchell Bryan, 1959–
DS143.J49 2011
305.892'4009041—dc23 2011034820

# Contents

# Foreword

It is with great pleasure that we present a volume of the Brandeis Library of Modern Jewish Thought devoted to Jews and racial thinking. Jews were famously the targets of racial thinking in modern times, but they also engaged in it. Mitchell Hart's fascinating and unprecedented survey of how they did so offers rich materials for teacher and student to engage this often forgotten chapter of Jewish intellectual history. Across Europe and the United States, as this volume thoroughly documents, Jews wrestled in different ways with the rise of this new scientific category, which assumed the status of a pervasive orthodoxy—one that is now thankfully a relic of the past. Hart's compilation, which is augmented by a wonderfully illuminating introduction, focuses on the sciences, but it is relevant to political theory as well. The volume helps expand the meaning of "modern Jewish thought," which was the preserve of anthropologists and statisticians as much as it was of the perennial thinkers that our other volumes address.

*Eugene R. Sheppard and Samuel Moyn, Editors*
The Brandeis Library of Modern Jewish Thought

# Acknowledgments

It is a pleasure to be able to thank the individuals and institutions that helped me complete this project. The generosity of Mr. Alexander Grass (*z"l*), who established the Alexander Grass Chair in Jewish History at the University of Florida, has allowed me the time and resources necessary to research, translate, and write. I am grateful to the staffs of the libraries at Columbia University, the Center for Jewish History in New York City, the New York Public Library, and the University of Florida for their assistance. Thank you to Shaina Hammerman for her fluid translations from the French. I owe an enormous debt of gratitude to Alexander von Thun, at Columbia University, for his assistance with the German translations. He has saved me from what would have been numerous embarrassing mistakes. My gratitude to Samuel Moyn and Eugene Sheppard for allowing this book to appear in their series, and to Sylvia Fuks Fried and Jeanne Ferris for their editorial assistance. Finally, as always, thanks to Nina for everything else.

# Jews and Race

## An Introductory Essay

Mitchell B. Hart

The well-known Israeli writer A. B. Yehoshua insisted some years ago that "Jews are not a race and never viewed themselves as such."[1] These claims are popular assertions, in all senses of the word. They are popular because they are widely held, and because they are appealing and satisfying. They reinforce some deeply rooted and comforting ideas held by Jews and non-Jews alike about Jewish history, culture, and identity. The first assertion, that the Jews are not a race, would appear at present to be fairly unproblematic, at least if we look to science as our guide in such matters. Since many biologists have told us that races in general do not exist in any "real" or natural way—that they are, rather, a cultural or social construct—then it seems patently absurd to consider the Jews a race. As Steven Kaplan has asked, if there are no races, how can Jews be a race?[2] Yet, it turns out that things are not that simple. Science, it seems, has not made up its mind on the issue of race. Some researchers in genetics now insist, as the philosopher Ian Hacking has written, "that stereotypical features of race are associated both with ancestral geographic origin and, to some extent, with genetic markers."[3] In other words, "race" might not be just a social construct after all, though it certainly is that. Race no longer exists in the older version of the nineteenth and early twentieth centuries, but modern genetic research may be in the process of redefining notions of identity that reanimate "the racial."[4]

The status of the Jews as a race surely depends in part on the ontological and epistemological status of races in general. If science tells us that races do not exist, then the Jews cannot be a race. On the other hand, to invert Kaplan's question, if there *are* races, can the Jews be a race—or, more precisely, a genetic community? Certainly many Jews as well as non-Jews continue to employ some sort of racial or quasi-racial language when they think and speak about Jewish identity (and many others, of course, reject such language). Many Jews in the past considered themselves members of a distinct race, one characterized by both positive and negative features. And Jewish thinkers employed the language and images of race to think about the Jewish past and present. Thus, Yehoshua's assertion that the Jews never understood themselves as a race is, despite what many wish to believe, patently incorrect.

The collection of source material that makes up this volume is but a small sample of a large group of texts, written by Jews about Jews, that engaged the vexed question of Jews and race. These are texts written in a number of languages and in different contexts, by Jewish scholars and community leaders living in different countries.[5] Their work was published in a variety of media: in books, academic and popular journals, newspapers, and magazines. It was aimed at both Jewish and non-Jewish audiences. Although the differences among these Jewish thinkers and writers were surely important, it is nonetheless possible to identify a common set of questions and issues that drove their inquiries into "the Jewish race."

Are the Jews a race? If so, are they a pure race? If so, what accounts for this purity? If not, which of the various racial branches contributed to the makeup of the Jewish race? Do the Jews possess particular, even unique, traits or qualities that set them apart from other groups? If they do, what accounts for these traits? Are they biological and hereditary, or cultural and environmental? Are they the product of a Jewish nature or essence, or the vicissitudes of historical and contemporary external forces?

These broad, foundational questions led, in turn, to more specific questions. If the Jews are a race, then what is the impact of assimilation on the collective Jewish body and mind? Is intermixture—including intermarriage—with other races and peoples a boon, or does it produce decline and degeneration in the Jews? Do Jews suffer from certain illnesses more than other people? Are Jews immune to certain disorders? Are they prone to certain types of criminal behavior and other social pathologies? Are they naturally an urban rather than a rural or agricultural people? Are Jews predisposed to certain occupations or economic systems, such as capitalism?

How much does Judaism have to do with shaping the Jews physically and mentally? What, in other words, does religion have to do with race?[6] Judaism, as a system of ritual observances issued as commandments or *mitzvot*, dictated every aspect of an observant Jew's life. Racial thinkers queried the impact of the *mitzvot* on the "Jewish body," both individual and collective. For instance, what is the relationship between the observance of the kosher dietary laws, circumcision, or sexual purity laws and the makeup of the purported Jewish body, or levels of Jewish health and disease? What role does the ban on intermarriage play in the history of the Jewish race? Have Jews actually adhered to the practice of endogamy,[7] and thus kept their blood relatively pure from foreign influence (to phrase the question in the terms that were used much of the time)? Or is the historical reality different from the religious and cultural demand and expectation? Is endogamy a healthy or unhealthy practice, considered from a racial and eugenic viewpoint? Does it lead, for example, to a decline in fertility—that is, to fewer and unhealthier offspring? Many scientists believed this was the case, and as the selections included in part 5, "'Racial Mixing,'" illustrate, Jewish racial thinkers took up this question in their own work.

Framing and undergirding the particular queries into purported Jewish traits and the relationship of Judaism to Jewishness was the larger question of causality: how might we account for such characteristics? By the middle of the nineteenth century, at the latest, it was a common belief—even a cliché—that Jews were predisposed to certain ways of thinking and acting because of their "racial nature." At the same time, others insisted that Jewish traits were due mainly to external factors: dispersion, repressive legislation, concentration in certain occupations such as money lending, enforced residence in ghettos, and periodic outbursts of anti-Jewish violence. As we shall see, the question of biology versus environment—a question that seemed to preoccupy almost everyone who wrote about race—was central as well to the debate over the Jews and race.

Race or culture, biology or environment? Perhaps both external and internal forces worked together, so that certain physical and moral traits initially caused by external pressures or practices became hereditary over time. In the words of Felix Theilhaber, a prominent German Jewish racial scientist, "what originally was social or religious-hygienic practice could very well cause acquired traits to become part of the racial disposition."[8] Sigmund Feist asserts that certain physical deformities and gestures traditionally associated with Jews—crooked backs, the rocking back and forth of the upper body, the frequency of bowleggedness—are not racial traits per se, "but rather characteristics that have been acquired due to external conditions (sitting in a stooped position for long periods of time, traditional habits of prayer, rachitis [inflammation of the spine] due to deficient diet, and so forth)." These, Feist assures his readers, "will immediately vanish with a change in adolescent habits or behaviors."[9] This notion of "acquired characteristics" extended back to ancient times, but in the modern period it had come to be associated with the eighteenth-century French naturalist Jean-Baptiste Lamarck. This Lamarckian approach to biological or physical attributes proved to be quite popular among Jewish thinkers, a point to which we will return later in this essay.

Such questions about anatomical and physiological traits and their causes, asked specifically about Jews, were being asked in one way or another about all races and nations. Jewish racial thinkers employed the common intellectual tools of the day to address what they understood as the fundamental issues of Jewish history and contemporary Jewish life. Those Jewish scholars who engaged with race drew on material from a wide variety of fields, including history, anthropology, biology, medicine, statistics, economics, and sociology. They created narratives that provided evidence and interpretations governed by a more or less clear sense of contemporary critical, academic questions and themes. In other words, this was genuine interdisciplinary work carried on with all the tools and methods of academic scholarship. As such, the writings included in this volume constitute a chapter in the intellectual and political history of modern Jewish studies and modern Jewish thought, and the history of the racial and social sciences—even if, for the most part, they have yet to be written into the normative histories of these intellectual traditions.

Jewish scholars who began publishing in the 1880s were joining a debate about "the Jewish race" that had already been going on for decades. To a large extent, non-Jewish scientists and thinkers set the terms of the debate, though of course Jewish scholars brought their own particular research interests and—perhaps more important—their own political or ideological agendas to their work (a matter to which we will return). The selections included in part 1, "General Overviews," are intended to introduce the contours of the discourse about the Jews as a race, including the extent to which Jewish scholars based their arguments on an already well-established set of themes and questions.

Thus, Jewish and Christian scholars did not inhabit two distinct and separate mental worlds when it came to matters of race, including the matter of Jews and race. It is worth emphasizing in this regard that "race" was then commonly used as a conceptual framework with which to confront the vital questions of the day. Certainly all Jews did not adopt racial ideas and images, at least when thinking about their own group. The essay included here by the French Jewish scholar Salomon Reinach offers powerful testimony to this. But for those Jewish thinkers who did employ such ideas in their scholarly or popular writings, this use by no means placed them outside the bounds of respectable academic or Jewish society.

In pointing out the accepted and respectable nature of racial thought in the past, the aim is certainly not to build a case for the truth or accuracy of this research, or to suggest that Jews do, in fact, constitute a race. Rather, it is merely to insist that we acknowledge the legitimate or normative status of this work in its own time and its own particular context. It is insufficient, to say the least, to label this material "pseudoscience" or "pseudoscholarship," as if that explains anything that is not already obvious. It certainly does not help us understand how and why so many highly educated individuals embraced these ideas over such a long time and in so many places.

### *Race and Modern Jewish Thought*

Thus, rather than ask how Jews could have become involved in such unpalatable and potentially dangerous ideas (or deny that they ever did), we might ask: What did Jews stand to gain by engaging with racial thought? Why was the idea of a Jewish race attractive to many Jews? What purposes did Jews serve by making "the Jews" into a race? And why does it matter for us to know that Jewish scholars and writers were actively engaged in debates over the racial history and identity of the Jews? Why, in other words, is it important to call attention to the fact that, at certain times and places, Jews believed in race; used the methods of the social sciences and of the systematic scholarly study of races that came to be known as racial science to analyze Jewish history and contemporary life; put this scientific knowledge to particular political purposes; and even at times engaged not only in racialism but also racism?

Part of the answer to the latter set of questions lies with the incompleteness of the historical record, and the urge to fill this in to the extent possible. Historians of Jewish life, as well as historians of racial thought, have told the story of the relationship between Jews and race largely within the framework of victimhood. And without a doubt, Jews have been victims of racial science and racism. Racial science in the nineteenth and twentieth centuries was one of the chief weapons used against Jews. Until recently, then, scholars for the most part have paid little attention to how race was used by Jewish thinkers, academics, and writers who took race and the idea of "the Jewish race" seriously.[10]

The subject of Jews and racial thought is of historical interest and importance not least because it forces us to reorient the way we think about the normative narrative of the Jewish past. In the context of this series, for instance, we are forced to ask, or to ask again, "What is modern Jewish thought?" Or, more precisely, of what exactly does modern Jewish thought consist, and how should the history of modern Jewish thought be written? Is it limited to philosophy and theology, traditionally understood? Or must we broaden the scope of our definition? Granted, individuals included in this volume—such as Arthur Ruppin,

Ignaz Zollschan, Samuel Weissenberg, and Maurice Fishberg—are, to say the least, far less well-known and celebrated than Moses Mendelssohn, Hermann Cohen, Martin Buber, Franz Rosenzweig, Hannah Arendt, Abraham Joshua Heschel, and Emmanuel Levinas. The canon of modern Jewish thought consists of the latter set of figures (and many others, of course), while the former are all but forgotten. And, to be sure, one could reasonably argue that the philosophers and theologians have been and remain more significant for the course of modern Jewish thinking and self-perception. But then the historian wants to know why this is so. Is it due to some intrinsic quality of the various scholars and thinkers? Are philosophy and theology necessarily more important and of more lasting interest and value than anthropological, biological, or social scientific thought? Or do the reasons have more to do with external forces or pressures, such as political and social developments, or events and trends that shaped the contours and definition of Jewish thought? In sum, what are the factors that determine the answer to the question, "What is Jewish thought?"

Jewish racial thinking, in fact, contains many, if not all, of those components that may be identified with Jewish thought: exegesis of Jewish texts, including sacred texts—both the Bible and the Talmud; exploration of the meaning of, or reasons for, the commandments (*ta'amei mitzvot*)—that is, the effects on the purported Jewish body and mind of the observance of the commandments or, conversely, the impact of their neglect; contemplation of the importance of the interaction of Jewish with non-Jewish society and culture; apologetics and polemics; the relationship of the Jewish past to the present and future; the meaning of Jewish history, both for Jews and more generally; the survival of the Jewish people, both historically and in the future; and the impact of key historical developments and structures—such as capitalism, emancipation, assimilation, and integration—on the lives of individual Jews and on Jewish collectives. Questions related to God's existence and role in the world are, as one might expect, mainly absent from these writings. Nature, society, and history, rather than God, are understood to be the primary forces acting on individuals and collectives.

Thus, we ask, again, what qualifies as modern Jewish thought? What, if any, are the criteria of validity, legitimacy, and inclusion in the master narrative, if such a thing still exists? Are there recognized boundaries to the definition of modern Jewish thought? If a particular Jewish thinker employs the same scholarly methods as his or her contemporaries, invokes classical Jewish texts while at the same time citing the most current scientific literature, and seeks to contribute to the ongoing development of the collective scholarly endeavor by querying the Jewish past and present, is this sufficient? Or is there a necessary ethical component, a boundary set not by form or content but by morality? In other words, is the fact that the thinkers included in this volume, or at least most of them, took race seriously as a reality and a conceptual category enough to disqualify them? If so, Buber and Rosenzweig—both of whom took race, and the notion of a Jewish race, quite seriously—would have to be cast out as well.

In another context, the preeminent Jewish historian of the twentieth century, Gershom Scholem, insisted that "there is no way of telling a priori what beliefs are possible or impossible within the framework of Judaism . . . The 'Jewishness' in the religiosity of any particular period is not measured by dogmatic criteria that are unrelated to actual historical circumstances, but solely by what sincere Jews do, in fact, believe, or—at least—consider to be legitimate possibilities."[11] This sort of nonessentialism with regard to religion holds just as true for questions about other expressions of Jewishness or Jewish identity. The Jewish thinkers we are considering were sincere, and a Jewish racial identity was one legitimate possibility when Jews imagined who and what they are. Thus, the complex relationship of Jews to racial thinking and imagery offers another, though less well-known, side of modern Jewish thought. Knowledge of this relationship contributes to our understanding of the full range of possible realms and avenues of thought available to and taken by some Jews over the past few centuries.

The value or significance of Jewish racial texts, however, lies not only in the reconfiguration of modern Jewish thought that such texts suggest. In a recent work on Jewish historiography, Moshe Rosman has suggested that one of the values of Jewish history resides in the different perspective that knowledge of the Jewish past might bring to other historiographies.[12] I would argue that the subject of Jews and race promises to make a similar contribution. How might this history impact the narratives produced about racial thinking and racism in Europe and North America, to take only the two parts of the world covered in this book?

Jewish racial thinkers ought to be of interest not only to students of Jewish history but also to students of racial thought and racism more generally. This is so especially because including Jews necessarily complicates the history of racial theory and practice; if nothing else, it shows that at certain moments, in certain places, the objects of a racialized discourse appropriate the idioms of science and employ that science to analyze and criticize their own group. As

Nancy Stepan and Sander Gilman have shown, this appropriation process is highly complex and often treacherous, since it entails the internalization—the acceptance at a profound emotional as well as intellectual level—of many of the negative images produced about one's "self."[13] Nonetheless, the use of racial imagery by Jews involves a significant shift, a redefinition of agency in which the object becomes both subject and object of analysis.

The Jewish engagement with race offers historians of race, and of the social and biological sciences, a different set of ideas and images with which to analyze the broader history of their subject. As many historians have pointed out, race—particularly in the United States—is more often than not defined in terms of skin color, especially black and white. Even those who insist on greater complexity often achieve this by simply adding other "colors." Yet, as studies of Jews and race have amply demonstrated, historically race has not only or even mainly been about skin color. In Europe and the United States, Jews were often considered to be "white" and yet could still be seen as a race apart. In Europe especially, definitions of racial traits and racial groups included components far beyond skin color, although this certainly was also an important ingredient. The "Jewish body," as Sander Gilman has shown, was in its entirety an object of fascination for scholars and popular writers.[14]

### *"The Jews" in Racial Thought*

This fascination, as we have said, also extended to many Jewish thinkers. In one respect, the Jewish engagement with racial discourse can be understood as a natural or normal development, a result of more general intellectual trends in the sciences that eventually attracted many educated and acculturated Jews. At the same time, such intellectual trends alone are not sufficient to explain this Jewish interest in the racialization of the Jews. The question of Jewish racial identity was also a question of politics: the politics of Jewish emancipation and assimilation, of antisemitism, and of Jewish nationalism (mainly Zionism) and its opponents. The last part of this volume is devoted to highlighting the political or ideological impulses behind Jewish racial writings, efforts that included both polemics and apologetics.

Thus, the Jewish engagement with race must be understood as the result of multiple forces, irreducible to one historical factor. The politics of antisemitism and nationalism were immediate driving forces, and we will return to these. Longer-term intellectual developments were also central in producing the conditions for a Jewish racial discourse. By the middle of the eighteenth century, at the latest, naturalists and philosophers had begun to include human beings in the classificatory systems applied to the plant and animal worlds.[15] Although not racial or racist per se, this sort of classification was instrumental in the development of racial thought. And more often than not, it did come with a fairly pronounced bias, creating not only divisions but also hierarchies that assumed white Europeans to be the apex of civilization and culture.

For example, in 1758 the Swedish naturalist Carl von Linné—generally known as Linnaeus—published the tenth and last edition of his great work *The System of Nature*. In it, Linnaeus classified *Homo sapiens* as a specific category of primates and then further divided it into six main categories, each with its own particular characteristics:

> 1. *Ferus* or Wild Man: on all fours, mute, hairy.
>
> 2. American (Indian): reddish, choleric, erect. Hair: black, straight, thick; Nostrils: wide; Face: harsh; Beard: scanty. Obstinate, merry, free. Paints himself with fine red lines. Regulated by customs.
>
> 3. European: white, sanguine, muscular. Hair: flowing, long. Eyes: blue. Gentle, acute, inventive. Covered with close vestments. Governed by laws.
>
> 4. Asian: sallow (ashen or pale), melancholy, stiff. Hair, black. Eyes, dark. Severe, haughty, avaricious. Covered with loose garments. Ruled by opinions.
>
> 5. African: Black, phlegmatic, relaxed. Hair: black, frizzled. Skin: silky. Nose: flat. Lips: tumid (bloated or puffy). Women without shame, *Mammae*; lactate profusely. Crafty, indolent, negligent. Anoints himself with grease. Governed by caprice.
>
> 6. Monstrous: Troglodytes.[16]

This classification includes many, though certainly not all, of the fundamental components of modern racial theory as it took shape in the eighteenth century. Human identity and development are approached in terms of natural science, and this classificatory framework demands that humans be described and defined, at a minimum, by their physical traits. Beyond this, though, already in Linnaeus we can see the link between science and aesthetics, between racial classification and judgments about beauty and ugliness, that was to become so central to racial thought. Moreover, we can see the link between science and morality, between racial classification and judgments about character and worth, as well as about the levels of civilization and culture—what philosophers used to call the "moral economy." Thus, Europeans have long, flowing hair and blue eyes, and are possessed of a gentle temperament; they are acute in judgment and inventive; finally, they are governed by laws. The other human races—red, yellow, and black—fall short of this white European ideal.

Where did the Jews fit in this early scheme? Linneaus does not mention them. But the logic of classification and hierarchy suggests, even demands, that Jews too be categorized. And indeed, very quickly Jews became of particular interest to naturalists, anthropologists, and others involved in the classificatory project. The "naturalization" of Jewish traits became far more widespread, a mainstay not only of literature and popular culture but also of science. "The Jews," conceived of as a distinct entity or collective with their own essential physical and mental traits, became an object of research for scholars—including Jewish scholars—in the human sciences. In this sense, they constitute a vivid example of the social or cultural construction of race; we can see the Jews being made into a race through the discursive analyses produced about them.

The Jewish involvement with racial thought certainly must be understood as a response to, and participation in, this objectification or racialization of the Jews themselves—a process that began, many have argued, in the fifteenth century at the latest, only to reach its peak in the first half of the twentieth.[17] Of course, racial thinking and racial science cannot be reduced to the discourse on Jews and race. The Jews were just one of the many "races" studied by social scientists. Nonetheless, given the long history of Jewish difference in Christian Europe, the Jews were also not just any other group. They were the objects of a racial science and mythology created in large measure by Christian European and American thinkers, who identified themselves as members of various racial subgroups that constituted the white or Caucasian race. Jews, obviously, were not Christians, and for most racial thinkers Jews also were not white—at least, not fully white. In Europe, historically, Jews were often cast as the embodiment or incarnation of the negative, the dangerous, and the degenerate. If the ideal of the good and the beautiful derived from, and was represented by, the art and ideals of the ancient Greeks, then the Hebrews represented the opposite.[18] They were ugly and malformed, with long and beak-shaped noses, hunched backs, concave chests, and flat feet. Their physical deformities were said to have been accompanied by a host of mental and nervous disorders, everything from neurasthenia and idiocy (the former due to an excessive involvement in every form of modern, unhealthy economic and social activity; the latter a result of centuries-long inbreeding) to diabetes (known as a "Jewish disease"), gastritis, and hemorrhoids (the first two due to the purported inadequacies of the traditional Jewish diet, among other things; the last to the long hours Jewish boys and men were required to sit on hard benches studying the Torah and Talmud). These physical, mental, and neurological disorders were taken, in turn, as evidence of a more fundamental moral degeneracy of the Jews.

It is important to note that not every researcher into issues of race who took up the question of the Jews did so in a spirit of hostility or antisemitism. There were many non-Jewish social scientists and thinkers who saw in the Jews a healthy, even superior, people—a racial or eugenic model for contemporary Christians. Had the Jews not maintained their collective identity over thousands of years? Had Moses not recognized thousands of years earlier the central importance of rules of hygiene and purity and set these forth in his laws? What were the laws of *kashrut*, circumcision, female hygiene, and the other rules found in the books of Leviticus and Deuteronomy if not the means by which the nation insured its physical as well as spiritual purity? Ezra, so the argument went, clearly understood the crucial role endogamous marriage plays in the maintenance of racial and national health and identity, and thus forbade intermarriage between Jews and others. Indeed, the Jews had raised the ideal of their separate identity and purity to a divine commandment. Thus, for many Christian as well as Jewish thinkers, the Jews were a perfect example of a racial or eugenic people.[19]

Thus, a racial analysis of Jews was not necessarily antisemitic. But as science assumed an authority and power to establish truth, antisemites increasingly invoked scientific language to frame their theories and to give their ideas a patina of objective rigor. Thus, one can speak of a scientific antisemitism, akin to a racial science, that employed the methods and arguments of anthropology, biology, statistics, medicine, economics, and history to construct a "truth" about the Jew. In seeking to understand the Jewish engagement with race, it is important to recall that a number of motives or impulses were at work, and racial antisemitism is only part of the explanation. Nonetheless, antisemitism, as it developed over the course of the nineteenth century, did indeed play a crucial role in eliciting a Jewish racial discourse. Racial science and racist mythology, when taken up by antisemites, became fundamental components of a larger ideological struggle to define the Jews as essentially different, and to limit or ban their participation in the modern nation-state. The idea of the essential or natural difference between the Jew and the Christian was nothing new. However, revolutionary transformations in intellectual, political, social, and economic life meant that the naturalization of the Jews would increasingly be framed in a different language, and the meaning and significance of that naturalization would change.

### *Racial Thought and Modern Jewish Identity*

By the last half of the nineteenth century, some Jewish thinkers began to respond to the ongoing debate about "the Jewish race" and to racial antisemitism by producing scientific studies of their own.[20] These Jewish racial thinkers wrote about Jewish bodies and minds, and about Jewish social, economic, and cultural behavior. Like their non-Jewish counterparts, Jewish scientists took seriously what the statistics purportedly revealed about collective Jewish life. As the texts included in part 2, "Anthropology," show, Jewish thinkers wove narratives from the data on the size of crania and chests; the shape of noses and the color of skin; and height and weight. Part 3, "Medicine and Biology," takes up the issue of the susceptibility or resistance to particular diseases on the part of Jews, and the relevance of this to their racial identity. The texts contained in part 5, "'Racial Mixing,'" address historical and contemporary questions of sexual relations directly, though the issue of intermixture was so central to the concerns of Jewish racial thinkers that it is not surprising to encounter it in texts included in other parts.

Indeed, intermarriage, or what was often referred to as "racial intermixture," went to the heart of the question of Jewish racial identity. Did the ancient Hebrew tribes that conquered parts of the land of Canaan intermingle sexually with the indigenous tribes? If so, to what extent? And what was the impact of such intermixture on the genetic makeup of the Jewish people? Similar questions have also been asked about later periods of Jewish history, up to and including the present. A related concern was the impact of conversions to Judaism, since this entailed the importation of "foreign blood" into the Jewish body. What impact did conversions to Judaism have on the Jewish collective—most famously, the conversion, sometime in the eighth or ninth century, of the Khazars to Judaism?

Jewish racial thinkers also took up the question of purported Jewish racial traits as they related to social and economic activities. Part 4, "Society and Economy," offers examples of the debate over Jews and crime. Statistics seemed to show that Jews committed certain types of crime in greater numbers than their non-Jewish neighbors. Was this due to a racial predisposition, as many had argued, or should it be explained by sociological and historical factors? A similar debate ensued over Jewish economic or occupational patterns. The Jews were believed to be racially predisposed to capitalism, and thus to certain forms of making a living that revolved around the lending of money at interest, or buying and selling for profit. Again, was the claim that the Jews were genetically programmed for capitalist behavior accurate, or were certain occupational patterns better explained by the history of the Jews in Europe and their relation to church and state?

From the myriad pieces of evidence produced about the Jewish body and mind, Jewish scholars sought to answer not only historical questions, but also larger questions about Jewish identity and difference, about the effects of modernity on the Jewish body and Jewish consciousness, and about the future of the Jewish collective.

Thus, by 1906, Arthur Ruppin, one of the most prominent and important Jewish social scientists writing in the first three decades of the twentieth century, could assert: "Almost all inquiries into the social, intellectual, and physical differences between Jews and Christians address the question of whether these differences have their root in the particular racial makeup or in the unique economic and political conditions of the Jews over the past two thousand years. One might, in fact, designate this question [the racial question] as the fundamental problem or issue of research about the Jews."[21] This does not mean that all Jewish researchers and writers on the subject agreed on the fundamentals, let alone on the implications of racial theory for interpretations of Jewish history and contemporary Jewish life. At a time when the principles of heredity, of the transmission of traits over generations, and of course, of the relationship between nature and nurture, or biology and environment, were highly contested, Jews, too, could differ in their basic assumptions and approaches. We do, in fact, find examples of a biological or racial determinism within Jewish social scientific literature. This was the assertion that Jews possessed particular traits, and that such traits were better understood or explained as a product of race or biology than by culture or environment. Not surprisingly, perhaps, we usually see this when the author is discussing a purported positive or superior trait of the Jews: superior intelligence, talent, ability; the disinclination to alcoholism or physical violence; or immunity from particular diseases.

It was easier, of course, to subscribe to some sort of biological determinism, to a view of Jewish history based on heredity, when you were focusing on the purported positive or superior qualities of your people, and there is evidence of this scattered throughout the documents collected here. However, Jewish thinkers were confronted with a large body of scientific literature that had claimed to demonstrate objectively that the Jewish body and mind were diseased and degenerate. And it was this negative imagery that mattered more, since it undergirded a long-standing ambivalence on the part of many non-Jews toward Jewish emancipation and assimilation, a hostility to the presence of Jews that found its way at certain times into the platforms of political parties and contributed to the continuing restrictions on the full participation of Jews in the workings of the state.

Thus, the discussion and debate over the Jews as a race was one element of a much broader debate about the identity of the Jews more generally, and the configuration of the modern nation-state, society, and culture. From the beginning of the debate over the place of the Jews in the modern nation, in the eighteenth century, those thinkers and public figures involved in it had to address a number of interrelated questions: What is a nation? What components or factors determine national belonging and identity? What are the Jews? What ultimately defines and determines their distinct identity and difference? Can they become full subjects or citizens of the nation-state, or is their difference from the majority so profound or essential as to make full membership impossible?

Matters of racial, religious, and national identity, and the interconnections between these, were fundamental to debates over Jewry. There was no one unequivocal answer to the questions raised above, either from Jewish or non-Jewish quarters. Indeed, each country in which Jews lived responded to the question of Jewish identity and difference in its own way, bringing to bear its own developing national traditions. At the same time, even within particular countries the approach to the Jewish minority was hardly homogeneous. A wide range of opinions could be found on the issue of the Jews as a race and nation, and whether or not Jewish integration and full equality were possible or desirable.

As Jews identified with their community or people, Jewish writers about race felt compelled to respond to those who employed racial ideas to construct an image of the diseased and dangerous Jew, and then used this negative image to make a case for reversing Jewish emancipation and assimilation. Jewish racial scientists assumed what the historian John Efron has called the role of "defenders of the race."[22] At the same time, they were critics, and their critique of "the Jews" was often severe. As scientists and scholars, or rabbis and public figures participating in a scientific debate, they accepted the data presented by science on the modern Jewish condition, including the data that showed Jews in a less than favorable light. Thus, in much of the Jewish racial writing, the Jews are represented as unhealthy, as a race or nation in decline.

At times, then, the images put forth by Jewish writers can seem surprisingly close to those used by antisemites at the time. However, while many or even most antisemitic writers embraced some version of an immutable or "eternal" Jewish racial identity, Jewish thinkers could not accept the idea that the explanation for the damaged condition of Jewry resided in the nature of Jewry itself. They embraced an environmental and historical explanation for so-called racial traits. The vast majority of Jewish social thinkers in the decades before the 1930s did not reject biological determinism because it was scientifically wrong, or because it was politically incorrect or dangerous—that is, because it was frequently, though not always, aligned with right-wing, often antisemitic political movements. Rather, they rejected it because it could not serve their own particular political and social purposes.

Unlike a strict or strong hereditarian explanation for collective traits, the environmentalist tradition within the social and biological sciences opened up the possibility of progressive, meliorative change at the collective level. Theories of degeneration, it should be noted, also relied on a strong environmental framework; progress and decline were two sides of the same racialist coin, and Jewish thinkers employed both related ideas in their work.[23] An environmental determinism allowed Jewish thinkers to admit the contemporary deficiencies of the Jews while simultaneously holding open the possibility of improvement in the future. And it cast the Jewish racial thinker in the role of expert, indispensable in this historical process of Jewish improvement. Jewish scientists would fill the roles of apologist and reformer, defending their own people from attacks by antisemites while offering suggestions for positive transformation based on their expert knowledge and the insights of science.

In other words, with regard to questions of race, Jews could accept the notion of a Jewish racial identity, rooted in common origins and even typical physical and mental characteristics—though they clearly recognized that Jews were not always identical in appearance. And they could accept the statistical and anecdotal evidence that demonstrated that contemporary Jewry had suffered a decline, that much of Jewry was "degenerate." But what most Jewish social thinkers could not accept was a causal explanation for the Jewish condition rooted in a fixed, immutable racial or biological essence or identity. They could not accept the view that the Jews were degenerate *because they were Jews*. That, of course, would have made improvement impossible. It would have made social and racial scientific research into the Jewish condition nothing more than a quaint, antiquarian pastime, and it would have marked the social and political programs of reform—those of liberal integrationists or of Zionists—as futile and utopian.

### *Race and Jewish Politics*

Racial texts were almost by definition politically charged, if not politically motivated. As we have seen, Jewish thinkers engaged with race partly in order to respond to a racialized antisemitism. Yet this was only one of the political or ideological uses to which racial thought could be put. Racial thought also played a role in intra-Jewish politics, most notably in the arguments between Zionists and so-called assimilationists.

The idea that the Jews constituted a race seemed especially attractive to Zionists. Embracing this notion allowed Zionists to redefine the Jews as more than just a collective held together by a common religious faith; they were a people, a Volk,[24] in the anthropological sense. If the Jews were a race, that meant that their identity hinged not solely on the subjective willingness of individuals to remain tied to the group but on objective, material realities, on bones and blood.

However, racial ideas offered Zionists more than just a way to demonstrate Jewish identity and unity. It also helped them clarify the urgency of the nationalist cause. The Jews were an ethnic group, a nation, a race essentially different from other nations with whom they had been asked, or forced, to integrate or assimilate. Yet Jewish identity, continuity, and survival were seen as under attack. The source of the threat was not, however, the traditional enemies of the Jews, the antisemites. The gravest danger now, in Europe and the United States, was not animosity but benevolence; not the distance and isolation that came with religious or racial antipathy, but the social and sexual mixing that came with the breakdown of barriers. Jewish elites were now not only being forced to confront the age-old problem of hatred of Jews—though this remained a palpable threat—but the recent, and for some far more difficult, challenges of freedom, acceptance, and material well-being or affluence.

The answer to this challenge or problem of assimilation, at least for the Zionists, was the re-isolation of Jews socially and culturally, in their own land, within their own commonwealth or state. This, Zionists insisted, would guarantee the continuity and survival of the Jewish people, while at the same time allowing the Jewish Volk to take its rightful place in the community of nations as a fully independent people. Zionism, in fact, was proposed as the only viable solution to the threat to Jewish collective survival. And race was seen as a necessary component of this national revival. Not all Zionist thinkers embraced such racialist notions, as the selection in this volume by Robert Weltsch testifies. Nonetheless, racial ideas and images proved quite attractive to many Jewish nationalists, offering them a language with which to define Jewishness as an objective fact, a matter of biology and history as well as subjective will. Moreover, the fact that racial thinking was closely aligned with science, that it drew much of its content—as well as whatever claim it had to mainstream legitimacy—from the natural and social sciences, was also attractive to Zionism, a movement that portrayed itself as scientific.[25]

In defining the Jews as a nation with its own particular—even unique—physical and mental attributes, Jewish nationalists believed they had refuted the older emancipationist assertion that Jewish identity and difference consisted almost entirely of religious adherence and sensibility. The Jews, in this view, were a *Glaubensgemeinschaft*, a community defined by a shared faith; religious faith was, in the end, the only thing that separated Jews from non-Jews. This notion had been central to the emancipatory and integratory project that Jews had made their own since the late eighteenth century. The modern nation-state, rooted in the commitment to breaking down the older forms of corporate identity and communal structure, demanded that Jews become citizens, that they fully embrace their identities as members of the nation-state and society—in other words, Germany, France, Italy, and so on. This demand left little room for a concomitant attachment to an ancient homeland and a dream of resurgent Jewish sovereignty. Thus, Jews set about becoming citizens. This did not occur overnight, nor did it happen in a uniform or homogeneous manner. As Todd Endelman, a historian of British Jewry, and others have shown, different national Jewish communities integrated in different ways.[26] Yet in each case, it did entail some emendation of the traditional Jewish belief that living outside of the Land of Israel constituted exile; that Jewish life in the Diaspora was a temporary and deficient condition, a product of either divine punishment or political defeat; and that at some future time a messiah would appear to lead the Jews back to the Land of Israel and return them to an independent nation-state. Why, many non-Jewish commentators wondered, would the Jews continue to believe in their own exile and pray to be returned to the Land of Israel if, as they insist, they love their new motherland or fatherland as much as they claim? Does insisting on a continued Jewish national identity not fly in the face of their identities as citizens? The argument that the only thing that differentiated Jews from their fellow citizens was religion—that in all other ways, Jews were as French or German or English as any other citizen—solved the problem of national identity. Or so the majority of Jews believed.

Regardless of the subjective belief of the Jews that they were, despite religious differences, just as German or French as their Christian neighbors, many of their non-Jewish compatriots disputed this. The civic or legal emancipation of the Jews in Europe that began in France in 1789 and continued into the late nineteenth century did not do away with the challenge of Jewish integration; rather, it produced the conditions for this challenge. And for those opposed to Jewish equality, race became a critical tool in the anti-egalitarian arsenal. Racialism offered purportedly objective markers of collective identity and difference that would counter the subjective self-understanding of "inferior" groups and their advocates. Racial antisemitism, like racism in general, posited that difference lay in the blood, the body and mind, the physiological and nervous systems. You can change your religion, but you cannot change your ancestry, your blood, what today we would call your genetic makeup. Thus, race was a particularly useful weapon for those who insisted that the Jews remained, and ought to remain, separate and inferior despite all their efforts to assimilate, and despite all the rhetoric of equality.

At some level, Jewish nationalists accepted the argument that the differences between Jews and their non-Jewish neighbors were so vast, and anti-Jewish sentiment so deep, that the dream of Jewish integration and equality was a chimera (though, as we shall see, Jewish nationalists firmly rejected the antisemitic belief that the Jews were racially inferior). Other Jewish social thinkers, committed to Jewish integration into the larger, non-Jewish society and culture, obviously disagreed with the nationalist, particularly Zionist, analyses. Yet this in no way meant that non-Zionists were not also involved in researching and analyzing Jews along racial lines.

A Jewish racial identity could and did serve a liberal or integrationist agenda just as well as a nationalist one. The Anglo-Jewish scholar Joseph Jacobs, for instance, insisted that the Jews were a pure race, and he believed that this purity helped guarantee the Jews' nobility and thus their qualification for full participation in English society. (In this belief, Jacobs was echoing to some extent an argument made in the middle of the seventeenth century by the Amsterdam rabbi Menasseh ben Israel. In writing to Oliver Cromwell, urging him to readmit the Jews into England, Menasseh lists "the nobleness and purity of their blood" as one of the three attributes that recommend the Jews as trustworthy and productive inhabitants of a country.[27])

Others, such as Isidore Loeb in France and Maurice Fishberg in the United States, repudiated the idea of a pure Jewish race, arguing instead that the Jews were the product of a two-millennia-long process of intermixture with the various populations in whose midst they lived. Loeb insisted that all groups or nations were the product of racial mixing that reached back to prehistory. The idea and ideal of racial purity were pernicious errors. National and cultural superiority came not from purity but from diversity, from the amalgamation of as many different races as possible. Accordingly, the argument that the Jews could not and should not fully integrate into Europe because they constituted a distinct race was baseless: "There is not a single people in Europe whose race is absolutely pure. The racial objection [to equal rights] pitted against the Jews is thus without merit and self-defeating."[28] Loeb did not reject the reality of distinct races in general, or the idea that Jewish identity was in part racial. He spoke of "Jewish blood" and "Aryan blood" as if they actually existed. Rather, he rejected the argument that the Jews were a pure race, and that their racial identity prohibited them from becoming full-fledged Frenchmen, Germans, and so forth.

Nor did Maurice Fishberg altogether reject the idea that the Jews constituted a race; rather, he too insisted on the fluidity of this identity. For Fishberg, whose work came to be seen as representative of the integrationist position, the Jews' strength and health as a race or people resided in their ability to assimilate, to adapt and thrive in new and different environments. In Darwinian terms (which Fishberg, like many other Jewish thinkers, readily employed), the Jews were a model of adaptation and survival. Assimilation, therefore, was not a danger, but a necessity and a virtue.

Thus, as important as the defensive or apologetic impulse was for Jewish thinkers engaged with questions of race, it alone cannot explain the lure that racial ideas held for many Jews. Intra-Jewish politics, especially the ideological struggles over the most pressing questions of modern Jewish collective life, also played a substantial role in making racial ideas attractive. Although some political or ideological impulse can be identified in almost all of the texts included here, those contained in the final part of this book, "Politics," were chosen for their explicitly political engagement. These offer a glimpse of the role that race played in contemporary debates between Jewish thinkers and antisemitic racialists or nativist opponents of immigration, between advocates of Jewish integration and nationalists committed to Zionism, and, in some cases, between individuals or factions within the same political movement.

### *Race and Cultural Worth*

There are a number of things, therefore, that help explain the attraction of racial ideas for many Jews. Yet, as noted repeatedly, Jewish racial thinking in the period between 1880 and 1940 cannot be understood without reference to antisemitism. Jewish thinkers considered racial language and imagery to be a powerful weapon that Jews possessed in the struggle against antisemitism. Thus, Jewish racial thinking was born of both self-defense and self-criticism—of the intellectual and political engagement and struggle of Jews with the wider world and of ideological battles waged among Jews themselves.

Racial antisemites posited a natural, innate difference and hostility between Jews (or Semites) and so-called Aryans. Moreover, they insisted on the natural superiority of Aryans. Central to the argument was the insistence on a connection between race and culture, and the idea that only Aryans—particularly Teutonic or Germanic Aryans—were capable of producing genuine culture. Jews, these antisemites asserted, could mimic culture and could buy and sell cultural products, but they could not produce it in any meaningful way. They lacked the capacity for "genius" in the arts, as the nineteenth-century composer Richard Wagner put it in his famous essay on Jews and music.[29] In fact, according to one strain of this argument, anything of worth or value in the history of civilization could only have been brought forth by Aryans. Civilization, then, became synonymous with one particular race.

What followed from this was that other races—particularly the Jews, at least in Europe—represented the antithesis of all that was civilized and cultured. The antisemitic argument about racial nature and culture had a comforting circularity about it: As naturally inferior, Jews by definition could not have participated in the development of civilization; that they have contributed nothing to civilization demonstrates their natural inferiority. This all went to prove, in the minds of antisemites, that the granting to Jews of their civic rights and efforts to integrate them into European society in the name of equality were dangerously naive and misplaced.

Of course, Jewish racial thinkers, like Jews in general, could not accept this notion of a natural Jewish inferiority and inequality. They might argue among themselves about the desirability of assimilation and the feasibility of the Zionist enterprise, but they agreed that the Jews, as a historical people or Volk, were equal, if not superior, to all other civilized nations—especially Anglo-Saxons and Aryans. Jewish thinkers, whether Zionist or integrationist, took it on themselves to refute the widespread and popular notion of Aryan superiority.

Indeed, a driving force behind the production of Jewish racial texts was the need that many Jews felt to address the question of the value or worth of the Jewish people. Again, these Jewish racial thinkers did not challenge the legitimacy of the intellectual enterprise itself; in this case, they did not dispute the category of racial worth. Rather, they sought to overturn the judgment that the Jews were an unworthy or inferior race. The terms of the debate over national character and national survival and worth had been set by non-Jewish thinkers and can be traced back in large measure to the German philosopher Johann Gottfried Herder—though Herder, it should be made clear, was not a racial thinker, at least not in the nineteenth-century mode. Herder certainly evinced a highly ambivalent attitude toward the Jews. Yet he did articulate in the eighteenth century a philosophy of culture and of national or Volk identity that rested on an appreciation of what was unique about different groups, the Jews included. He advanced an alternative to the Enlightenment universalism that had left little room for protracted or permanent difference. Herder embraced difference at the collective level and understood difference or particularism as a necessary component of the universal. He put forth the idea that the Hebrews had indeed contributed something unique and valuable to the world.

For Jewish thinkers engaged with this question of national or racial worth, the notion that the ancient Hebrews, together with modern Jews, had something unique to offer the world, and that this justified their continued survival as a distinct Volk, held enormous power and appeal. It was a position that Jewish thinkers accepted a priori but also felt compelled to demonstrate scientifically.

As a number of the selections in the final part show, one important element of Jewish racial thought came to be the articulation of the Jews' uniqueness, their distinct collective identity, and the specific contributions to civilization that flowed from this. This was supposed to provided evidence of the Jews' racial and cultural worth, point to the likelihood of their future contributions, and thus justify their continued existence as a collective with a distinct identity.

### *Jews and Race into the Present*

Jewish racial thinking was hardly universal: many Jews were undoubtedly ignorant of it, and many actively repudiated it. Nonetheless, it was a far more widespread phenomenon than most general histories of either modern Jewish or racial thought acknowledge. And it was normative, accepted by Jews as well as non-Jews as a valid means by which to discuss Jewish identity and difference, and their political and social implications.

Still, it must be admitted that the idea of Jews being involved in racial thinking produces an initial disorientation, a sense of incompatibility of categories. Jews were victims of racial ideas and racist actions; modern antisemitism is constructed out of racialist principles about the Jews' immutable body and spirit. Ultimately, of course, it is the Holocaust that gives Jewish racial thinking, especially when it emerges in Europe, its strange—even paradoxical—quality. We have a sense of almost inherent contradiction, of an inversion that somehow doesn't quite make sense. How could Jews, who at least in Europe were the ultimate victims of racial discourse and practice, also have been believers in and practitioners of this way of looking at the world? And yet they were.

If we are going to arrive at an adequate understanding of Jewish racial thinking, we need to bracket the Holocaust—set it aside, or move behind or before it. All of the documents contained in this volume were produced before the Holocaust, and most before the Nazis' rise to power. They need to be read and interpreted with this fact constantly in mind.

We might imagine that the central role played by racial antisemitism in the ideology of Nazism and in the Holocaust would have placed any notion of a Jewish race entirely out of bounds in the post-Holocaust world. And this does seem to have been the case for about half a century. Invoking the Jewish race so soon after the revelations of the death camps to talk about Jewish identity could only invoke the enormous crimes committed in the name of racial difference. Even the scholarly efforts represented in this volume, in which Jews engaged seriously with arguments about the Jewish race, have seemed to be too incongruous and problematic, and thus for the most part have been ignored.[30]

Yet, as scholars such as Susan Glenn and David Biale have argued, it would be a mistake to imagine that "blood narratives have lost their relevance to discussions of modern Jewish identity." Some remnant of racial thinking appears to have survived among many Jews. Even though such thinking may have been submerged or made invisible for fifty years, many Jews still "think with blood" about Jewish belonging. What Glenn calls "blood logic" still seems to be at work: "Throughout all of the de-racializing stages of twentieth-century social thought, Jews have continued to invoke blood logic as a way of defining and maintaining group identity."[31]

The matter of Jews and race is, therefore, of contemporary as well as historical significance, certainly for Jews. We began with A. B. Yehoshua's assertion that the Jews are not a race and that they never considered themselves as such. As even a denial of this sort indicates, the relationship of Jews to race continues to play some role in Jewish self-perceptions. In Yehoshua's case, it is the negation of such a connection that is desirable. This is understandable, given the injustices and horrors committed against Jews in the name of race. However, as others have demonstrated, the notion of a Jewish race nevertheless continues to appeal to many Jews today; interestingly, it is no longer an idea that demands to be immediately dismissed or denounced.

The question "What are the Jews?"—a religion, a nation, an ethnic group, a race, or some combination of all these and more—continues to preoccupy many people, Jews and non-Jews alike. And biological and genetic arguments possess a power for many Jews as they seek to explain to themselves and others just what it is that constitutes Jewishness. This genetic understanding of identity has been validated or reinforced for many by the numerous studies that appear to demonstrate a connection between specific genetic communities or subcommunities, such as Ashkenazic Jewish women, and certain diseases such as breast cancer, or the studies that purport to show a genetic link between the ancient Jewish priestly class, *Kohanim*, and Jews living today who claim priestly descent (a notion already present in the essay by Redcliffe N. Salaman reproduced in this volume). In this sense, "race" is a significant component not only of scholarly or academic modern Jewish thought, but also of popular or everyday Jewish thought. It is one of the building blocks of contemporary Jewish identity construction, even if there are many who would dispute the applicability of biological or racial categories to Jews. To be sure, given the enormous developments in genetic and biological knowledge over the past eighty years, the information and analyses contained in the primary sources presented here can offer little to those who believe in and seek illumination about the genetic identity of Jews in the present. What these documents offer, instead, is evidence of a time when the shapes of skulls and noses and the colors of eyes and hair; questions of racial purity and mixture; and hereditary predispositions to certain types of social, political, and economic behavior were central to the most pressing questions being asked about the place of Jews in the modern world.

A final, brief remark about the selection of documents. The writings included here represent a small percentage of the material published by Jewish thinkers on race. As such, these texts are intended to be suggestive, not exhaustive—chosen to provide an introduction to the major themes and arguments. For the most part, they are rather obscure and not readily available. This is intentional. Most have not been translated into English before. Numerous texts have been omitted (including works of fiction), most because of limitations of space, and some of the better known because they are already available in English. Thus, selections from the works of Moses Hess, Benjamin Disraeli, Franz Rosenzweig, and Franz Boas all deserve a prominent place in any discussion of Jews writing on race. Yet these were either originally written in English or have already been translated and are relatively easy to obtain. This is also true of less well-known pieces such as Max Reichler's essay "Jewish Eugenics," which is now available on the Internet (as are the two selections by Joseph Jacobs). Maurice Fishberg is an exception. His *Jews, Race, and Environment* is in print. Yet Fishberg's voice was such an important and influential one that it seemed necessary to include him in this volume.

Almost all the selections were written by individuals (all male) who were publicly identified as Jews. In two cases, I could not determine the background of the writer but included the pieces nonetheless, both because of the interest of the material contained in them and because they appeared in a journal, *Zeitschrift für die Demographie und Statistik der Juden* (The journal of demography and statistics of the Jews), that was explicitly identified as a Jewish journal. In their own way, then, they constitute a specific sort of Jewish thought or knowledge—or at least, they raise yet again the question of the limits or contours of these categories. Finally, in order to distinguish notes in the original from my own, I've placed my notes in square brackets.

Unless otherwise indicated, all translations are by the editor.

## Notes

1. A. B. Yehoshua, "Who Is a Jew?," *Contemplate* 3 (2005–6): 73.

2. Steven Kaplan, "If There Are No Races, How Can the Jews Be a 'Race'?," *Journal of Modern Jewish Studies* 2, no. 1 (2003): 79–96. On the argument that there are no biological races, see also James C. King, *The Biology of Race* (Berkeley: University of California Press, 1981); Alain F. Corcos, *The Myth of the Jewish Race: A Biologist's Point of View* (Bethlehem, Pa.: Lehigh University Press, 2005); Colin Kidd, *The Forging of Races: Race and Scripture in the Protestant Atlantic World, 1600–2000* (Cambridge: Cambridge University Press, 2006), 1–18.

3. Ian Hacking, "Genetics, Biosocial Groups, and the Future of Identity," *Daedalus* 135, no. 4 (2006): 86. For a recent example of a "genetic history" of the Jews, see David B. Goldstein, *Jacob's Legacy: A Genetic View of Jewish History* (New Haven: Yale University Press, 2008).

4. See Nadia Abu El-Haj, "The Genetic Reinscription of Race," *Annual Review of Anthropology* 36 (2007):283–300.

5. It is important to note that the sources collected here are limited to the nineteenth and twentieth centuries and largely, though not entirely, to Central and Western Europe, the United Kingdom, and the United States. (The selections by Elkind and Weissenberg, though translated from the German, were written by Jewish social scientists living and working in Eastern Europe.) Jews, however, were deeply engaged with questions of race and identity in earlier centuries, and in many different parts of the world during the early modern and mod-

ern periods. Jonathan Schorsch has provided a wealth of evidence demonstrating the Jewish engagement with racial thinking in the early modern period, in both Europe and the Americas. See his two major works, *Jews and Blacks in the Early Modern World* (Cambridge: Cambridge University Press, 2004) and *Swimming the Christian Atlantic* (Leiden, the Netherlands: Brill, 2009). Eugene Avrutin explores the racialization of Jews, by both non-Jewish and Jewish intellectuals, in late imperial Russia in "Racial Categories and the Politics of (Jewish) Difference in Late Imperial Russia," *Kritika* 8, no. 1 (2007): 13–40. Robert Weinberg has examined the uses to which Jewish scientists put racial and eugenic ideas in the 1920s in the Soviet Union. See his "Biology and the Jewish Question after the Revolution: One Soviet Approach to the Productivization of Jewish Labor," *Jewish History* 21, nos. 3–4 (2007): 413–28.

6. The more general question of the complex relationship between race and religion is taken up by Gil Anidjar in *Semites: Race, Religion, Literature* (Stanford: Stanford University Press, 2008), a work that brilliantly explores how the categories of "race" and "religion" came to be constituted, and for what purposes and to what effects.

7. Endogamy, or marrying only within one's own group, was often called "inbreeding" in the racial literature. This has nothing to do with incestuous relations, a connotation that the English word "inbreeding" may carry.

8. See the selection by Theilhaber in this volume.

9. See the selection by Feist in this volume.

10. See the section on further readings at the end of this book for a list of those scholars who have explored Jewish thinking on race. Of particular importance has been the work of Sander Gilman, who has done the most to set the terms of discussion and to demonstrate that Jewish racial thought extended far beyond a few Jewish thinkers.

11. Gershom Scholem, quoted in David Biale, *Gershom Scholem: Kabbalah and Counter-History* (Cambridge: Harvard University Press, 1979), 154.

12. Moshe Rosman, *How Jewish Is Jewish History?* (London: Littman, 2007), 47.

13. Nancy Leys Stepan and Sander Gilman, "Appropriating the Idioms of Science: The Rejection of Scientific Racism," in *The Racial Economy of Science*, ed. Sandra Harding (Bloomington: Indiana University Press, 1993), 170–93.

14. Sander Gilman, *The Jew's Body* (New York: Routledge, 1991).

15. The use of the animal world as a model for thinking about human traits and differences in ways that we might call "racial" reaches further back, at least into the sixteenth century. On the influence of animal breeding on the emergence of racial thought, see Charles de Miramon, "Noble Dogs, Noble Blood: The Invention of the Concept of Race in the Late Middle Ages," in *The Origins of Racism in the West*, ed. Miriam Eliav-Feldon, Benjamin Isaac, and Joseph Ziegler (Cambridge: Cambridge University Press, 2009), 200–216.

16. Carl von Linné, excerpt from *The System of Nature*, in *Race and the Enlightenment: A Reader*, ed. Emmanuel Chukwudi Eze (Cambridge, Mass.: Blackwell, 2008), 13. I have slightly amended the original wording.

17. Just when to begin the history of this racialization process is a difficult question, since historians do not agree on when the idea of race began. Many now believe that racial thinking existed in the ancient world; others continue to insist that true racial thinking began only in the early modern or modern periods, in the sixteenth century or later. For a few examples

of the naturalization of Jewish traits in the Middle Ages, see Peter Biller, "A Scientific View of Jews from Paris around 1300," in *Micrologus* 9 (2001):137–68. On the larger question of when racial thinking and racism began, see the essays collected in *The Origins of Racism in the West*, ed. Eliav-Feldon, Isaac, and Ziegler.

18. On the relationship between racial thinking and aesthetics, see George L. Mosse, *Toward the Final Solution* (Madison: University of Wisconsin Press, 1978).

19. See Mitchell B. Hart, *The Healthy Jew: The Symbiosis of Judaism and Modern Medicine* (New York: Cambridge University Press, 2007).

20. Jews were not the only minority group to do this. Native Americans and African Americans also produced studies in which they accepted fundamental aspects of racial thought while using it to respond to negative images and evaluations of their group. For instance, the African-American writer Martin Delany linked the Hebrew word for man, *adam*, with the word for red, *adom*, and saw this as scientific evidence that the original man was "clay color or yellow, more resembling that of the lightest of the pure-blooded North American Indians." This allowed Delany, as Colin Kidd has argued, to refute the dominant narrative of a white Adam and thus "undermine white pretensions." On Delany and others who argued in a similar vein, see Kidd, *The Forging of Races: Race and Scripture in the Protestant Atlantic World, 1600–2000* (Cambridge: Cambridge University Press, 2006). The quotation from Delany and Kidd's comment appears on pages 31–32. See also Gilman and Stepan, "Appropriating the Idioms of Science."

21. Arthur Ruppin, "Begabungsunterschiede christlicher und jüdischer Kinder," *Zeitschrift für Demographie und Statistik der Juden* 2, nos. 8–9 (1906): 129.

22. John Efron, *Defenders of the Race: Jewish Doctors and Race Science in Fin-de-Siècle Europe* (New Haven: Yale University Press, 1994).

23. For a detailed discussion of the theory of degeneration in the Jewish context, see Todd Samuel Presner, *Muscular Judaism: The Jewish Body and the Politics of Regeneration* (London: Routledge, 2007). For the history of the idea of degeneration more generally, see Daniel Pick, *Faces of Degeneration* (Cambridge: Cambridge University Press, 1989).

24. Throughout the German-language texts translated in this volume, I have chosen to retain the original word "Volk" (plural: "Völker"). It is one of a number of German terms whose resonance in the original does not carry over into English. In this case, the English word "folk" fails to capture the nationalist and racialist components of the German. And though "Volk" can refer to "nation," "race," or "people," none of these English words quite captures the fullness of "Volk."

25. See Amos Funkenstein, *Perceptions of Jewish History* (Berkeley: University of California Press, 1993), 338–50.

26. See Endelman's groundbreaking *The Jews of Georgian England, 1714–1830: Tradition and Change in a Liberal Society*, 2nd ed. (Ann Arbor: University of Michigan Press, 2002). This edition contains a valuable preface in which Endelman articulates the historiographical contribution of his work and its impact on our thinking about how integration unfolded. See also the essays collected in *Toward Modernity: The European Jewish Model*, ed. Jacob Katz (New Brunswick, N.J.: Transaction, 1987) and in *Paths of Emancipation: Jews, States, and Citizenship*, ed. Pierre Birnbaum and Ira Katznelson (Princeton: Princeton University Press, 1995).

27. Menasseh ben Israel, "How Profitable the Nation of the Jews Are" (1655), in *The Jew in the Modern World*, ed. Paul Mendes-Flohr and Jehuda Reinharz, 2nd ed. (Oxford University Press, 1995), 10.

28. See the selection by Loeb in this volume.

29. Wagner's "Das Judenthum in der Musik" (Jewry in music) was published anonymously in 1850. Selections of this essay can be found in English in *The Jew in the Modern World*, ed. Mendes-Flohr and Reinharz, 327–31.

30. The major exception to this was the eminent historian George Mosse. See his "The Influence of the Völkish Idea on German Jewry," in *Studies of the Leo Baeck Institute*, ed. Max Kreutzberger (New York: Fredrick Ungar, 1967), 1:81–114. See also Michael Marrus, *The Politics of Assimilation* (Oxford: Oxford University Press, 1971), chapter one; and the writings of Joachim Doron, who produced a doctoral dissertation in 1977 at Tel-Aviv University that dealt with the appropriation of racial ideas and images by Zionism. For a summary of Doron's arguments, see his "Classic Zionism and Modern Antisemitism: Parallels and Influences (1883–1914)," *Studies in Zionism* 8 (Autumn 1983): 169–204.

31. Susan Glenn, "In the Blood? Consent, Descent, and the Ironies of Jewish Identity," *Jewish Social Studies* 8, nos. 2–3 (2002): 139–40. See also David Biale, *Blood and Belief: The Circulation of a Symbol between Jews and Christians* (Berkeley: University of California Press, 2007).

# I | General Overviews

The scholarly debate about the Jews and race emerged as one part of a much broader scientific inquiry into race. The Jewish scholars who thought and wrote about "the Jewish race" necessarily did so using the categories and methods of science at the time. In addition, they sought to make their work scientifically acceptable, so they engaged with the existing scholarship. This scholarship, however, was not unified in its opinion about the racial definition of the Jews.

Were the Jews, in fact, even a race? If so, had they maintained themselves as a "pure" race—that is, had they succeeded in eliminating or minimizing the amount of "foreign blood" that had entered into the collective Jewish body? If they were a mixed race, what were the constituent elements of that race? What tribes or nations, either in the biblical period or later, had contributed to the Jewish race? What are the main racial divisions within the modern Jewish people? What is the relationship between biology and faith when it comes to defining the Jews racially? Are the Jews of Ethiopia, India, and China linked to other Jews by anything more than common religious beliefs?

The articles in this initial section are intended to introduce students to these overarching issues and themes. They highlight the fact that Jewish scholars were joining a discussion about Jews and race that, by the late nineteenth century, had been going on for close to a century. And these introductory texts make clear just how extensive the evidence invoked could be, ranging from the ancient world through the present.

# 1 | Racial Characteristics of Modern Jews

## Joseph Jacobs

"On the Racial Characteristics of Modern Jews," in *Jewish Statistics: Social, Vital and Anthropometric* (London: D. Nutt, 1891).

Joseph Jacobs (1854–1916) was born in Australia and educated in England and Germany. He was professionally involved in a number of academic disciplines, including folklore, anthropology, statistics, history, and archaeology. Jacobs lived in England until 1900, when he traveled to the United States to become one of the editors of *The Jewish Encyclopedia*. He was one of the earliest advocates and practitioners of a systematic, scientific study of Jews along statistical and racial lines, and he published numerous books and articles related to Jews and race. This selection is from a paper he read before the Anthropological Institute of Great Britain and Ireland on February 24, 1885. See the entry in the *Encyclopedia Judaica*, 9:1235–36.

In the following research I have endeavored to bring together all the data, scientific or historical, which bear on the question of the purity of the Jewish race. I have found it necessary for this purpose to scrutinize somewhat closely many Jewish qualities and habits that have hitherto been regarded as peculiarly the results of race. Most of these, however, have been found to be due to social causes, and cannot therefore be regarded as primarily racial. Nevertheless I trust even the discussion of the secondarily racial qualities of Jews with which this paper opens may not be without interest to students of anthropology. They exhibit, I conceive, a striking example of the influence which the social life of man has on his physical qualities. For a decision on the main question, I have been forced to turn to history, which is on this occasion more than usually Janus-faced.

We have first of all to determine which are the Jews whose racial qualities we are to determine. I have made the following estimate, necessarily rough, of the various classes of persons now living, who may claim to be Jews by religion or by birth, or by both [see table 1.1].[1]

1. The best enumeration of Jews is by M. I. Loeb, art. "Juifs," in Saint Martin's *Dictionnaire de Geographie*; his chief errors are making the number of Russian Jews too low by a million, and the Falashas 200,000 instead of 50,000.

[TABLE 1.1]

| Name | Country | Number | Percent of whole |
|---|---|---|---|
| A. *Jews both by religion and by birth* | | 6,925,000 | 98.9 |
| Ashkenazim | Teutonia and Slavonia | 6,500,000 | 92.8 |
| Sephardim | Romance, Levant, Africa | 425,000 | 6.1 |
| Samaritans? | Nablus | 150 | |
| B. *Jews by religion, but not by birth* | | 75,000 | 1.1 |
| Falashas[a] | Abyssinia | 50,000 | |
| Karaites | Crimea | 6,000 | |
| Daggatouns, etc.[b] | Sahara | 10,000 | |
| Beni-Israel[c] | Bombay | 6,500 | |
| Cochin[d] | Cochin | 1,600 | |
| C. *Jews by birth, but not by religion* | | 12,000 | 0.2 |
| Chuetas or Anussim[e] | Balearic Is. | 6,000 | |
| Maiminen[f] | Salonichi | 4,000 | |
| G'did al Islam[g] | Khorassan | 2,000 | |

*Notes*

[a]Rohlfs in Petermann "Mittheil," 1883, p. 213.

[b]Serour, "Les Daggatouns," 1880. I include in this number the Mavambu or Negro-Jews of the Loango Coast (*vide* Andree, "Volkskunde d. Juden," 1881, p. 90).

[c]Census of India, 1881, gives 7,952 Jews in British Bombay.

[d]"Jüd. Littblt," 1883, No. 36. The number of Jews in China is unknown.

[e]Descendants of Spanish Jews still isolated. Lewin, *ibid.*, No. 30.

[f]Descendants of followers of the Jewish "Mahdi," Sabbathai Zebi. Graetz in "Monatsft," 1884, Feb.

[g]Jews forcibly converted to Islam thirty years ago, "Vesillo Israel," April, 1884.

Besides these, there exist a large number of persons, mostly in Europe, who have Jewish blood in their veins as descendants of Jewish converts. This is specially the case in Spain, where Jewish blood has filtrated through all ranks of society up to the very highest, and the same is said of certain districts of mid-France. The anthropology of Jews can never be satisfactorily settled till careful examination of these various data has shown their resemblances and differences. From the common qualities of classes A and B we can determine qualities due to religion; from those common to A and C, but differing in B, we might draw valuable conclusions as to influences of race. As a matter of fact, for the second and third classes we have practically no data to work with, except the vague impressions of travelers, and we must therefore confine our attention to the two chief divisions of Jews: (1) Sephardim, mostly descendants of the refugees from Spain in 1492, and now residing on the littoral of the Mediterranean;[2] and (2) Ashkenazim, dwelling in all the countries inhabited by Teutons or Slavs. The latter form an overwhelming majority (93 percent), and our information about them is tolerably extensive and reliable.

What are the qualities, if any, that we are to regard as *racially* characteristic of Jews? Much vague declamation has been spoken and written on this subject. All the moral, social, and intellectual qualities of Jews have been spoken of as being theirs by right of birth in its physical sense. Jews differ from others in all these points, it is true, as I have partly shown elsewhere.[3] But the differences are due, in my opinion, to the combined effect of their social isolation and of their own traditions and customs, and if they have nowadays any hereditary predisposition toward certain habits and callings, these can only be regarded as secondarily racial, acquired hereditary tendencies which cannot be brought forward as proof of racial purity. If all the Johns and Maries of Europe were to be shut up in ghetti for a couple of centuries they would undoubtedly show peculiarities in habits and thought; they would develop a Johannine psychology, as it were, and most probably, as we shall see, a Johannine biostatics. And there is another reason why the psychological traits of Jews must be omitted for the present from any research which claims to be scientific. Science was to Condillac a hundred years ago only a well-constructed terminology (*une langage bien faite*); nowadays science is measurement accurately calculated. Now though I hope to show on some future occasion that the intellectual capacity of Jews, if not absolutely, is yet relatively measurable as compared with that of other Europeans, I should still hesitate to qualify these distinctions as racial in a strict sense. They seem more a matter of temperament, which is at best but the tone of race, and is much more modifiable by education and environment than purely racial characteristics, so that it may happen that widely diverse races—for example, Jews and Frenchmen—may have much the same temperament. Under any circumstances it would be difficult for a Jew to avoid subjective bias in dealing

2. I have reckoned in [*sic*] with the Sephardim the Italian Jews and those under Moslem rule.

3. *Vide* my "Studies in Jewish Statistics" (*Jewish Chronicle* Office). [That essay was published in the same volume—*Jewish Statistics*—as this selection.]

with these matters, and where that bias leads to any assertion of superiority the result is as unsatisfactory from the point of view of science as it is from that of taste. It remains then to consider those qualities of Jews which depend on physical properties, and these have the further advantage of lending themselves to accurate measurement. These are (1) the vital statistics of Jews—marriages, births, deaths, diseases; and (2) their anthropometry or bodily measurements.[4]

[. . .]

## DISCUSSION

The Rev. Dr. Hermann Adler[5] (Delegate Chief Rabbi) congratulated the President on having chosen a subject of such profound interest to the student of anthropology. He agreed with the view propounded by Mr. Jacobs in his exhaustive paper, that on the whole there had not been any large foreign admixture with the Jewish race. As a theme for further inquiry, he drew attention to the copies in Dr. Wright's *Empire of the Hittites* of the representations discovered near Carchemish of the ancient inhabitants of that country. Their features bore an extraordinary resemblance to the inferior Hebraic type, with low forehead, hooked nose, and thick lips. If the hypothesis of Professor Sayce and Dr. Wright were accepted as correct, might the existence of this type, which argued kinship with the Mongolian race, and which differed so materially from the characteristic features of the Semitic race—the expanded forehead and symmetrical lineaments—be traced to intermarriage with the Hittites who are represented in the Bible as descended from Ham?[6] The dark and the blond type [*sic*], the speaker believed, should be regarded as original, dating from Bible times and described respectively in Canticles 5:11 and 2 Samuel 6:12. That the existence of the blond type was not due to intermarriage might be proved by the fact that it was to be found among the Jews of North Africa, Syria, Arabia, and Persia,

4. [Omissions from selections are indicated by ellipsis points within square brackets. What follows is a report of the discussion of Jacobs's paper by members of the audience.]

5. [Hermann Adler (1839–1911) was the chief rabbi of Great Britain from 1891 to 1911.]

6. *Note by Mr. Jacobs.*—These Jewish-looking "Hittites" were probably the Semitic vassals of the genuine Hittites. Mr. T. Tyler has pointed out to me at the British Museum two types on the monuments, one of Mongolian features and a kind of Chinese tail [queue], the other of the ordinary Semitic type. The latter he conjectures to be the vassals of the former, and thus their Jewish appearance is simply another example of the identity of the Jewish and the Semitic type.

where, owing to the prevalence of fanaticism, mixed marriages had rarely, if ever, taken place. Goethe, a man of science as well as a poet, had pithily summed up the main anthropological characteristic of the Hebrew race in the words: "Es ist das beharrlichste Volk der Erde. Es ist, es war, es wird sein" ["This is the most tenacious Volk in the world. This is how it is, how it was, and how it will be"].

Dr. Behrend[7] observed that M. Littré had well said that all springs of human conduct arose from two instincts, that of self-preservation, and the reproductive instinct for the preservation of the race. The rightful cultivation of these two instincts led to the primary desire of all humanity—happiness, and the chief element in human happiness was health. Health, both of body and mind, depended mainly on conduct, not only of the individual, but also from heredity. Therefore we should expect that as conduct (and through conduct, health; and through health, happiness) was the object of religion, a code of religion should lay down laws, which would be a guide of conduct, and thereby conduce to health and happiness. These primary instincts, that of self-preservation and the reproductive instinct, were mainly regulated in the Jewish code by laws concerning diet, circumcision, and sexual relations. The speaker had shown elsewhere at length (in a series of papers "On the Communicability to Man of the Diseases from Animals Used as Food") that the Hebraic dietary laws preserved [the Jews] from the transmission of such diseases, and especially from the ravages of tuberculosis, which in its various forms was accountable for at least one-fifth of the entire mortality in this country. Sexual relations were regulated in the Hebrew code by laws which aimed at conserving the highest attainable degree of virility, by restraining undue indulgence and ensuring procreation only at a specially healthy period. We need hardly pause to dwell on the enormous advantages [that] such a start in the battle of life must give toward the "survival of the fittest."

The special biostatic privileges of Jews might be summed up in the proven facts that they married less, had fewer births, died less (that is, lived longer), increased at a greater rate, and had fewer stillborn and illegitimate children than any other race. It was quite unnecessary to repeat the statistics upon these points: they had been given over and over again, by Hoffmann, Kolb, Bergmann, Legoyt, Bernouilli, Lagneau, Loeb, and many others; but it was interesting, and to the Jews vitally instructive, to note that in proportion as they mixed with other races—either of their own accord or by the spread of social tolerance—they

7. [Henry Behrend (1828–1893) was an Anglo-Jewish physician, medical researcher, and hospital adminstrator.]

lost these biostatic privileges, and the differences became effaced. Thus M. de Bergmann ("Beiträge zur Geschichte der Bevölkerung in Deutschland") showed that the relation of the sexes among the Jews in Posen had of late become much modified: that while from 1819 to 1864 it was as 111.94 boys to 100 girls, it fell to 106.39 to 100 from 1864 to 1873; similarly, the proportion of illegitimate births among them had increased, showing a relaxation in their adherence to the Mosaic code. In every one of the biostatic privileges they enjoyed, the penalty had to be paid for laxity of observances, and either in their own persons or in their descendants, those who transgressed had to submit to the inexorable law of "being cut off from their own people," as far as was concerned in their share of the physical advantages of their race.

Mr. F. D. Mocatta[8] remarked that in addition to the two greater divisions of the Jewish race, Sephardim (Spanish) and Ashkenazim (German), not to mention the Italian Jews, there were various other families of Jews, such as those of the interior of Morocco, speaking Arabic, and not Spanish; those of Persia and of Yemen; and others. Besides these were large numbers of Jews in various countries, who might be considered not to be of the seed of Abraham, or only to be to a greater or lesser degree crossed with it. Such were the Beni-Israel of Bombay, those of Foo-Choo-Foo (now nearly obliterated), the Riff Jews of the north of Morocco (an armed, warlike set, loosely adhering to Judaism, but differing in physique and habit from other Jews), the nearly black and crispy Malabar Jews, etc. Also the Jews of Southeast Russia in Europe, who speak Russian and are a well-developed, hardy, and generally ruddy race, are probably a different family from those of Poland and Central Russia, who still speak a dialect of German, their ancestors having been driven out of Germany at the period of the Crusades. This family might possibly represent, as the Karaites of the Crimea were often supposed to do, the descendants of the Khozars, a tribe on the Caspian, who about the seventh century founded a state and maintained it for the best part of two centuries, adopting the Jewish religion. All these, so to speak, outlying families of Jews might be regarded as descendants of proselytes, but as they had blended but very little with the general mass of the Jews, they did not much affect the subject then under consideration. In biblical times the Jews frequently made matrimonial alliances with the surrounding populations, and this was a constant theme of the reproach of prophets and reformers, notably of

8. [Frederick David Mocatta (1828–1905) was a prominent communal leader of London Jewry, a philanthropist, and a scholar.]

Ezra and Nehemiah. Later on, at the time of the conquest of Titus, when Christianity was only dawning on the Latin world, many Jews were carried to Rome, the bulk being the common people, who were put to labor on public works and often devoured at gladiatorial shows; but some of whom, being scholars and persons of refinement, were admitted into Roman society, and by the purity of their doctrine won over to their philosophy and religion many of the higher classes, notably women, who were becoming tired of the superstitions and worldliness into which the pagan religions had degenerated. This probably led to alliances, and such is M. Renan's opinion.[9] The Jews also, ever prone to adopt the habits and manners of surrounding nations, became lax; Romanized and Hellenized their names, as was evidenced in the Jewish catacombs at Rome; and probably contracted marriages with the people around them. All these sources might have led to an admixture of non-Jewish blood, [but] the extent of such admixture (the alliances being at all times exceptional rather than general, and having become rarer with the persecutions which set in the earlier ages of the Christian Church) was not likely to have essentially modified either the type or the physical or moral characteristics of the Jewish race, which might therefore be regarded for all practical purposes as pure. This was all the more probable since a large number of the issue of such mixed alliances naturally fell back to the dominant religions of the various times and countries, and ceased to have anything to do with Judaism. The speaker said he had not alluded to alliances made between Jews and Oriental peoples, Mohammedans, etc., in earlier times, first because it would be difficult to prove their frequency or the contrary, and second because, these peoples being for the most part Semitic themselves, the changes thus induced would have been far less accentuated.

Sir Joseph Fayrer[10] had no criticisms to make on the erudite papers which had been read that evening, but would ask one or two questions, first remarking that he had known Jews in Calcutta where one member of the family had light hair and gray eyes, another dark hair and complexion. It struck him that the Armenians presented those peculiar characteristics of physiognomy which were usually attributed to the Jew. Was this not simply a question of race, both being Semitic, and should not the so-called Jewish physiognomy rather be called

9. [Ernest Renan (1823–92) was a French philosopher, historian, and theorist of nationalism.]

10. [Joseph Fayrer (1824–1907) was an English physician known principally as an expert on medicine and disease in India.]

Semitic than be regarded as the special attribute of the Hebrew, as distinct from other Semitic races such as the Armenian? The speaker would ask the learned author of the second paper (Mr. Jacobs) if he could give any information as to the relation of the Afghans to the Jews? They undoubtedly had the physiognomy strongly marked—it was often said they were descendants of the lost tribes, and there was a tribe among them calling themselves Beni-Israel. What was known and accepted among erudite Jews as to the origin of the Afghans? Again, what was the origin of the race of Black Jews on the Malabar coast? Were these not a mixed race, and were they not the result of admixture with the Teluigan races of Southern India? Pure as the Jewish race is, it would seem that it must be recognized that evidences of such admixture with other races did exist, and it would also seem that they had taken more or less of an impression from their surroundings and from the character of the races among which they had settled.

Mr. Lucien Wolf[11] did not agree with Mr. Jacobs's view of the physiological characteristics of Jews. Mr. Jacobs practically denied the existence of these characteristics, whereas the speaker felt inclined not only to assert their existence, but to assert that they were so well defined as to form real race distinctions. This view could be proved by statistics, and figures could also be given to prove the immunity of Jews from phthisis, which Mr. Jacobs contested. The purity of the race could not be demonstrated by anthropological measurements, for, physically, Jews varied enormously. It was different with their vital characteristics, and while we found that these were maintained at a high average, we might rest assured that the race was being conserved. The evidence brought forward by Dr. Neubauer in favor of his view that the Jewish race had not kept itself pure told against the proposition it was intended to support when it was tested by other evidence. Thus it might be asked how was it that, notwithstanding these large accessions to Judaism, the race had not increased, and that in spite of these large infusions of alien blood, so important a vital characteristic as its high reproductive power has not become modified. It must be obvious that had the remarkable multiplying power of the Jews been left unchecked, they must have increased far beyond their present numbers, and if they could receive accessions from other races without diminishing this power, then by this time they ought to have peopled the world. The conclusion must be then that the mixed marriages referred to had not affected the purity of the race. By their tendency to sterility

11. [Lucien Wolf (1857–1930) was a noted Anglo-Jewish journalist, historian, and activist on behalf of the Jewish community.]

they have periodically carried off the perpetually growing fringe of Judaism, leaving always a pure nucleus to repropagate itself. Thus by bringing to light the fact that mixed marriages were generally sterile, the evidence cited by Dr. Neubauer, instead of telling against the purity of the Jewish race revealed the most powerful argument in its favor. Nor was this theory of sterility a theory only. The speaker had investigated a large number of cases of mixed marriages—not quite so many as Mr. Jacobs—and in every single case he had found, if not absolute sterility, at least a falling off in the vital power of the offspring, placing them far below the average obtaining in the Jewish community. This falling off was only postponed sterility, as he had had occasion to prove himself by investigating the history through several generations of a few mixed marriages.

# 2 | Reflections on the Jews

## Isidore Loeb

"Réflexions sur les Juifs," *Revue des Etudes Juives* 27 (1893):1–31.

The essay is preceded by a note from the editors of the journal, in which they tell readers that what follows is an unpublished draft, dated 1885, discovered on the death of the author. Isidore Loeb (1839–92) was a French rabbi and scholar. He published on a wide variety of topics, including the Bible and Talmud, medieval history, the history of Jews in modern Europe, and mathematics. He held the post of secretary of the Alliance Israélite Universelle, and he also published works directly related to the situation of Jews in Turkey, Serbia, Romania, and Russia. See the entry in the *Encyclopedia Judaica*, 11:438.

The idea of emancipating the Jews and according them, in the state, the same rights as all other men, is an entirely modern idea, but the idea is so just that in less than one hundred years, and despite inveterate prejudices, it has imposed itself on every spirit by the unique force of its truth. The principle of equal rights applied to Jews was a ray of light concerning policies affecting them, hitherto so obscure and so unrealistic. It appeared with the obviousness and certitude of an axiom.

Any proof for this principle is therefore superfluous. This question, discussed in the past, is answered today.

It is absolutely impossible to find any reason to justify exceptional laws for a group of people, in particular, for the Jews. The principle of human brotherhood, of equal rights for all men, is the foundation of every modern state. Outside this principle, there can only be arbitrariness and injustice, and a state that is not founded on justice cannot even be conceived of.

The word "emancipation," as it is officially used, is an inexact word that only imperfectly renders that which humanity, civilization, and fairness demand for the Jews. "In general, I do not like this word 'emancipation,'" said [Ferenc] Deák to the Hungarian Chamber [of Deputies] in 1866, "it shames us; it is as if the Jews were once our slaves. The Jews have the law on their side, and if we accord it to them, we are not obeying feelings of sympathy or antipathy, but only principles of justice."[12]

12. Wertheimer, *Jahrbuch für Israeliten*, 5627 (Vienna, 1867), p. XIII.

"If we continue to refuse human rights to the Jews," Wolfgang Menzel said, "we deserve to lose ours forever."[13]

On what grounds, in a modern state, could exceptional laws for Jews be based?

Religious grounds? Religion certainly still accounts for a large part of the prejudices and malicious sentiments that prevail against the Jews in certain parts of Europe, and it can even exercise its influence on the conduct of statesmen regarding the Jews; but none of them would dare to invoke religion today to justify Jewish inequality. There is not a government that would want to or could oppress the Jews for the reasons cited in the Middle Ages; for example, that the Jewish crime [of deicide] is indelible, that God wants the Jews to be abased in order that their humiliation bears eternal witness to their fallacy and to the glory of Christianity. These reasons, which seemed excellent in the past and which were even invoked seriously in the English Parliament in the first half of this century, have lost all credibility today. Theology is definitively banished from politics.[14]

"European culture of late," says [Johann Caspar] Bluntschli,[15] "has little by little escaped and been delivered from places that joined the law with a circumscribed religion. It became clear to present-day peoples that religion is a question of internal conscience that cannot be submitted to external force. They conceive of the law as an external organization established by men, serving a human goal that men must uphold and yield to, and that, consequently, given the same circumstances, should be the same for everyone. This is why modern law was separated from the terms of a circumscribed religion and was established as common law, equal for all of the inhabitants of a country."

It is true that in the years 1820 and 1850, a Christian state was much talked about in Germany and that, all the while recognizing that Jews should be emancipated and treated as equals under the law, there was, however, a will to keep them from politics, from high administrative functions, from the police force, and from teaching, because, it was said, the German state was essentially a "Christian state." But the followers of this theory never managed to explain

13. *Literaturblatt*, 1833, n. 120; *Ersch and Grüber Encyclopedia*, article "Judenemancipation," p. 237, n. 24.

14. Those persons who remain under the influence of theological ideas and who would wish to apply them politically should not forget, in any case, that Christianity was born out of Judaism and that Jesus was Jewish.

15. Bluntschli, *Der Staat Rumänien und das Rechtverhältniss der Juden in Rumänien*, Berlin, 1879, p. 10.

what they meant by this phrase. The remarkable discussion at the Diet of Prussia assembled in 1847, which we'll have occasion to talk about more than once, pointed out the contradictions and impossibilities that this phrase contains. One saw then that the formula was hollow or absurd; from that moment on, the phrase was definitively condemned.

The modern state is destined to settle a certain number of material and intellectual or moral questions that are absolutely foreign to religion; religion is a question for the individual, purely a question of conscience, and one with which no legislator should occupy himself. "The expression of an essentially Christian government," [Thomas Babington] Macaulay says, "is as sensible as that of an essentially Protestant cuisine or essentially Christian horseback riding. The government is in place to maintain peace, forcing us to settle our disputes by way of arbitration instead of settling them with blows, forcing us to compensate for our needs through work instead of compensating for them through plunder."[16] It has nothing to do with religion.

It is true that the objection was raised against the Jews, that they would be strangers everywhere and that they would consequently never be treated as indigenous.

This objection can have two meanings:

It can signify that Jews are not the same race as the peoples among whom they live;

Or, in putting aside the question of race, independently of human will, that the Jews would everywhere voluntarily form a nation apart, a state within a state, a closed corporation that distinguishes itself by its physical particularities (type, muscular strength, etc.), by legislation, language, customs, and the fact that they would regard every country they reside in as a temporary homeland, always ready to abandon it for the Holy Land, the definitive homeland toward which all of their aspirations are turned.

The first objection rests on the idea that every nation has at its foundation racial unity and that the Jews, being a race apart, cannot take part in any nation. But this conception is absolutely false.

It is without a doubt difficult to find a precise and clear definition of the word or the idea of a nation, but all scholars agree that the unity of a nation is not

16. Macaulay, *Essais politiques et philosophiques*, translated by Mr. Guillaume Guizet, Paris, 1872, p. 382.

founded on the unity of race. A nation is a group of people united by the same allegiances, the same historical memories, the same aspirations for the future, attaching all of these feelings to a common homeland, real if not ideal, and having a defined political existence.[17] "Following certain theories," says Mr. Topinard,[18] "nationality is determined by language, a purely ethnographic and radically false doctrine; as Mr. Abel Hovelacque said most fortunately, this is but *a social reason*. Coming from accidental events more so than the geographic disposition of places, [nationality] asserts itself through a community of interests, of suffering, and of glory; bloodshed for a single cause cements it; hearts beating in unison from one end of a territory to the other are its characteristics."[19]

Whatever the merit of these formulas, it is certain that race does not enter into the idea of a nation as an indispensable factor. There are races that are divided into several distinct nationalities, as for example, the Slavic race, and inversely, every nation is composed of diverse races. A nation made of a pure and unique race does not exist. Nowhere in the world, or at least in the civilized world, is there a single race of absolutely pure blood.[20] "Races are divided, dispersed, blended, crossbred in every way, in every direction, for thousands of centuries . . . We speak of an Anglo-Germanic and Latin race, a German race, English, Slavic, as if there were in these epithets something other than a political denomination, an accidental conglomeration of anthropological elements from diverse sources."[21]

Already before historical time, the races mixed their blood, and the already altered races that existed at the origin of historical time have since then crossbred and mixed ad infinitum. All European nations are formed of an amalgam of diverse races, and those generally seen as the most gifted are the nations where the greatest number of races have merged their different qualities and corrected, through a sort of intellectual and moral crossbreeding, their primitive defects. The French nation is composed of the most diverse races: Iberians, Ligurians, Celts, Germanic peoples, Romans, Greeks, and even Arabs.[22] Italy is a mixture of

17. See, for example, Maurice Block, *Dictionnaire général de la politique*, 2nd vol., Paris, 1874, p. 374.

18. [Paul Topinard (1830–1911) was an eminent French anthropologist.]

19. Topinard, *L'anthropologie*, 3rd ed., Paris, 1879, p. 10.

20. Topinard, *L'anthropologie*, 3rd ed., p. 458: "Gerdy rightly affirms that there are no longer pure races."

21. Topinard, *Ibid.*, p. 456.

22. Lagneau, *Anthropologie de la France*, Paris, 1859, p. 572–752; compare with Topinard, p. 457–458.

ancient Latin races, Etruscans, and Greeks, to which Ligurians, Celts, Germanic races (Lombards, Goths), and Arabs have been added. In Spain, a mix of Romans, Iberians, Ligurians, Celts, Germanic races like the Visigoths, Muslim Arabs, and Berbers can be found. In England, one finds Iberians, Ligurians, Celts, Anglos, Saxons, Danish, Normans, etc. We know the incredible mixture and juxtaposition of races from Austria-Hungary. Germany is, in large part, populated by Celts, who are not a Germanic race; in Mecklenburg, in Prussia, one recognizes Slavic and Finnish elements. The Germans of our day are essentially a mixed race. "In Germany," says Mr. Topinard, "it would be yet more difficult (than in France) to discern a Germanic type. Every invasion from the Orient to the Occident has passed through this country, including those that ended in northern and central France. Neither the depths of prehistory nor the successive currents that followed have succeeded in forming a type so far from homogeneous . . . If they (the Germans) are a federation of people, they are not an anthropological race."[23]

"The Hungarians or Magyars," says the same author, "are altered by their having mixed with the Turks, the Khazars, with the Bulgarians and the Romanians . . . Linguists attribute to them a Finnish language . . . A slight slanting of the eyes and cheekbones that jut out among some of them, makes one think not of the Finnish type, but of a Mongolian influence."[24] In Russia, one finds to the north (and even farther, in the center), Finnish or partly Finnish populations; here and there, populations more or less Mongolian; among the peasants, who have the best chance of representing the primitive element, there are physiognomies that recall the pure Enez people or the Todas people.[25] The Russian nation can be considered to be formed of Slavs, Lithuanians, Celts, Germanic peoples, Mongols, Finns, Lapps, Ugrians, and Tartars, not to mention Jews.[26] There is not a single people in Europe whose race is absolutely pure. The racial objection pitted against the Jews is thus without merit and self-defeating.

This is not all: nothing proves that the present-day Jews who reside in most of the European states are the descendants of the ancient Jews of Palestine and strictly of the Semitic race. Several ethnographers have already remarked on the considerable difference that exists between certain types of Jews, for example

23. Topinard, *Ibid.*, p. 470.

24. Topinard, *Ibid.*, p. 470.

25. Topinard, *Ibid.*, p. 468, 480, 481, 522.

26. Eliseé Reclus, *Europe scandinave et russe*, p. 853, and *Mittheilungen* by Petermann, 23rd vol., p. 141–143.

those Jews called Spanish and those called German. There are historians who maintain that a large number of modern Jews from our countries descend from pagans who converted to Judaism in the first centuries of the Christian era. Very particularly, in Russia and Germany, one may assume that many present-day Jews descend from the famous Khazars, of the Tartar race, who settled on the banks of the Volga and on the border of the Caspian Sea around the seventh or eight century, embraced Judaism, and were later subjugated by the Russians. Without wanting to take this thesis too far or attribute too much importance to it, one could say along with Mr. Renan: "This race (the Jewish race), considered the ideal pure *ethnos* for having conserved the prohibition against mixed marriages over the centuries, was deeply penetrated by foreign infusions, not unlike those that took place in other races . . . Considerably large quantities of populations with non-Israelite blood embraced Judaism, so that the significance of this word from the ethnographic point of view became highly dubious."[27]

And earlier:[28]

> Without doubt, in Gaul, there were Jewish émigrés (of the Semitic race), but there was also a mass of people who connected with Judaism through conversion but who did not have a single ancestor in Palestine. And when we reflect on the fact that German and English Jews came from France, we find ourselves regretting that we do not have more data about the origins of Judaism in our country. We would probably see that the Gallic Jew at the time of Guntram and Chilperic was more often than not only a Gaul professing the Israelite religion . . . But there is a more important historic event, closer to our days and seeming to have had very grave consequences: it is the conversion of the Khazars . . . Could a Jew of Palestinian origin ever be called Tokhtamysh (as Jews are named on Hebraic inscriptions in the Crimea), instead of being called Abraham, Levy, or Jacob? Evidently, no; this Tokhtamysh was a Tatar, a converted Nogai. This conversion of the kingdom of Khazars has considerable importance for the question of the origin of the Jews who live in the Danubian countries and central Russia. These regions contain great masses of Jewish people who probably have no or almost no Jewish ethnographic [traits].[29]

27. Renan, *Le Judaisme comme race et comme religion*, Paris, 1883, p. 24 and following.

28. *Ibid*., p. 22–23.

29. Regarding the Jewish Khazars, see d'Hosson, *Des Peuples du Caucase*, (Paris, 1828); Vivien de Saint-Martin, *Les Khazars*, Paris, 1851; Harkavy, *Discussions des écrivains juifs au sujet*

We could go back even further in the history of crossbreeding between Jews and non-Jews. Pagans who were converted to Judaism in the past in Syria, Palmyra, and Hadiab were without doubt not entirely Semitic. Those from Rome or Alexandria, more numerous perhaps than is thought, were most certainly not Semitic. It is known that as early as the first centuries of the Christian era, a rather active Jewish propaganda was in practice in Rome and surely in other parts of the Roman Empire as well.[30] "In almost every part of the known world at that time, *a very large number of persons* had ties to Judaism. Proselytism, little by little, underwent extraordinary growth . . . For already quite a long time," says Josephus, "many people took to the way in which we (the Jews) worship God with great zeal, and there is not a single city, among the Greeks as well as among the barbarians, there is not a single people for whom the observance of the seventh day as a day of rest is not widespread, where the fast and the lighting of torches and several of our precepts relating to diet [literally, delicacies] have not been adopted. They also aspire to imitate the harmony that reigns over us, our ardor for manual labor . . ."[31] Here we see, therefore, in our countries, and as far back as ancient times, many Jews who do not come from Jewish blood.

One may observe that there are, among European Jews, two distinct types, certainly from different origins, the Spanish type of Jews and the German type of Jews. Among the Jews of Persia, one also notices two types that differ from one another, indicating a diversity of origins.[32] Neither the Falashas of Ethiopia, who are Jews, nor the Bene-Israel of India, nor probably the nomadic Jewish tribes who are scattered deep into the Sahara, south of Algeria, have Semitic blood.[33] From all directions, Jewish blood received infusions of Aryan or other blood that profoundly modified it.

To return to our Occidental countries, considerable quantities of Aryan blood

---

*des Chazars* (in Russian), Saint Petersburg, 1874; Harkavy, in *Russische Revue*, 1875; P. Cassel, *Der Chazarische Kœnigsbrief*, Berlin, 1877.

30. See Renan, *Histoire des origines du christianisme.*

31. Kuenen, *Judaisme et Christianisme*, in *Revue de l'histoire des religions*, 4th year, vol. VII, n. 2 (Paris, 1883), p. 208–209.

32. Polack, *Persien*, Leipzig, 1865, I, p. 21 and following.

33. On the Falashas, see principally Philoxène Luzzatto, *Mémoire sur les Juifs d'Abyssinie*, in *Archives Israélites*, years 1851–1854; J. Halévy, *Travels in Abyssinia*, in the volume of the Miscellanies of the *Society of Hebrew Literature*, 2nd series, 2nd vol., London, 1877. For the Bene-Israel, see Benjamin II, *Cinq années de voyage on Orient*, Paris, 1856; *Archives Israélites*, 1855, p. 273–275. On the Jewish farmers of the African desert, see *Univers israélite*, II, 503.

mixed there with Jewish blood, during the entire Middle Ages, through marriage between Jews and Christians and through the conversion of slaves. It is known that slave commerce flourished in the Middle Ages, and that the Jews occupied themselves with it as much as the Christians. One of the great preoccupations of the councils and popes was to prevent the conversion to Judaism of slaves who were in Jewish hands.[34] It is thus incontestable that these conversions were numerous. Marriages between Jews and Christians were also frequent, as the canons of the councils again prove.[35] Conversely, there is not a population of Christians in Europe that did not receive an infiltration, at times a rather important one, of Jewish blood. Who can say how many thousands of Jews were baptized in Germany during the persecutions of the first Crusades, during the horrible scenes of the Black Death, and in a hundred other circumstances where they were forced to choose between baptism and death? In Spain, the Visigoth kings of the first centuries, the persecutors of 1391, and finally the Inquisition pursued, by fire and sword, the systematic conversion of the Jews. Jewish blood flows freely through the veins of the Spanish people, and this is so well known that a cardinal composed *The Firebrand of Spanish Nobility*,[36] when the greatest families in Spain were stigmatized as Jews. We see that Jewish blood was mixed in every way with the blood of other races. It has by turns received from and brought to others considerable quantities of foreign blood. The German who today attacks a Jew under the pretext that they are not of the same race is doubly mistaken. The Jew can descend from an Aryan or a Finn who converted to Judaism; his Christian adversary can descend from some Jew from the Middle Ages, a victim of the antisemitism from that era. Nothing guarantees that this Jew whom he pursues with his hatred is not a man of his blood and of his race.

Then wherein lies the difference between the Jewish race and the Aryan races?

34. See, for example, the Synods of Elvira (305), Laodicea (397), Chalcedon (451), Agde (506), Auvergne (535), Reims (630); the Bull of Gregory IX, from March 5, 1233; see also Baronius, vol. XXI, p. 91, ad annum 1233. On the general conversion of Christians to Judaism, see, for example, the Council of Bourges in 1276 (Baronius, vol. XI, p. 1026), the Bull of Nicolas IV, from September 5, 1288, and the very curious letter from the same pope to the archbishops of Arles, Aix, etc., in 1290 (Baronius, vol. XXIII, p. 92).

35. For example, the Council of Toledo in 589 (Labbe, tome V, p. 1012), the Council of Toledo in 633 (*Ibid.*, p. 1719). The Theodosian Code, chapter *De Judæis*, title: *Ne quis*, already defends marriages between Jews and Christians; Cf. The Bull of Benoît XIV, tome III, p. 4.

36. *El tizon de la nobleza espanola*, por el Cardenal de Francesco Mendoza; Barcelona, 1880.

Everyone agrees that the Jewish race or the Semitic race, in general, is connected to European types.[37] Mr. Renan explained very well how Jews in the ghetto have a certain particular physiognomy, a result of their oppression; but since the emancipation of the Jews, the particular characteristics of this physiognomy have disappeared. They are already no longer visible in a large number of French and Italian Jews. This physiognomy is, in the natural history of the Jews, an accident that is fading away; it does not constitute a type. The Jews are a part of the white type, whose various species or varieties populate our countries. Between a French or German Jew and a French or German Christian there is assuredly less of a difference, if there is one at all, than between a Frenchman and a German, a German and a Slav. But even if this difference were more obvious, there would be no reason to drive Jews out of a country and to refuse them civil and political rights. Every nation is composed of different races, and therein the Jewish race can find a legitimate place.

*Translated by Shaina Hammerman*

37. Topinard, *Ibid.*, 469.

# 3 | Preface from *Jews, Race, and Environment*

Maurice Fishberg

*Jews, Race, and Environment* (1911; New Brunswick, N.J.: Transaction, 2006).

Maurice Fishberg (1872–1934) was a physician, professor of medicine, and anthropologist. He was born in Russia and emigrated to the United States in 1889. Fishberg authored an important textbook, *Pulmonary Tuberculosis* (1916), and worked and taught at numerous New York City hospitals, as well as for the United Hebrew Charities. He was regarded as the leading American Jewish authority on the subject of Jews and race, having published numerous articles on the subject in both general and Jewish journals and newspapers. *Jews, Race, and Environment* was a comprehensive collection of contemporary research as well as a statement of Fishberg's belief that Jewish traits had social, rather than biological, origins. The book was reprinted in 2006.

This volume is an attempt to present the results of anthropological, demographic, pathological, and sociological investigations of the Jews. Considering that one-fifth of all the Jews in the world live at present in English-speaking countries, and that the migrations of Eastern European Jews tend toward the United States and England with its colonies, I believe I need not apologize for claiming attention to this subject. The facts presented are not available in any book, and it may safely be declared that the whole world is interested in the subject of the Jews as a race, and the getting into closer touch with the ethnic relations of the Jews. Moreover, the perennial problem, whether it is possible to assimilate the vast number of Southern and Eastern immigrants to the United States and British colonies has been applied more to the Jews than to any other white people. It has even been questioned whether there is ever a probability of incorporating the Jews into the body politic of Anglo-Saxon communities.

That anthropology only is competent to answer this question is agreed. Yet there is no book in English treating of the race traits of the Jews. The literature on the subject in English consists mostly of investigations by special parliamentary commissions, containing opinions of statesmen, social workers, educators, etc. It appears that the prevailing opinion is that the Jews, alleged to have maintained themselves in absolute racial purity for three or four thousand years, may prove hard to assimilate. On the one hand we have those Jews who take great pride in the purity of their breed, and, on the other, the people among whom they live who see a peculiar peril in the prospect of indefinitely harboring an alien race which is not likely to mix with the general population. This apprehension is confirmed by the Jewish nationalists, who look for repatriation in Palestine, or some other territory, thus corroborating the opinion that they are aliens in Europe, encamped for the time being, and waiting for an opportunity to retreat to their natural home in Asia. Indeed, the problem has of late been given official recognition in Anglo-Saxon countries. When bills were introduced in Parliaments aiming at the exclusion of Asiatic immigration, it was questioned whether Jews might not be considered Asiatics under the law; and in the United States a bill was recently introduced in Congress specifically declaring that the law prohibiting immigration and naturalization of Asiatics does not refer to Jews, Armenians, and Syrians.[38]

This inquiry into the race traits of the Jews could not be carried out by a study of these people in any one country, because we find at the outset that they present significant differences depending greatly on their birth-place, social and political conditions, and, in general, the environment in which they find themselves. Their anthropological characteristics could best be studied in New York City, where exist a million Jews from Europe, Asia, and Africa; and we have taken advantage of the material thus offered by obtaining anthropometric measurements of about three thousand Jews in this city. The conclusions as to the anthropological types of the Jews are based on these measurements, as well as on a collation of the scattered literature on the subject. The demography of the Jews could best be studied from official government publications in those countries where the censuses classify the population by religious confession. The changes in the physical, social, and economic conditions of the Jews under emancipation could best be studied in Western Europe and America, and this study involved a careful search into the literature on the Jews to bring out certain points which might have practical social bearings, especially on the problem of assimilation.

While speaking of the changes which the contemporary Jews have been undergoing within the last fifty years, we have avoided taking the position of partisan or advocate, and have treated the subject objectively. Books aiming at sympathetic apologies, defending, often excusing, Israel's existence among the

38. [The bill (H.R. 24,993) was introduced in April 1910 by Representative Everis Hayes of California. The House of Representatives passed the bill on May 2.]

nations, are on the same plane as those containing venomous diatribes full of scurrilous invectives against the Semites. It should also be understood that while pointing at the process of assimilation of the Jews, we by no means advocate their absorption by the surrounding people of different faiths. We do not find it important for the welfare of the remnants of Israel, or of those around them, that Jewry should commit race suicide. What is aimed at, however, is to point out what appears to be the tendencies, the *Zeitgeist*, of the Jews at the threshold of the Twentieth Century. Showing that while discarding the greater part of their separative ritualism the modern Jews commit suicide as Jews, because they cease to be peculiar, it is difficult to avoid describing in detail the metamorphosis this change works on the children of Israel. The large number of mixed marriages, which keeps on growing, could only take place among Jews who have discarded the separative tenets of their religion. People obeying the dietary laws religiously could not come in close and intimate contact with those whose table they could not share. The fact that the differences between Jews and Christians are not everywhere racial, due to anatomical or physiological peculiarities, but are solely the result of the social and political environment, explains our optimism as regards the ultimate obliteration of all distinctions between Jews and Christians in Europe and America. This optimism is confirmed by conditions in Italy, Scandinavia, and Australia, where anti-Semitism is practically unknown. When intermarriage between Jews and Christians will reach the same proportions in other countries, and the facts presented in Chapter IX clearly show that the time is not distant, anti-Semitism will everywhere meet with the same fate as in Italy, Scandinavia and Australia. Both Jews and Christians have been contributing to this end, the former by discarding their separative ritualism, and thus displaying willingness to bridge the gulf which separated them from others, and the latter by legalizing civil marriage. Whether this means that ceasing to be peculiar may prove deadly to Judaism can only be conjectured. All I could do was to present the facts.

[. . .]

# 4 | Jewish Race
## Fritz Kahn

"Rasse, Jüdische," in *Jüdisches Lexikon* (Berlin: Jüdischer Verlag, 1930), vol. 4.

Fritz Kahn (1888–1968) was born in Halle, Germany. Trained as a physician, he published a number of medical works, including the four-volume *Das Leben des Menschen* (Human life; 1922–29). He served as editor of the *Sammelblätter jüdischer Wissens* (Occasional papers on Jewish knowledge) and of the natural science section of the *Encyclopedia Judaica*. He published *Die Juden als Rasse und Kulturvolk* (The Jews as a race and a cultural people) in 1920. See the entry in the *Universal Jewish Encyclopedia*, 6:287.

### 1. GENERAL

In zoology, race is defined as groups of individual beings that can be considered to have a common origin and blood relation on account of a unity of identifiable physical and mental traits. Human groups, to which the zoological notion of race applies, today are to be found only within those areas untouched by world history and the mixing of peoples that it produces. Among world historical peoples there are no pure races, on account of the countless occurrences of mixing that took place in prehistoric and historical periods. Certainly, there is the ideal concept of "the Teuton," and there are numerous individuals of this Germanic type; but there is no larger or more coherent ethnological group of Germans. So-called Teutonic or Germanic Völker, such as the Germans, English, and Scandinavians, emerged out of numerous mixings of Saxons, Celts, Slavs, Mediterranean peoples, Jews, and others, and only over the course of many centuries of inbreeding and adaptation (sharing climate, ways of life, language, education, political forms, religions, and historical fate) were they blended together into Völker of a certain unified character. Nonetheless, one cannot identify this as race, but at most as ethnoculture (approximately identical to the idea of nation). Within the nation, the different constitutive races appear to a degree pure, but to a much greater degree in mixed form. Thus, they provide a particular nation with a particular "racial" stamp vis-à-vis other nations, while these Völker themselves are made up of other components. For instance, the German Volk is characterized by the relative frequency of the Teutonic type, the Russian by the Slavic, and the Italian by the Mediterranean; at the same time, however, there is also often found to a not inconsiderable degree all other types of races mixed in: for instance, the Slavs in the eastern part of Germany, the Alpine type in the south; in Russia the Teutonic type in the west, in the east, the Mongolian; and so forth. Truly, one ought not to speak of a homogeneous or immutable racial character among any of the great nations within the European or Near Eastern cultural spheres.

## 2. THE JEWS AS A RACE

The Jews, too, considered as a cultural phenomenon, emerged out of a mixture of many different races and cultural peoples. They are made up of certain human groups of various origins who were joined together first as a religious, then as a cultural, and finally as a political unity; and through a centuries-long process of inbreeding and reciprocal physical and intellectual assimilation, and through the leveling influences of a common environment and a common fate, were melded into one coherent group characterized by a distinct and unified type: the Jew. According to the, on the whole, reliable evidence found in the Bible, the Jews were constituted from the following identifiable groups:

(a) The families of the patriarchs, "the descendants of Terach," who came from southern Babylon (Ur in the Chaldees), and around 2200 wandered from north Babylon (Haran in Padan-Aram) to Canaan. As Babylonians, they belonged—in terms of biological race—in all probability to the Arab-Iranian mixed contingent of the Mediterranean race (*mittelländischen Rasse*).

(b) The Hittites who, during the period of the entry of the patriarchs (into Canaan), made up the ruling class within the Canaanite population and intermarried with the patriarchs—the conversion of slaves and mixed marriage being legal. In antiquity the Hittites were representative of the Armenian type [. . .] and transmitted to the Jewish Volk certain elements that in Europe—especially in caricature—are deemed particularly Jewish: slight stature; smooth skull; a bent, birdlike [literally, candle-snuffer] nose; a minor slanting of the eyes; a tendency toward obesity; and short, slightly bent limbs. [The transmission of these elements] began at the time of the patriarchs and continued with the second conquest of the land of Canaan; it occurred through an intensive process of intermixture of Hittites with Jews.

(c) Egyptians from the period of the "Egyptian enslavement" (around 1200 [BCE]) and through intermarriages, the purchasing of slaves, and slave conversions that are testified to in numerous places in the Bible, Arabic-Negroid elements became part of the Jews (large eyes, a dark complexion, black woolly hair, protruding lips, large teeth [. . .]).

(d) Arabs, through the union of the patriarchal tribes, who came out of Egypt, with the "Hebrews" (the tribes of Israel around the year 1000 [BCE]) who were nomadic Bedouins of the Arabic type; they are today often designated as the "beautiful Orientals" among the Jews, and are found above all among the Jews of Spain and North Africa.

(e) Canaanites, who were a population that mixed Arabic Semites of an older cultural stratum (the so-called Amorites) with more recently immigrated Babylonian, Egyptian, and Hittite transmitters of culture (*Kulturträger*), who came there by virtue of colonization and foreign rule. These latter were only gradually absorbed by the Judah-Israel tribes invading Canaan, through military means (enslavement, conversion of military captives, concubinage of captured women), and later through peaceful means of assimilation and intermarriage (1000–800 BC). (This, according to the theory of [Felix] von Luschan.[39] [. . .]).

(f) Blond Germanic elements, absorbed over many centuries, first through military means (enslavement), then through peaceful assimilatory intermarriage with the Philistines, who were quite likely of Nordic origins and who belong to the blond type (900–400 BC).

(g) Greeks and Romans, through intermarriage and the absorption of slaves during the centuries of Hellenism and Roman rule in Judea (300 BC to 70 BC).

(h) Converts from all of the peoples who made up the civilized world at the time, during the centuries of the decline and decay of antiquity, the conversion of pagans, and the abolishment of slavery (from 1 to 1000 [CE]): peoples such as the Arabs, Egyptians, Babylonians, Syrians, Persians, Armenians, Greeks, Romans, Berbers, Germans, Celts, Slavs, Hungarians, etc.

### 3. ASHKENAZIM AND SEPHARDIM

After the destruction of Jerusalem, the Jewish Volk was dispersed, through exile, into the Diaspora as two distinct groups: a Northeastern group that spread

39. [Felix von Luschan (1854–1924) was an anthropologist and professor at the University of Berlin.]

out through Turkey, the Balkans, northern Italy, Germany, Hungary, Austria, Poland, Galicia, and southern and western Russia; and a southwestern group that settled in the greater Arabian cultural spheres, in North Africa and in Southern Europe from the Bosporus to Spain. Due to completely different historical trajectories, milieus, intellectual and physical developments; through intermarriage and assimilation with and into two thoroughly different ethno-racial and cultural spheres; and on account of the different realities of the northern and southern climates (the brightness of the north), these two groups developed into two distinct types, the German or Ashkenazic, and the Spanish or Sephardic Jew. The Ashkenazim are Germanized and Slavicized, the Sephardim are Mediterraneanized Jews. Of the Sephardim, a large number disappeared after the expulsion from Spain (1492) on account of persecution, forced baptism, and assimilation in later periods.

### 4. FOREIGN TRIBES

Of the various components or elements of the Jewish Volk mentioned thus far, which have been completely integrated into the body of the Jewish Volk through hundreds of years of assimilation, intermarriage, and inbreeding, it is necessary to strictly differentiate those "Jews" who, in all likelihood, have accepted the Jewish faith as outsiders and call themselves Jews. These remain distinct autonomous Völker, without actually having mixed through intermarriage [with other Jews], and thus retain their anthropological and ethnological distinctiveness. Such foreign races of the Jewish faith are:

(a) The Yemenite Jews of Arabia, believed to be descendants of southern Arabian (*himjarish*) tribes, and who around 450 [CE] became Jews.

(b) The Falashas in Abyssinia [Ethiopia]—a mixed group living by the Red Sea, made up of whites and Negroes (?) and numbering approximately 50,000 (?) individuals.[40]

(c) The Caucus Jews on the Caspian Sea, Georgian (*Grusinich*) tribes of Iranian racial descent, who later mixed with the Kyrgyz (Mongolians of the Volga region); they were, probably, converted to Judaism by Persian Jews. The latter intermarried with the converts, so that the Georgian Jews are a combination of three different races: Semitic Jewish, Aryan Iranian, and Mongolian Turanian.

40. [Question marks in the original.]

(d) The black Jews of the *Kallah Israel* in Bombay. [. . .] These are Hindustanis who were probably converted to Judaism by Spanish Jews, and today live as "black Jews" in proximity to the "white Jews" (descendants of the Spanish) on the Malabar Coast (compare to Negro Jews).[41]

(e) The Chinese Jews in the province of Hunan.

(f) The Mawambu Negroes, of the Loango Coast, who follow Jewish ritual (compare to Negro Jews).

(g) The Chazars.

These foreign tribes were brought to Jewry, though not to the Jewish Volk, through conversion. They belong today to the Jewish community of faith; however, they are in no way a part of the Jewish Volk. Through their relatively vibrant participation in the recent colonization efforts in Palestine, there could possibly occur there in the future a consolidation of these racial elements, as new components of the body of the Jewish Volk, and thus influence the contemporary type of Jew.

## 5. ANTHROPOLOGY

The general genealogy of civilized Völker from various races, a history we have sketched above, and in particular the abundant transformations found in the racial history of the Jews, is the reason that all attempts to characterize contemporary civilized Völker anthropologically remained without result. Aside from the facts that the criteria of anthropology (cranial measurements, body size, skin and hair color, hair texture, etc.) are in the main unreliable and insufficient, and that statistical results tend to be exploited and interpreted in a wide variety of ways, it is the multitude of components and the great number of intermixings that make it impossible to establish indices for any civilized Volk, let alone for the Jews—whose racial history is more multifaceted and problematic than that of any other Volk. All of the theories put forth by race theorists about "the Jews as a race" are premature and untenable. There still is no methodological scientific (*fachwissenschaftlich*) basis for building such theories. The few anthropological investigations carried out on Jews thus far [. . .] can be considered only as precursors to a future anthropology of the Jews, which requires large-scale, systematic, decades-long inquiries. And one can predict the results of such investigations

41. [The reference is to Aron Sandler, "Negerjuden, schwartze Juden," in *Jüdisches Lexikon*—also the source for this selection—(Berlin: Jüdischer Verlag, 1930), 4:447.]

with a fair amount of certainty, given the evidence already accumulated and the theoretical assumptions that will be brought to bear: there will be considerable anthropological differences among the groups investigated, produced by variations of environment. Whether these differences ought to also be interpreted as "racial"—that is, as a matter of historical antecedents—or as secondary environmental influences will be difficult, if not impossible, to decide. In general, the interpretation of established facts of anthropology, once these facts had been established, has thus far always proved itself to be very problematic. It [interpretation] is to be initiated and conducted with utmost caution. One really ought not to expect anthropology to arrive at a solution to the racial problem as racial theory conceives of it, given that it [racial theory] associates the notion of race with cultural worth. The former [anthropology] only grasps the somatic aspect, which in general possesses only a very limited value for judgments regarding psychological, moral, and cultural characteristics.

# 5 | On the Origins and Race of the Jews

## Arthur Ruppin

"The Composition of the Jews in Palestine," chapter 1 of *Soziologie der Juden* (Berlin: Jüdischer Verlag, 1930), vol. 1.

The work's title page informs readers that the material in the two-volume *Soziologie der Juden* (Sociology of the Jews) derives from lectures delivered at Hebrew University in Jerusalem. Arthur Ruppin (1876–1943) was born in Posen, then a district of Prussia. He studied law and national economy at the Universities of Berlin and Halle. After a short stint as a lawyer, in 1904 he accepted the position of director of the newly founded Bureau of Jewish Statistics in Berlin. In this capacity, Ruppin was responsible for the publication of the *Zeitschrift für Demographie und Statistik der Juden* (The journal of the demography and statistics of the Jews), which he edited with his assistant Jakob Thon. Ruppin was keenly interested in the question of the Jews as a race, and the theme appears in almost all of his most important writings. His most influential work was *Die Juden der Gegenwart* (The Jews of today), published first in 1904 and then in a revised edition in 1911. See the entry in the *Encyclopedia Judaica*, 14:430–31.

### 1. THE THREE VOLK ELEMENTS: CANAANITE, BEDOUIN, PHILISTINE

The Jewish people emerged during the fourteenth and fifteenth centuries before Christ, when Palestine was controlled by Egypt, and its cities ruled by the nomarchs of the pharaoh. During this time, according to the biblical account, a nomadic people—the "sons of Jacob"—came from the desert, advancing into the eastern part of Jordan, and then went on to western Jordan. They were perhaps identical to the "Chabiri" (= Hebrews?) who had invaded from the East, mentioned in fourteenth-century reports made to the pharaoh by Palestinian landlords, and discovered at Tel-el-Amarna. These sons of Jacob subjugated the inhabitants of Palestine, the Canaanites or Amorites.[42] In the ensuing period,

42. According to Kautzsch (*Das Alte Testament*, Tübingen 1922, commentary on Genesis 15:19), the Canaanites and the Amorites are identical; in his view, the name "Amorite" was used by the Elohistic writer, and the name "Canaanite" by the Jawhist biblical source. Ac-

the sons of Jacob gradually amalgamated with the other inhabitants of the land and became one Volk, which has commonly been named the Israelites, the sons of Israel. Later, the Israelites engaged in fierce battles with the Philistines. The Philistines had launched an attack by sea against the Egyptians from their dwelling place in Caphtor (Crete) in the year 1196 BC. They were, however, fended off by Ramses III, and then settled on the Mediterranean coast of Palestine—giving it its name (Philistina = Palestine). The struggles between these two peoples, which lasted for centuries, ended with the Philistines losing their ethnic unity and being amalgamated into the Israelite Volk.

Thus, there are three Volk elements out of which the Jewish people in Palestine were composed: the sons of Jacob, the Canaanites, and the Philistines. The Philistines belong—like the Greeks of antiquity—to the Aegean cultural circle, and brought the highly evolved Cretan culture (for example, iron tools and chariots of war) to Palestine. Considering that Palestine was a small land without permanent natural borders, and that for thousands of years it had been a point of entry (a bridge) for the Aramaeans living to the north and for the Bedouins living to the east and to the south, the Canaanites have to be seen as a cross between Aramaeans and Bedouins. The same goes for the sons of Jacob. The Bible reports that the *heros eponymos* [founder of a people or nation] of the Israelites, Abraham, came from Haran in Aram-Naharajim[43] and identifies Jacob explicitly as an Aramaean (Deuteronomy 26:5). On the other hand, it appears that before their entry into Palestine, the sons of Jacob united and intermixed with a Sinai Bedouin tribe, called the Kenites.

It has been claimed repeatedly that already in the second millennium before Christ, or even earlier, a blond Volk, belonging to a Northern European race, made its way from Northern Europe to Palestine during a period of great migration. Various researchers think they can prove, on the basis of visual depictions found in Egyptian tombs, that the Amorites were blond and blue-eyed,

---

cording to Albright (*Journal of the Palestine Oriental Society*, vol. 8, p. 255, Jerusalem, 1928), the name "Canaanite" refers to the inhabitants of the coastal plains, the name "Amorite" to the inhabitants of the mountainous regions and the lands east of the Jordan. In any case, in terms of origins and language, the Canaanites and the Amorites are closely related.

43. The claim that Abraham came from Ur in the Chaldees is a later addition. Aram-Naharijm is not the land of the two rivers, Mesopotamia, but the Egyptian Narina or Naharin: northern Syria with Aleppo as the capital. (Kautzsch, et al., commentary on Genesis, 24:10).

belonging to this Northern European race.[44] However, this proof has turned out to be unsound, since the blond and blue colors on the visual images were not originally present, but emerged only as a result of the flaking off of a black top coat.[45] It is, however, conceivable that in the seventh century BCE a part of the invading Scythian tribes, who are of Northern European descent and appear to have been related to today's Kurds, had settled permanently in Palestine. The name Scythopolis, which Josephus gives for the city of Beisan in the upper Jordan Valley, indicates the settlement of Scythians in that place. Given such proximity of a population of a Northern European race, a sporadic influx of Northern European racial blood (*Rassenblutes*) into the Jewish Volk is generally conceivable. However, we know that although at all times half-nomadic peoples such as the Scythians displayed in their [campaigns of] conquest enormous force and speed, their actual numbers were nonetheless small. It is therefore not very likely that the Scythians influenced the Jews racially in any discernible way, especially since their dominance in Palestine lasted for such a short period.

## 2. THE THREE RACIAL COMPONENTS

Thus, the three elements of the Jewish people originate in northern Syria (Aramaeans), in the Arabic-Sinaitic steppes (Bedouins), and in Southern Europe (Philistines). The Völker who lived in these regions in antiquity were differentiated from one other on account of physical characteristics or, as we might also label them, racial traits.[46]

44. Hans Günther, *Rassenkunde der jüdischen Volkes* (Munich, 1930), p. 56.

45. On this see the report of Max Burchardt, who shortly before the World War led a scientific expedition to Egypt to research the visual depictions of foreign peoples by Egyptians, in *Zeitschrift für Demographie und Statistik der Juden*, Berlin, 1927, p. 7.

46. Among the abundant literature on the Jewish race, see the following: R. Andree, *Zur Volkskunde der Juden* (Leipzig, 1881); Joseph Jacobs, "On the Racial Characteristics of Modern Jews," in *Journal of the Anthropological Institute*, vol. 15, London, 1893; A. H. Sayce, *The Races of the Old Testament* (London, 1893); S. Weissenberg, "Die südrissischen Juden," *Archiv für Anthropologie*, vol. 23, p. 348; Elkind, *Evrei* (Moscow, 1902), in Russian; M. J. Judt, *Die Juden als Rasse* (Warsaw, 1902; German edition Berlin, 1903); Maurice Fishberg, *The Jews* (New York, 1911); F. v. Luschan, *The Early Inhabitants of Western Asia* (London, 1911); I. Zollschan, *Das Rassenproblem* (Vienna, 1912); Fritz Kahn, *Die Juden als Rasse und Kulturvolk* (Berlin, 1920); F. v. Luschan, *Völker, Rassen, Sprachen* (Berlin, 1922); Wagenseil, *Beiträge zur physischen Anthropologie der sefardischen Juden und zur jüdischen Rassenfrage* (Stuttgart, 1922); S. Feist, *Stammeskunde der Juden* (Leipzig, 1925); H. Günther, *Rassenkunde des jüdischen Volkes*

FIGURE 5.1

The first component, the Aramaeans, were political heirs to the ancient Hittite Empire, which reached the heights of its power around approximately 2000 BC, and whose sphere of influence reached from its capital Hattusas (today, Boghaszköi, near Angora) deep into the Near East and Syria, and eastward far beyond the Euphrates. When this empire started to decline, sometime around 1500 BC, a part of it was preserved under the rule of the Aramaeans in northern Syria, with Sendschirli[47] (near Alexandrette) its capital; they remained an independent empire until the eighth century, an empire whose southern border, at the time of Solomon, reached Damascus. Judging from the stone monuments found in Sendschirli, the Aramaean type possessed a small, thickset stature, with short limbs; a thick, curved nose; a broad face; and broad skull (see plate 1 [fig. 5.1]). Even the excavations made by Baron von Oppenheim in the city of Tel-Halaf (east of the Euphrates), which was founded by Hittites, and inhabited by Aramaeans, show this same type (see plates 2 and 3 [figs. 5.2 and 5.3]). This type was rather preponderant throughout Syria and Assyria in the first pre-Christian millennium, just as the Aramaic language at this time dominated the entire

(Munich, 1930). Aside from Weissenberg and Wagenseil, who are mentioned above, anthropometric examinations of Jews have been conducted by Miss Dr. Lipieç (Warsaw), who published her results in numerous publications.

47. [Zincirli or Zinjirli, was an ancient city in what is today southeastern Turkey.]

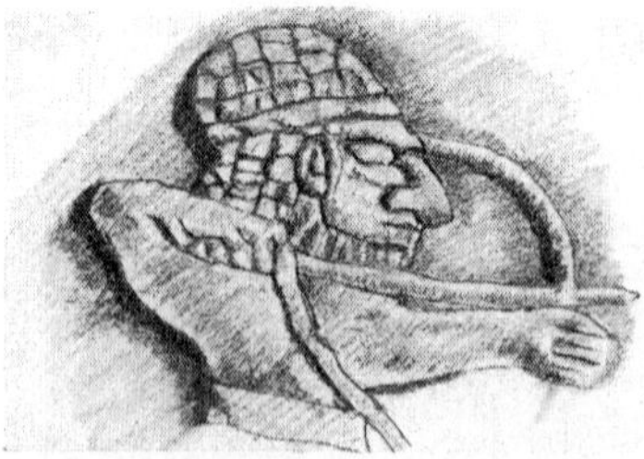

FIGURE 5.2

FIGURE 5.3

region. When today's anti-Semitic caricaturists portray Jews with thick, curved noses and short limbs, they are actually showing the Aramaean or the Aramaic component within contemporary Jewry.

However, another type with such a prominent, protruding, very large, straight nose was to be found in Sendschirli (see plate 4 [fig. 5.4]). This type appears to have been dominant among the Hittites proper, in Asia Minor—as the findings in Boghaszköi demonstrate—remnants of which survived within the Aramaean Empire.

We are also taught about the appearance of the Aramaeans (North Syrians) by Egyptian representations; for example, a relief from the Temple of Ramses, in Medinet Habu, from approximately the year 1350 [BCE] which shows Ramses[48] slaying his Syrian enemies (see plate 6 [fig. 5.6]); and a mural from the grave of Sebekhetep in Carnak from the fifteenth century [BCE], which shows a legation from Rethen (northern Syria) bringing tribute to the pharaoh (see plate 5 [fig. 5.5]).

In racial theory, the type that possesses the anatomical traits of the Aramaeans is designated as a "Near Eastern race" (*vorderasiatische Rasse*). The Assyrians also belong to this race, as the statues of Assyrian kings from the ninth and eighth centuries [BCE] show; these display with particular prominence the broad skull, the curved nose, and the massive physique (see plate 7 [fig. 5.7]). It is possible that the Assyrian sculptors have even exaggerated the curvature and thickness of the nose somewhat, since, like the "eagle's nose" of the Prussian nobility, this was perhaps considered a mark of [social] distinction. The Jewish nose is different from the noble nose in that the noble nose proceeds straight out from the base

48. [Ruppin is referring to the Temple of Ramses II. The date 1350 here, however, is not correct, as Ramses II reigned in the thirteenth century BCE.]

FIGURE 5.4

FIGURE 5.5

FIGURE 5.6

of the nose, and the bend or curve begins only in the middle; the bridge of the nose is small. The Jewish nose, in contrast, displays the curvature throughout, from the base of the nose to the tip, which is usually thick. Interestingly, a small Egyptian statuette, from the period around 1700 BC,[49] shows an Egyptian Hyksos king in the shape of a sphinx and with a characteristic "Jewish nose," pinching the ears of an Egyptian [subject] kneeling in front of him.

49. In the British Museum, 5th Egypt Room, Vitrine F, No. 54678.

FIGURE 5.7

The second component of the Israelite Volk, the Bedouins, were the equivalent of today's Bedouins of the Arabic steppes and the Sinai Peninsula. This is to say that they were of tall, slender stature, with long limbs; a narrow, straight nose; and narrow face; and were dolichocephalic. If one can say about the Aramaeans that their anatomies tend toward being thickset and large, so the Bedouins' tend toward the long and slender. Eugen Fischer[50]—and, following him, H. Günther[51]—have recently introduced the designation of "Oriental" race into racial theory to designate those of this Bedouin type. Both scholars describe this race as closely akin to the Mediterranean race, which constitutes one of the three major branches of the white race. It is, therefore, arguably preferable to speak of this race as a variant (a racial branch) of the Mediterranean race, which in turn then would have to be divided into an Oriental (what Günther calls "eastern") and Occidental ("western") racial branch.

The Philistines, the third component, were of medium stature, with a rather narrow, straight nose and a narrow face, and were dolichocephalic. They constitute, along with the other Mediterranean peoples, the occidental (western) branch of the Mediterranean race. On Egyptian reliefs, they are represented with a head ornament of bird feathers (see plate 8 [fig. 5.8]). In contrast to the other Völker we have mentioned here, they did not wear beards.

All three components had white skin of various tones, from the fair white of the Aramaeans to the brownish white of the Philistines and the light brown of the Bedouins. They had dark hair and dark eyes.

The Jews of Palestine, who were constituted out of these three components, accordingly also displayed the bodily traits of these three components, either in a pure way or as a mixture of one with another. Redcliffe N. Salaman identifies the Philistines as a significant element in the racial composition of the

50. *Menschliche Erblichkeitslehre* (Munich, 1927), vol. 1, p. 162.

51. *Rassenkunde des jüdische Volkes* (Munich, 1930), p. 68.

FIGURE 5.8

Jews.[52] He seeks to explain the frequent presence of the Greek type among today's Jews, which he calls "Pseudo-Gentiles," with reference to this impact [of the Philistines]. The question, however, is whether these Pseudo-Gentiles cannot just as well be traced back to the influence of the Oriental racial branch. Felix v. Luschan—who, in a multitude of works, has engaged with the issue of Jewish racial composition[53]—noticed, during his research trips through the Near East and northern Syria, the surprising similarity of the European Jews with many Near Eastern Armenians, with the Syrians of north Syria, and with the representations of the Hittite Aramaeans found on the reliefs of Sendschirli; he has concluded from this that the majority of Jews belongs to this Near Eastern–northern Syrian type, which he calls "Armenoid." Other authors, in contrast, have found an unexpected similarity between the Jews and many Arabian (Bedouin) tribes. All three hypotheses have some truth to them. It is correct, as v. Luschan claims, that one finds individuals among today's Jews who are similar to Syrians and Armenians. But it is also correct that among the Jews there exist individuals who display a great similarity to the Bedouins or Southern Europeans. Had v. Luschan made his research trips not in the Near East, but in Arabia or southern Italy, he would perhaps not have called attention to the similarity of the Jews with the Syrians or Armenians, but rather with the Arabian Bedouins or the Southern Europeans. Still, he did come closest to the truth as, in terms of percentage, the

52. "Racial Origins of Jewish Types," in *Transactions of the Jewish Historical Society of England*, vol. 9, London, 1920; in addition, "What Has Become of the Philistines?," in *Qua[r]terly Statement of Palestine Exploration Fund*, vol. 57, p. 37, London, 1925.

53. See especially "Die Rassenstellung der Juden," in *Korresp.-Blatt der Anthropol. Gesellschaft*, 1892; in addition, *Zeitschrift f. Demogr. und Statistik der Juden*, 1905, p. 1, Berlin. [Felix von Luschan was one of Ruppin's teachers at the University of Berlin.]

Near Eastern–north Syrian type is most strongly represented among today's Central and Eastern European Jews.

Beyond this, v. Luschan's contribution has been to save the racial study of the Jews from the false path onto which linguistic researchers had led it. Heretofore, on account of the closeness of Hebrew to other Semitic languages, the Jews have been linked mainly with other Semitic-speaking peoples, and in particular with the purest representatives, the Bedouin Arabs; the most "authentic" Jews, in this view, are racially related to the Bedouins, and must be dolichocephalic. Von Luschan's theory stood in direct opposition to this, since the "Armenoids" were decisively brachycephalic and both in antiquity and today belonged linguistically not to the Semites, but to the Indo-Germans. Only through this repudiation of the "Semite theory" was the way cleared for the first time for unbiased research into the Jewish race.[54]

When, after the destruction of the Kingdom of Judea (586 BC), a considerable portion of the Jews were led from Palestine to Babylonia, they maintained their religious particularity; yet they also absorbed converts from among the inhabitants of Babylonia and later from Persia, after the Persians conquered Babylon. However, this absorption of foreign blood should have had no influence, particularly on those Jews who, after seventy years of exile, returned to Palestine from Babylonia under the leadership of Ezra and Nehemiah. The relative short time of their stay in Babylonia, and the fact that it was precisely those pious, esteemed Jews who were careful to separate themselves from the pagans who returned to Palestine appears to justify the assertion that they returned from Babylonia with nearly the same racial traits that they had [originally] brought with them from Palestine. In Palestine itself, Ezra placed particular importance on keeping the pure families clear from intermixture with foreign elements, and made sure that foreign Volk elements would be purged. Therefore, at the time of the Second Temple's destruction, the Jews in Palestine were racially constituted more or less as they had been at the time of the destruction of the First Temple. The absorption of the Bedouin Edomites that occurred in the meantime only led to a certain strengthening of the Bedouin element.

Following the results laid out above, the racial lineage (genealogical tree)

54. In an article on the racial status of the Jews, which v. Luschan wrote in 1905 at my request for the journal *Zeitschrift für Demographie und Statistik der Juden*, he declared: "It is as great a confusion of terms to speak of a Semitic race as to speak of a dolichocephalic language. The word 'Semitic' belongs to linguistics, not to the study of race." *Zeitschrift für Demographie und Statistik der Juden*, 1905, p. 1.

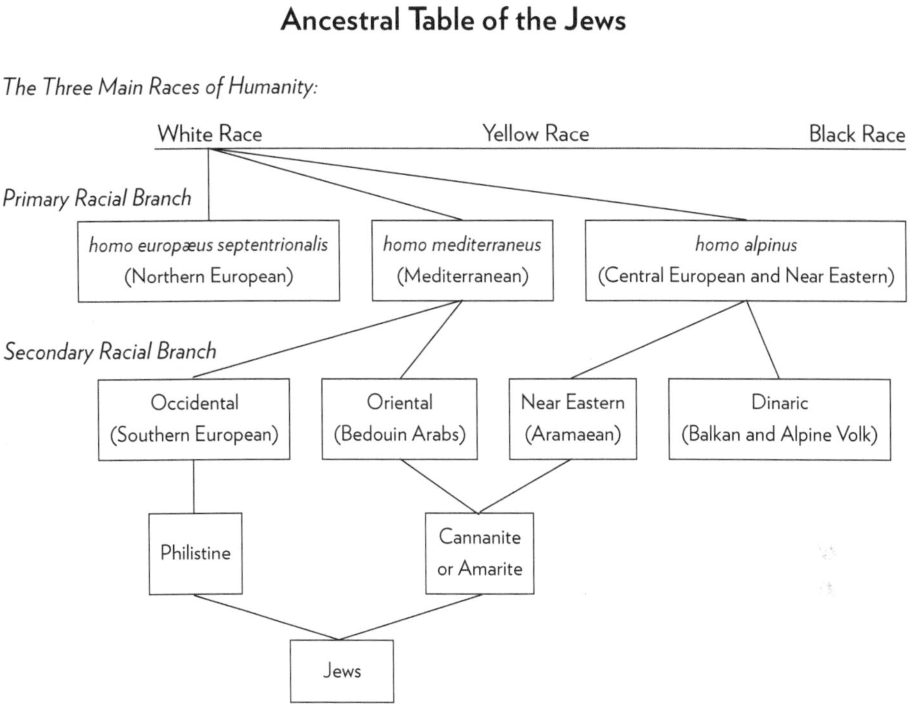


FIGURE 5.9

of the Jews in Palestine at the time of the destruction of Jewish sovereignty is offered in [figure 5.9 above]. We avail ourselves of the most commonly used racial categories in anthropology. Let it be noted, to avoid any misunderstanding, that this racial classification—like every subdivision of race—is of course purely arbitrary. Instead of invoking skin color, hair and eye color, or the shape of the head, which are used here as the most important differentiating traits, one could employ any other anatomical characteristics as the foundation for such classification.[55] The decisive factor employed by zoology to distinguish between species (the only absolute distinction that can be drawn to divide species and to maintain their idiosyncrasy)—namely, the capability of reproduction within

55. Botany progressed from the arbitrary system of Linnaeus, which took into consideration only one trait (the filament), to a "natural" system that bases itself on the different structural forms (designs) of nature that are evident in plants, and seeks to make that the foundation of its classifications. Anthropology has still not been able to leave the arbitrary system of classification behind.

the same species and the lack of that capability between different species—is of no use in distinguishing human races, since all humans are capable of reproducing with each other. The division of human beings into races and subraces also remains incomplete, insofar as the various races are connected to one another through crossings, leaving the racial identity of certain individuals in doubt. Nonetheless, the concept of races offers us a framework within which we may orient ourselves in regard to the chaos of individual differences by connecting that which is more closely related.

In racial theory, the most common racial division of humanity is that which classifies races into white, yellow, and black. The white race falls into the three branches of Northern European, Mediterranean, and Alpine. Within the Mediterranean branch, one finds the division between the Oriental (Bedouin) and Occidental branches; within the Alpine branch, the [subdivision between the] Near Eastern and the Dinaric. Within this terminological framework, the Jews are derived out of a mixture of the Near Eastern branch of the Alpine race with the Oriental and Occidental branches of the Mediterranean race.

# II | Anthropology

Anthropology was central to the discussion of race. And anthropology, as a discipline, was largely defined before the 1920s and 1930s by research into physical characteristics—rather than, say, cultural practices. Racialism, ultimately, posits a direct correlation between the external and the internal, between physical and nonphysical—for example, intellectual, spiritual, and moral—traits. Thus, skin color or head shape was seen not only or mainly as a physical attribute, but as an indication of a particular individual's or group's intellectual, political, and cultural capabilities.

Jewish anthropologists were also interested in the shape of skulls and the color of skin, hair, and eyes, and the texts in this section are intended to offer a small sample of this engagement with physical anthropology. Jewish racial thinkers, like almost all racial thinkers at the time, were also preoccupied with the ancient world, in particular with what the Bible could tell us about racial origins and history. Unlike racial theorists in general, however, Jewish racial thinkers did not appear overly interested in the earliest anthropological accounts in the Bible: the Genesis narratives about the creation of the first humans and the subsequent peopling of the earth. Jewish racial thinkers focused less on Genesis and more on Exodus and the other books that recounted the origins of the Jews as a people.

Thus, a number of the texts in this section are concerned with ancient history, with examining the relations between the Hebrew tribes that settled in Canaan and the native peoples already inhabiting the land. What was the extent of sexual intermixing between these tribes? Was it extensive enough to make a real difference in the racial makeup of the Hebrews, and thus the Jews? (Such questions will also, of course, be central to the texts in part 5, on "Racial Mixing.") What impact did dispersion in the Diaspora, and subsequent differences in climate and environment, have on the Jewish body and character? Are Jews today racially more or less homogeneous, or do they more closely resemble the non-Jews in whose midst they live than they do Jews on the other side of the world? Such questions were of interest in and of themselves to Jewish and non-Jewish thinkers; they constituted a crucial component of the scientific enterprise. But, as with almost all racial texts, they also bore on political and social issues that were never far in the background.

# 6 | Introduction to the Anthropological Study of the Jews

## Édward Goldstein

"Introduction à l'étude anthropologique des Juifs," *Revue d'anthropologie*, series 3a, 8 (1885): 639–75.

Édward Goldstein (1844–1920) was a Polish Jewish anthropologist and author. The *Revue d'anthropologie* was the preeminent anthropological journal in France in the late nineteenth century. Its editors in chief were Paul Broca (1824–80) and Paul Topinard (1830–1911), France's leading anthropologists in this period.

The Jews appeal to the anthropologist in a very special way: that of an experiment conducted century after century on a people who would have been submitted to the most varied climatic conditions and social surroundings. They are, in effect, a unique example of what differences in habitat, on the one hand, and isolation, on the other hand, as well as the intermingling of blood with other human groups, can do to men whose origins and filiations have been better recorded than those of any other known people.

For the linguist, the Jews also present conditions of particular interest, for their history is written in the idiom typical of the family of Semitic languages, and moreover, the variations of this idiom may be pursued through the ages, which has enabled the establishment of the chronology of Hebrew texts.

When the Jews ceased speaking this language in order to adopt others, they transcribed their documents in all of these languages: they contributed in this way to the linguistics of new sacred texts.

On the other hand, the different dialects observed among them in Palestine, and in modern times the development of their jargons in certain countries, allow for the study of the various laws that govern the phonetic transformations and the different modes of modification of the language.

The linguists themselves, through the analysis of the language and all of its variations, have supplied precious information about the history of this people's migrations; and history in turn thus was able to become a mine of information for anthropology.

As for the statistician, he can, in studying the Jews, establish with a certain precision the influence of social surroundings on the prosperity of a human group, on marriage, birth rate, death rate—in short, on what was called demography and what can, it seems, be named more rightly biostatistics.

Given therefore that the study of Jews is equally appealing for the anthropologist, the historian, the linguist, and the statistician, it is not surprising that numerous important works in each of these fields of study have been published quite recently.

Before beginning personal research on the anthropology of the Jews, it seemed to us that beforehand, it was indispensable to spell out clearly the results already acquired.

The complexity of the subject demands that, for more clarity, we establish divisions. These present themselves quite naturally in the following manner:

(1) Successive phases through which the study of the Jewish race has passed.

(2) Formative elements of Jewish nationality before the dispersion.

(3) Dispersion of Jews on the surface of the globe and influence of local elements, social surroundings, and intersections on the remnants of this nationality.

(4) Research to begin on the study of the anthropological problems concerning the Jews.

We will approach the various aspects of our subject in this order. This manner of dividing it will permit us to classify all of the material scattered here and there. Once the terrain is cleared, we will easily see where all of the research has led us, and this, in turn, will allow us to recognize the problems that remain to be resolved.

## 1. SUCCESSIVE PHASES THROUGH WHICH THE STUDY OF THE JEWISH RACE HAS PASSED

From the very beginning of anthropology, we have been preoccupied with the Jewish type, with all the characteristics of which the Jew is composed; but with this comes the preconceived idea that the Jewish race, preserved by its isolation, was for anthropology the pure race par excellence. In this way, we began to assume as dogma the purity and integrity of the Jewish race to such an extent that this alleged racial purity, which we never even considered challenging, was invoked as an argument by partisans of diametrically opposed ideas, such as the champions of the unity of the human race, as well as those who champion the plurality of the origin of humanity—by monogenesists as well as by polygenesists.

Taking this preconceived idea as a point of departure, the monogenesists make use of it as an argument in favor of their doctrine. Their most authoritative representative, Prichard,[1] presents the following thesis:

> The Jews took their physical characteristics from the nations in the midst of which they resided long-term, and even so, they can still be identified by certain particular traits of their physiognomy.
>
> In the northern lands of Europe, they have white skin; the English Jews generally have blue eyes and blond hair; in some parts of Germany, one may see many with a red beard; in Portugal, they are dark-skinned . . .
>
> The Jews who have settled in the province of Cochin seem to have established their residence there long ago. Today, they are black and so completely similar in coloring to the natives that Dr. Claudius Buchanan says that he cannot always distinguish them from the Hindus. (In Mattancherry, a city in Cochin, there is a particular colony of Jews who arrived in this country at a later time and who are called Jerusalem Jews or white Jews.) This leads to the understanding that the black color of the Jews, found in different parts of India, could depend upon mixing with the Hindus through marriage; but there is no proof that this supposition is well-founded; and on the contrary, it is probable that the conservation of Jews in these lands as a distinct people is due, there as elsewhere, only to their constant distance from any mixing with the natives.
>
> The Jesuits who were in China say positively that the Jews of Henan who have resided in this province for a good many centuries, still form a separate society, and marry only among themselves. There is reason to believe that the ancient Jewish inhabitants of the Cochin province were part of the same migration as those in China, and it is unlikely that they differed from their brothers as regards their relations with the natives.

We see that, for the monogenesists, all of the differences observed among the Jews of Europe concerning skin, eye, and hair color, and even the differences

1. J. C. Prichard, *The Natural History of Man*, Paris, 1843, vol. I, p. 196. [James Cowles Prichard (1786–1848) was an early-nineteenth-century English anthropologist and physician, and the author of the highly influential *Researches into the Physical History of Mankind*.]

as characteristic as the black Jews of Cochin present compared with others, are entirely due to the influence of their surroundings.

The polygenesists make use of the same argument, the purity of the Jewish race, in order to demonstrate the opposite thesis.

Rudolphi,[2] one of the most senior of the German representatives of polygenesis, says, for example, that which follows here:

> Despite their diverse habitats, their faces and their skulls have maintained their specific character. Blumenbach[3] represented this perfectly in his *Dec. Cran.*, figs. 28 and 34, the skull of a five-year-old girl and that of a hundred-year-old man, both of them Jews. At first glance, their Jewishness is plain for all to see (*das Juedische spingt gleich in die Augen*). The Jewish character not only leaves its imprint on the exterior or soft tissue, it even marks the bone structure.

Edwards,[4] treating the question seriously, summarizes the polygenesist doctrine with such clarity that we would have done a great disservice to ourselves had we not cited him word for word:

> The Jewish traits are so blatant that it is difficult to be mistaken about them, and, as he [the Jew] may be found in almost all the countries of Europe, there is no national figure more generally known or more recognizable. One may regard them [the Jews] as colonies of the same race established in these lands. For centuries, they have made up part of the population of the countries in which they settled, and if they did not participate in the benefits of government, they were not deprived of the liberty of living on the same soil, of breathing the same air, of enjoying the same sun. As they conserved their religion, their customs, and their practices, making few alliances with the

2. K. A. Rudolphi, *Beiträge zur Anthropologie und allgemeinen Naturgeschichte*, Berlin, 1812, p. 153.

3. [Johann Friedrich Blumenbach (1752–1840) was a German anthropologist and one of the earliest and most important racial theorists. Goldstein's reference to "*Dec. Cran.*" is to Blumenbach's work on images of skulls, *Decas prima collectionis suae craniorum diversarum gentium illustrata*, published between 1795 and 1820.]

4. W. F. Edwards, *The Physiological Characteristics of the Human Races*, Paris, 1829, p. 15. [William Frederic Edwards (1776?–1842) was a Jamaican-born physician and anthropologist who became a member of French scientific circles in Paris. He was known as the father of French ethnology. See Claude Blankaert, "On the Origins of French Ethnology: William Edwards and the Doctrine of Race," in *Bones, Bodies, Behavior: Essays in Behavioral Anthropology*, ed. George Stocking (Madison: University of Wisconsin Press, 1990), 18–55.]

people among whom they lived, it would be difficult to find conditions more conducive to drawing out the effects of climate.

First of all, climate did not assimilate them to the nations among whom they reside; and what is more important is that they all resemble one another even in diverse climates. An English, French, German, Italian, Spanish, or Portuguese Jew is still a Jew based on features, regardless of the nuances he presents; that is to say that they all have the same characteristics of shape and proportion—in a word, that which essentially constitutes a type.

In this way, the Jews of these diverse countries resemble one another to a far greater extent than they resemble the nations among whom they live; and the climate, despite the extensive duration of its action, has lent them only diversities of complexion and of expression, and perhaps other modifications equally as slight.

In spite of the ways in which they resemble one another everywhere, perhaps it does not necessarily follow that who they were formerly is who they are today. But if you want to be contented with a three-hundred-year-old species, I can provide you with undeniable proof. In Milan, I saw Leonardo da Vinci's *Last Supper*; the Jews of today are painted there trait for trait. No one has represented the national character like this great painter, all the while conserving the greatest diversity among individuals . . .

What was the Jewish type at the time of their dispersion? This is what would be important to know. Thus we would have a period of more than 1,700 years, during which climate would have had time to have an effect, and we would know what we should expect in a space that encompasses nearly half of historical time.

We could content ourselves with less; but if you were more exigent and if you wanted to know what the Jewish type was at a more remote time, I can tell you what it was three thousand years ago.

On the tomb of an Egyptian king there are, next to Ethiopian Negroes, two other groups of foreign nations, one of whom we recognized in a rather striking manner as the Jewish nation. The day before, I had seen Jews strolling in the streets of London: I may as well have been looking at their portraits . . .

Belzoni describes the figures on this tomb in the following passages:

One can make out Persians, Jews, and Ethiopians there: the first by virtue of their costumes, which may still be recognized in the paintings that represent their wars with the Egyptians; the Jews are recognizable by their physiognomy and their coloring, and the Ethiopians by the color of their skin and their jewelry.

Here is, therefore, a people that maintains the same type for a long series of centuries, encompassing almost all of known history; in the course of the first half of this period, experiencing unheard-of disasters; during the other half, dispersed in diverse climates, persecuted, shamed, vilified, forming a caste of pariahs, the discards of mankind. A more ideal assemblage of circumstances for profoundly modifying the physical organization of a people could not be imagined; it is therefore necessary that human nature had a great power of resistance in order to triumph over [such circumstances].

This keen example seemed like a rigorous experiment conducted with a view to observe the influence of diverse climates on human shapes and proportions over the entire span of historic centuries.

We see that, for Edwards, there is but a single Jewish type, unchanging in time and in space.

The opinions of certain erudite thinkers concerning research about the ten lost Jewish tribes, who were claimed to have been recognized every time someone found himself in the presence of some little-known people, are to be indirectly linked to this period.

[. . .]

After these discussions between monogenesists and polygenesists, discussions in which the unity of the Jewish race was but an argument invoked by turns in the two camps, the Anthropological Society of Paris inaugurated serious discussions about the origins of the Jewish race.

If we compare all of the opinions proposed by the eminent scholars who compose this society, we deduce from them the following:

(1) There are two well-defined types of Jews: the northern type of Jew or German and Polish Jews, called Ashkenazim, and the southern or Spanish and Portuguese Jews, called Sephardim.

Mr. Boudin[5] says on this subject: "It seems to me that one has not distinguished the Jews of southern France, called Portuguese Jews, from the northern Jews, called German Jews."[6]

Mr. Lagneau,[7] on the other hand, expresses himself thusly: "The Jews are no-

5. [Jean-Christian M. F. J. Boudin (1806–67) was a French physician and anthropologist.]

6. *Bulletin de la Societé d'Anthropologie de Paris*, vol. II, p. 410.

7. [Gustave Lagneau (1827–96) was a French physician and anthropologist.]

ticeable by the black color of their hair, their beard, their long eyelashes, their thick eyebrows, prominent and well-arched; by their dark, large, sharp eyes; by their smooth complexion and by their nose, strongly aquiline and straight at its base. However, in our eastern provinces, numerous inhabitants professing Judaism are blonds or redheads and present entirely different anthropological characteristics from those of the other Jews."[8]

(2) The blond Jews from the northern countries come from a mixing of Jews from Judea with the Germanic peoples, the Slavs, and the Khazars. We took advantage of the historical documents to establish that these mixings are due to conversions to Judaism, which, until the tenth century, took place in southern Russia as well as the Germanic and Slavic countries.

Mr. Boudin explains his opinion, founded before anything else on anthropological considerations: "I believe that in England as in Germany, it is the result of crossbreeding; never have two individuals with black hair and eyes produced blond children, and I am persuaded that the same question can apply to skull shape."[9]

[Paul] Broca supports the opinion of Boudin with historical considerations:

> Mr. Boudin, I think, was right to attribute the blond hair of certain Jews from Alsace and Germany to the mixing of the Jewish race with the blond races of the North.
>
> What guides the Jews in their alliances is not the question of race, it is the question of religion, and the argument would be valid only if all Israelites were Jews. Now, to say nothing of the individual proselytism that may have introduced some Christian renegades into Jewish families, there is a fact that I take to be well-established, regardless of how little known it is, which is that around the ninth century, a part of the Slavic peoples who occupied Poland and southern Russia embraced Judaism; Christian missionaries, in the following century, gained numerous converts, and the Christian religion did not delay in becoming predominant; but it is not probable that all of the Israelites of Slavic origin were made into Christians; in any case, there was a rather long period during which the Jews could have and must have, without breaking the prescriptions of their religion, contracted numerous alliances with their Slavic coreligionists.[10]

8. Ibid., vol. II, p. 389.

9. Ibid., vol. VI, p. 515.

10. *Bulletin de la Societé d'Anthropologie de Paris*, vol. II, p. 416–417.

Mr. Pruner-Bey [Pruner Bey][11] insists upon the same considerations, and moreover, he clarifies a particular point: the question of the Khazars.

> The conversion of the Khazars to the Jewish religion is a well-known fact. Were they converted by missionaries coming from Hungary where the Jews had already been established for a long time, or by Karaite missionaries coming from Crimea? This question is undecided for me, but it is probable that the present-day Jews of Caucasia still descend in part from these Khazars.
>
> Judaism also gained, during a slightly less remote period, converts from among the Russians.
>
> In Poland, after the triumph of Christianity, the Jews maintained their great influence for a long time, and it looks as though they often married Christian women, since in 1092 the Christian King Ladislaus was forced to forbid these alliances. He also prohibited Jews from taking Christian servants.[12]

(3) It remains uncertain whether the blond element appeared only after the dispersion of the Jews, or whether this blond element made its appearance when the Jews existed as a nation.

Mr. Boudin considers that the crossbreeding took place later: "I did not see a single blond among the southern Jews, whether in France or in Algeria, whereas I saw many of them among the Jews of Alsace. This is what drove me to put forward the hypothesis of racial crossbreeding subsequent to the dispersion of the Jews."[13]

Mr. Rémusat appears to hold on to his opinion without looking favorably on the preceding thesis. He invokes the Bible: "Mr. Boudin, in speaking to us of blond Jews, put forth the thought that they became blond following their crossbreeding with the Germanic peoples; but there were already blonds among the Jews in ancient Judea. To say nothing of the characters with blond hair mentioned several times in the Bible, I will remind you that there should be true blonds among the Jews, since the most ancient traditions represented Jesus Christ as a blond man."[14]

Mr. Pruner-Bey shares the same sentiment as Mr. Rémusat. He invokes the

11. [Franz Ignaz Pruner (1808–82) was a German anthropologist and physician. In the 1830s he traveled to Egypt, where he began work in public health. In 1849 he was named personal physician to Abbas Pasha, and given the honorary title of *bey*.]

12. Ibid., vol. II, p. 418.

13. Ibid., vol. II, p. 412.

14. *Bulletin de la Societé d'Anthropologie de Paris*, vol. II, pp. 411–412.

observations made about living Jews and about paintings conserved on ancient monuments:

> But on the other hand, it is just as impossible to prove that those Jews of Egypt, Syria, and Italy who have blond, brown, or even red hair (the latter are rare) are all products of crossbreeding; in effect:
>
> The Hebrews, that is to say the descendants of Abraham, ordinarily belonged to the Aramaean branch of the Semitic line. The living remnants of this nation, who still speak Syriac, have a ruddy tint, even in Kurdistan, and they have for the most part blond hair and light eyes.
>
> The Canaanites are represented with red beards and hair on the most ancient monuments of Egypt.[15]

(4) There are entire populations who accepted Judaism, like the Falashas or Jews of Abyssinia; and there are, to the contrary, Jews who converted en masse to other religions.

The Jews of Abyssinia are well enough known that we did not provide citations. As for the second fact, it was presented to the Society by Mr. Topinard. He reminds us that there are some entire tribes of Israelites under negligible Kabylian influence: first, the Mehadjerids of Tuggurt, then a fraction of the tribe of the Zemoul near the Aïn-Feskia, the Wled-Zeiou, the Wled-Abdi, the Wled-Daoua, and the inhabitants of the villages of Mena and Mara. Moreover, he draws attention to the Hanenchas, parts of whom are composed exclusively of Jews who live as Arabs.

Mr. Topinard further cites the Beni-M'zab or Awbous, to the west of the Wed-R'ir and the Wargla. According to other authors, this Berber conglomeration descended from Israelites; it has retained a certain similarity in habits and characteristics.

They have the smooth brownish color, the intelligent physiognomy; blonds are rare among them; their beards are not thick; their eyes are black and almond-shaped; they are generally small in stature.

Mr. Topinard further indicates the existence of an Israelite tribe converted to Islam in the sixteenth century. They are the Mehadjerid of Tuggurt. They form a society apart, marry only among themselves, and have Jewish traits.

(5) Certain differences, with regard to birth rate, mortality, and the movement of the population in general, which characterize the Jews and distinguish them

15. Ibid., vol. II, p. 419.

from groups belonging to other religions, are due in large part to differences in conditions of existence.

We will limit ourselves to citing Mr. Lagneau, for these considerations are somewhat beyond our subject: "With Mr. Dally, the quite remarkable and morbid demographic differences that the Jews present, compared to the inhabitants of other races and other religions, seem to me to be caused less by their Semitic race than their general customs, their particular social conditions . . . Now, although ethnologically very different, the Jews of the Semitic race and the Judaized peoples of Russia, of Poland, and of the Danube provinces present rather analogous demographic movements . . ."

We have not completed here an account of all modern works, neither from French nor foreign scientists. There remained for us not only to finish the account, proceeding by trial and error in this period where scholars were searching to orient themselves, despite the few observations that they had at their disposal, but also to give an account of the present day. We had condensed all of these results in schematic tables and graphics that we intended to group together here. But we lacked the time to coordinate them. We are therefore forced to cut this chapter short and to move on without having finished this historical piece.

*Translated by Shaina Hammerman*

# 7 | Entry on Anthropology from *The Jewish Encyclopedia*

## Joseph Jacobs

"Anthropology," in *The Jewish Encyclopedia* (New York: Funk and Wagnalls, 1901), vol. 1.

For biographical information on Joseph Jacobs, see the note preceding the text of selection 1.

ANTHROPOLOGY: The science of man, especially in his physical aspects, and of the climatic and social environments determining those aspects. The anthropology of the Jews, who either racially or socially form a separate portion of mankind, should be of special interest to students of the science as bearing upon its central problem; namely, whether the similarities observed among different classes of mankind are due to "nature" or to "nurture"—that is, to common ancestry or to common environment. If Jews are wholly of one race, the difference produced among them by variations of social environment should form a suitable sphere of inquiry; if they are not of one race, it is of interest to the scientist to ascertain how the marked similarities between Jews of different climes have been produced. Much turns upon the preliminary question whether contemporary Jews are of the same race as those mentioned in the Bible.

### PURITY OF RACE

The general arguments hitherto advanced against the purity of the Jewish race are: (1) the evidence that in Bible times the Jews intermarried with surrounding nations; (2) the frequent reference to proselytes in early Christian literature; (3) the prohibition of intermarriage repeated in many of the councils of the church implies frequent infringements; (4) the conversion to Judaism of the Chazars, a Turanian tribe in south Russia, from whom, it is suggested, most of the Russian Jews, who form about half of contemporary Israelites, are descended; (5) the marked difference in type to be observed among contemporary Jews. To these arguments the upholders of the purity of the race reply: (1) the intermarriages mentioned in the Bible are few in number and with cognate tribes;

(2) proselytes were the chief sources from which the early Christian church drew its members, thus removing them from contact with Judaism; (3) the severity of the punishment attached by the church to intermarriage proves how infrequent intermarriages must have been; (4) the conversion of the Chazars was merely nominal, and it has left traces on only the few Karaites of south Russia—the other Russian Jews came from Germany, as is shown by the German dialect they use; (5) the differences of type may have been produced by social differences and are not so great when a series is taken into consideration. The upholders of the purity [of the race also] point out: (6) that *cohanim*, or members of the priestly caste, were and are not allowed to marry a proselyte, and must, therefore, have preserved their purity of descent; (7) that the marked resemblance of Jewesses throughout the world, showing as they do less variation among the females of the race, conforms to the biological test of purity of breed; (8) that mixed marriages in the present day are markedly infertile, which would reduce the influence of such intermarriages in an increasing geometrical ratio; (9) the rarity of instances in historical sources of proselytism in mixed marriages since the Middle Ages; (10) the prepotency of Jewish blood, as shown by the marked Jewish type of even the remoter offspring of Jews that have intermarried; (11) the stringent social separation, which can be historically proved throughout the Christian centuries; (12) the existence of marked Jewish type in the features and bodily measurements of contemporary Jews wherever found.

## ANTHROPOMETRY

Measurements of Jews have been taken sporadically in most European countries with the following results: The average height of Jews is 162.1 cm; span of arms, 169.1 cm; and girth around the chest, about 81 cm: so that they are the shortest and narrowest of Europeans. Their skulls are mainly brachycephalic; that is, the breadth is generally over 80 percent of the length. This has been used as an argument against the purity of race, as most Semites—like the Arabs and Syrians—are dolichocephalic, or long-headed. But, as Jewish skulls are almost the broadest in all Europe, it is difficult to say how this characteristic could have arisen from any mixture: it is probably due to cerebral development.

As regards complexion, Jews are darker than the surrounding peoples in Europe, except Galicia. The hair is also darker; on the average 15 percent having black hair as against 3 to 4 percent in the general European populations. Curiously enough, there is a larger proportion of red-haired men among Jews than in any other race; possibly due to want of nutrition. Jewesses seem to be more keen-sighted and to have greater strength of grip than other women. Among Jews about one-fifth have blue eyes, against one-third in the general populations. Altogether about one-fourth of the Jews can be described as fair, as against one-half of the populations among whom they dwell. The nose is generally considered the characteristic feature of the Jews, who have, on the average, the longest (77 mm) and narrowest (34 mm). Its characteristic shape is due to the accentuation of the nostrils, which gives it the "figure 6" formation. The lips of Jews are also characteristic, as large a proportion as 48 percent being thick. These features are the elements that go to make the marked Jewish type, which has been defined as "Semitic features with ghetto expression": it is found in the Assyrian bas-reliefs as well as in the ghetti of today. From composite portraits of Jewish lads, the Jewish face has been defined as possessing "accentuated flexible nostrils; largish mouth, with ends well marked, and pouting underlip; heavy chin; broad forehead with prominent superciliary ridges scantily covered with hair toward the outer extremities; and large, brilliant, dark eyes, set closely together, with heavy upper and protuberant lower lid, having a thoughtful expression in youth, transformed to a keen and penetrating gaze in manhood."[16]

The above results are averages taken from different numbers and different classes, and consequently vary in trustworthiness. The details as to hair, eye, and complexion are based upon the examination of no less than 120,000 individuals; those with regard to the nose, upon only 119. Differences in social position are found to affect results considerably; thus, while 12,000 Jews gave an average height of 162.1 cm, that of 130 English Jews of the better class was 170.8 cm. The predominantly narrow girth of Jews would give them what is technically known as the lowest "index of vitality," but statistics prove otherwise.

## BIOSTATICS

With regard to their vital statistics Jews show equal similarity among themselves and differences from the populations of which they form a part. Thus, as regards marriage, Jews in almost all countries have a lower marriage rate

16. [Here Jacobs is quoting his own essay, "On the Racial Characteristics of Jews." It is in that essay that he also discusses the caricature of the "Jewish nose" as a figure 6. See Jacobs, "On the Racial Characteristics of Modern Jews," in *Jewish Statistics: Social, Vital and Anthropometric* (London: D. Nutt, 1891): xxxii–xxxiii, selection 1 in this book.]

than Christians when reckoned upon their total population; their average being about six marriages to every 100 inhabitants. They marry earlier than Christians (in Russia one-half of Jewish marriages are between persons under twenty); and, as a consequence, there is a larger proportion of Jewish marriages between bachelors and spinsters. Jews marry their cousins more frequently than other people do—probably three times as often. The rate of intermarriage between Jews and Christians varies in different localities, from 1 percent in Algeria to 12 percent in Berlin. Jews appear to seek divorce in slightly fewer numbers than the rest of the population.

Estimated upon the total population, the birth rate of Jews is less—an average of about 33.5 per 1,000 per annum against 36.3 per 1,000 of the whole population—though this is opposed to the general impression, and appears to be contradicted by the fact that, as a rule, Jews have larger families than Christians. On the other hand, mixed marriages are remarkably infertile, resulting in only 15 births per 1,000. The sex of Jewish children is more predominantly male than in the general population, in the proportion of 112 to 105 (the female children being reckoned at 100); though, curiously enough, in Europe there is a larger proportion of Jewesses to Jews (106 to 100) than of other women to men in the general population (103 to 100). This predominance of male births among Jews has attracted the notice of naturalists, and appears to be due partly to the smaller number of illegitimate [births] and stillbirths. It is found that a larger proportion of males occur among the stillbirths, so that if there are less [*sic*] stillbirths, the larger is the number of males born. Jews show an average of about 3 percent stillbirths among all births as against 4 percent for the general population: this difference, though only of 1 percent absolutely, is 25 percent relatively. The comparative infrequency of stillbirths may be due to the small proportion of illegitimate births among Jews, which is, on the average, only one-fifth of the normal proportion. The superiority varies in different places, and is growing less marked as the pressure of ghetto opinion is becoming less effective: in Prussia, for example, there has been a perceptible rise in the rate of illegitimacy.

The death rate of Jews is lower than that of their neighbors—strikingly so in deaths under five years [of age]. This is the key to the whole of Jewish vital statistics, inasmuch as comparatively few deaths occur between five and twenty; hence, a relatively larger proportion of the Jewish population is living between these ages than is the case in general populations. Consequently when marriages or births are reckoned on the *whole* population, they appear less among Jews than among their neighbors; though if reckoned upon the population over twenty years of age—which would be the proper method—they would be really larger. Thus in Budapest, the percentage of the Jewish population under twenty was 45, while that of the Christians was about 34. The low death rate among infants is probably due to the fact that Jewish mothers rarely do anything but housework. A low death rate is shown in almost all the remaining ages until the very highest age, which implies that Jews are longer-lived than their neighbors. It has been suggested that Jews should claim special life tables and premium rates from the insurance companies. Owing to the early date of marriage and the viability of children, the length of a generation (= average age of males at marriage + 1 year + half the number of years of female fertility) of Jews is less than among Christians (about 31 years to 36); so that there are a larger number of generations living together; their increase is more rapid; and tradition holds a stronger place among them.

## MORBIDITY

Little has been done in the collection of details as to the special morbidity of Jews, either as regards the diseases to which they are most susceptible or as regards those from which they die. Jews have been credited with immunity from tuberculosis; but this has been disproved by the experience of the overcrowded immigrants in New York. They are undoubtedly freer than others from alcoholism, the number of such cases at Jewish clinics being phenomenally small. Jews are said to be more liable than others to diabetes and hemorrhoids—due probably to their sedentary habits. They are less liable to venereal diseases. They are undoubtedly more liable to disease of the nervous system, as is shown by the larger percentage of deaf and dumb, blind and insane among them than among the general population. Jews are markedly more [likely to be] colorblind than their neighbors, at least one-half as much again. Their neurotic tendency is due either to racial peculiarities or to the fact that they are mostly town dwellers and that they earn their living by relatively more brain work. Curiously enough, Jews, while showing inferiority compared with Christians in regard to nervous diseases, show superiority with regard to suicide, few of them resorting to self-destruction.

## SOCIAL CONDITIONS

The peculiarities of Jewish statistics may be due to racial unity or to similarity of social conditions. Even such measurements as those of height and growth may be due to nurture rather than to nature. It has been found, for example, that Jews in the East [End] of London reach an average height of 64.3 inches, whereas in the West End the average is 67.5. The social condition of Jews has thus a direct bearing upon their anthropometry, and the key to this is afforded by the fact that they live almost exclusively in towns, due in part to medieval persecution and in part to the needs of public worship. As a rule, only one-fifth of the Jewish population dwells outside of large towns, whereas two-thirds of the general population do so. This accounts in a large measure for their frail physique and shorter height, and for the larger proportion of mentally and physically afflicted. It also explains the small number of Jews in Continental armies, and, above all, the rarity of their employment as agricultural laborers. The peculiarities of their occupations are the predominance of commerce—over 50 percent of the adult workers being thus engaged as against only 6 percent of the general population—and the correspondingly small number of artisans, who are only one-half as numerous as among the Gentiles. Of the occupations most in vogue among Jewish artisans, tailoring and shoemaking take the precedence, as they do in the general population; and these have been the occasion of much "sweating" in the United States because of the long work hours which the Russian Jews are willing to accept. Owing to the prevalence of these ill-paid industries, Jews in the general mass are poorer than their fellow citizens, though a few exceptional persons have acquired great wealth. Taken as a whole, Jews are poorer than any European people. They appear to give more attention to the higher education of their children; and as a consequence are found among the professional classes in much larger proportion than their numbers warrant—for example, in Italy 8.7 percent of Jews against 3.7 percent of the general population. Here, again, correction has to be made, because of the fact that Jews are town dwellers, from whom the professions are almost exclusively recruited. This is especially the case with regard to medicine. Jewish doctors on the Continent of Europe are, comparatively speaking, three times as numerous as Gentile doctors. There are fewer clergymen: an average of 1 Jew to 1,500 of the population as against 1 Christian to 1,000.

[...]

Anthropologically considered, the Jews are a race of markedly uniform type, due either to unity of race or to similarity of environment. Their physical condition is mainly determined by their dwelling in towns. Their social position is the least fortunate, owing to the fact that they are crowded together, as in the Pale of Settlement in Russia, or are forced to immigrate to other countries, where they have to compete as foreigners. The general population is approaching the Jewish with regard to predilection for town life. The Russian Jews domiciled in other countries are bringing up a generation adapted to the newer environment. Jewish anthropological characteristics will therefore be likely to become more similar to that of the general population in the future. But the peculiarities due to race will still remain.

# 8 | The Jews as a Race

## J. M. Judt

Preface and Part 1 of *Die Juden als Rasse* (Berlin: Jüdischer Verlag, 1903).

J. M. Judt was a physician and anthropologist who lived and worked in Warsaw. The original Polish edition of *Die Juden als Rasse* was published in Warsaw in 1902.

### PREFACE

The present work was originally intended to be the introduction to a study of "the biostatistics and racial pathology of the Jews." However, as an analysis of the anthropological characteristics of the Jewish Volk brought to light numerous and significant issues, this separate monograph had to be devoted to addressing these.

Furthermore, the Jewish Volk, as a racial group with particular traits, deserves a thorough anthropological analysis. We are not dealing with an ethnic mass (*Völkerhaufen*) here, akin to that of other cultural peoples (*Kulturvölker*), because they [the Jews] do not possess a common soil; rather, they live in small communities scattered throughout the world. When we consider their separate and solitary fates, their centuries-long odyssey, and the most heterogeneous influences of their physical as well as their intellectual environments, it is easy to see that the Jews as a race make for extremely interesting research material.

The starting point for our analysis will be the questions: What are the Jews as a physical race, and what is their place in the overall anthropological racial scheme (*Rassentabelle*)? We understand by this a description defined or supported chiefly by anthropological data.

Naturally, an anthropometric description alone cannot provide a complete answer to our question, since it does not address the issue of the racial characteristics of ancient Jewry, but limits itself to contemporary Jews. Furthermore, it gives us little insight into the question if and to what extent the centuries-long wanderings influenced the physical traits of the Jews of antiquity. We therefore have supplemented this anthropometric data with those concerning the influence of milieu and history since the very beginnings of the Semitic races.

Along the obscure paths of these earliest wanderings, we went to Mesopotamia, Syria, and Canaan, and from there westward, into the realm of the Diaspora, striving to understand the origins of the Hebrew race, the relationship of the Jews to natives of the regions involved, as well as the nature and extent of racial crossings or intermixture.

[. . .]

## PART I: THE JEWS AS A RACE IN THE LIGHT OF CURRENT OPINION

Before we proceed to the solution of the problem of the Jews as a race, we will consider the currently prevailing views. We will thus mention quite a few theories, presenting them objectively, offering only their most characteristic or representative features.

### 1. *The Jews as a Pure Race*

Until the sixth decade of the last century, the prevalent opinion was that the Jews were a pure race, free from all foreign ethnic admixtures. The Volk, surrounded by an impenetrable wall of traditions, was supposed to have preserved not only a racial spirit (*Rassengeist*), but also uniform physical characteristics. The chief traits of the so-called Jewish type manifest themselves uniformly under all geographic conditions and in each and every world-historical era. Already Edwards (1829)[17] remarked on the great similarity between the Jews of today and their medieval representation in Leonardo da Vinci's painting *The Last Supper* and ancestral representations in pharaonic tombs. [. . .] Still, those who accept this general notion nonetheless are divided on many points. There are those, such as [Josiah] Nott (1850),[18] who endorse the notion of the immutability of the Jewish race, and who trace [the Jewish race] back to the anthropological type that emigrated from Mesopotamia four thousand years ago.[19]

17. [W. F. Edwards, *Des charactères phyisiologiques des races humaines considérés dans leur rapport avec l'histoire* (Paris: Chez Compère jeune libraire, 1829).]

18. [Josiah Clark Nott (1804–73) was an American physician and ethnologist.]

19. "From the time of Patriarch Abraham to the present the Jewish race has preserved its blood more purely than any other of antiquity. The original type brought by Abraham from Mesopotamia 4,000 years ago has been substantially handed down to the descendants of the present day" (*The Physical History of the Jewish Race*). [This footnote is in English in the German text.]

Others (Graetz[20]) find an analogy with the racial type of the Jews liberated from the Babylonian captivity (520 BC). Still others (Jacobs 1886) see the point of origin in the Roman Diaspora and trace the Jewish type only back to the 40,000 human souls who lost their homeland after losing their unfortunate struggle with the great world power of the day. The wandering masses did not, however, succumb to racial mixing. They remained isolated because of their firm religious beliefs, the power of common sentiments handed down through the generations, and also through the general misery and restrictions of the many years in the ghetto ("Jews are the lineal descendents of the Diaspora of the Roman Empire"[21]). According to Jacobs, the Jews also did not absorb any foreign ethnic elements during the epoch of their settlement in Palestine. They guarded the purity of marriage in the most stringent way while living among foreign peoples. This view is even today chiefly upheld by nationalists, who, by the way, unjustifiably see purity of race as one of the attributes of national solidarity.

Without reproducing all of the historical proofs and ethnological evidence, I want here only to mention one rather original claim of Buschan (1894),[22] which has been put forth to assert the alleged racial purity and unity of the Jews. This author observes differences in the pathological sphere, a greater hereditary immunity to some diseases, and takes these to be a sign of racial individuality. And since he finds an analogy between the different groups of Jews living in different lands, he believes himself to be justified in making the claim that today's Jews come in a direct line from those ancient Semitic tribes and that they contain no foreign elements.

In the following chapters of this study, we want to examine whether Jews are indeed a pure race. That is, have they really maintained the primordial characteristics of the Semitic tribe?

At this point we should merely like to remark that Buschan's claim has no rational foundation.

The pathological aspect of the Jews indeed exhibits a few quite peculiar nuances and differences, which, however, can in no way be traced back to aspects of race.

A higher percentage of nervous and mental disorders and a lower rate of

20. [Heinrich Graetz (1817–91), an eminent German Jewish historian, was the author of the most important work of Jewish history in the nineteenth century, the multivolume *History of the Jews*.]

21. [The quote is in English in the German text.]

22. [Georg Buschan (1863–1942) was a German physician and anthropologist.]

susceptibility to infectious diseases can be explained with reference to quite a different set of factors—namely, cultural and social forces.

Buschan is going too far in his conclusions.

### 2. *The Division of the Jews into Two Groups: Ashkenazim and Sephardim*

Only gradually did the former understanding of the Jews change. A great number of observations point to the inadequacy of the theory of a unified Jewish race. In particular, it was the craniological studies that contributed to lending this theory the power of scientific dogma.

Old legend already confirms the existence of two branches within the Jewish people: the Sephardim, from the tribe of Judah; and the Ashkenazim, who are supposed to have descended from the tribe of Benjamin. Having been separated by a multitude of historical events, the Ashkenazim are supposed to have accounted for the bulk of Jews settled throughout Northern and Middle Europe—that is, in Germany, Poland, and Russia. Conversely, a minority of the Jewish people—that is, about 10 percent of them, who were of Sephardic descent, made their way to Southern Europe, particularly Spain and Portugal. In a later period some fraction of Spanish-Portuguese Jews, the so-called Spagnoli, migrated to England, Holland, and the Balkans.

Even [Karl] Vogt (1863) has put forth a bold hypothesis in an attempt to explain this division. In his opinion, the Sephardic Jews must be considered the genuine descendants of the primordial Semitic tribe, while the Ashkenazim are related to the Aryans from the sources of the Indus River. At almost the same time, in the *Bulletin de la Societé d'Anthropologie de Paris* (1861 and 1865), these ideas also crystallized, though on a completely different basis. I refer to the famous discussions that took place in the then recently established anthropological society in Paris. The aura of fame that formed around Broca's school succeeded in bringing the problem [of explaining the division of Jewry] to the attention of a wider public. The most important discussions revolved around the question of the intermixing of the Jews in Europe with the [ancient] Germans and Slavs, as well as the Finns and Tartars. The timid voices of earlier researchers—for example, those of Nott and Gliddon (1857)[23]—only entered into the discussion when Broca made

23. "The votaries of Judaism may be divided into two broadly marked and distinct types, viz: the one above mentioned (Semitic type) and another distinguished by a lank and tall frame, clear blue eye [*sic*], very white and freckled skin, and yellow-reddish

the claim that in the ninth century of the new era, a Slavic tribe converted to Jewry. Let me quote now references to this particular debate, while I emphasize that this claim, which has so often been presented in consideration of the issue at hand, is in fact false.

> Following the triumph of Christianity in Poland, the Jews there exerted over a long period of time a significant influence, and, as we may suppose, often entered into marriages with Christian women. This state of things lasted until 1092, when the Christian King Ladislaus forbade such marriages. Jews now were also forbidden to keep Christian servants. And yet the influence of the Jews continued up to the thirteenth century. Only later did persecutions occur. Entire masses [of Jews] were robbed of their belongings, and forced into exile in foreign lands.[24]

Somewhere else we read "that even among the Russians many proselytes converted to Judaism."[25]

This sort of historical information provided the foundation for the emergence of a new set of views. The idea of the division of Jewry into Ashkenazim and Sephardim found many proponents. This claim quickly gained all the more currency when anthropological and statistical proof was produced. The Vrolik Museum in Amsterdam provided skulls of Dutch Jews; Prunen Bey (1865) did the same for North Africa, Quatrefages and Hamy (1882) for Algeria, and Ikow (1884) for Turkey.

The measurements consequently taken of these skulls of Sephardic Jews produced results completely different from those taken from the skulls of Ashkenazic Jews.

On the basis of these observations, two distinct anthropological types of Jews were posited. The Sephardic Jew is supposedly the descendant of the genuine Semites with elongated skulls, raven-black hair and eyes, dark skin color, and a long, elegant nose—a type approximating the beautiful form of the Arab Bedouins. This is the same type we encounter in Rembrandt's paintings of Amsterdam's Jews or in Alloris's *Judith with the Head of Holofernes* in the Pitti Gallery. In contrast, the Ashkenazic Jews represent a short-headed type, with a low

---

hair. Poland seems to be the focus of this fusion of Jews with German and Samaritan races" (*Indigenous Races of the Earth*, p. 580).

24. According to Tscherny, *Ethnographie de l'Empire d'Autriche*.

25. According to Hanthausen, *L'Empire Russe*.

forehead, brown or often blond hair and blue eyes, a thick nose, large mouth, a slightly protruding lower jaw, and prominent cheekbones.

This is the general outline of the characteristics of these two alleged types. Even now, this view is commonly held by anthropologists. I'll just mention their names: Blechmann (1881), Stieda and Dybowski (1883), Kollmann (1885), Topinard (1885), Hervé and Hovelacque (1887), Talko-Hryncewicz (1892), Deniker (1900).

*3. Division of the Jews into Three Racial Groups: Ikow's Theory*

The classification of the Jews as Sephardic and Ashkenazic discussed above left the problem unresolved. There exist a number of different groups within the Jewish population that could not be included among either the Sephardim or Ashkenazim. The various racial types of Jews in Western Europe, the Caucasus, south Russia, Poland, and Germany induced [Constantine] Ikow to put forth another grouping. Ikow's view is interesting insofar as he has shed light in an original way on the question at hand. This anthropologist's treatise, based on the vast amount of data on the historical mass migration, offers new motifs for our consideration and for that reason alone deserves great attention. By referring to, among other things, the evidence related to skull measurements, Ikow sets forth the following division.

> (1) The Jews from the East and from the South (the Balkans, Spain, Italy, Algeria, and the coast of the Mediterranean). They represent a genuine Semitic lineage, with a very weak or minimal admixture of alien elements. The analogy with the Arab as an anthropological type is striking: they are long-headed and brunet.
>
> (2) The Jews from Western Europe—a race that resulted from extensive crossing of the Semitic type with the native population [of Western Europe].
>
> (3) The Jews of Russia[26] display no signs of Semitic descent whatsoever; they are short-headed.
>
> [...]

We see in Ikow's hypothesis, besides its false anthropological foundation, a whole host of doubtful theories on which his conclusions rest. Among others one could mention the unfounded conjecture that the cradle of the Semites was

26. "The Jews of Russia (probably along with the Karaites) must be excluded from the number of Semites for good since they share no essential relation with them and belong to a completely different race" ("Neue Beiträge zur Anthropologie der Juden," *Arch. f. Anthrop.*, vol. 15, page 369 and passim.)

North Africa, and the merely hypothetical notion of a mass emigration of Jews to Slavic lands over the Caucasus, Crimea, and Dnieper.

### LAGNEAU'S THEORY

[Gustave] Lagneau offers another three-group division of the Jews (1891).

(1) The Jews of North Africa: the result of the intermixture of Jews who were natives of that region (Egypt, Carthage) with local tribes of Berbers, Copts, and Phoenicians; and later with Greek and Roman colonists; and finally, in the Middle Ages, with Arabs. Since this mixing occurred with predominantly dark-haired and dolichocephalic populations, the Jews there retain the notable traits of the Jewish type.

(2) The Roman Jews: from the northern coast of the Mediterranean Sea, mostly converts of Greek and Latin descent.

(3) The German, Polish, and Russian Jews: they are the product of a mixing with the ancient German, Slavic, and Cossack races.

The author has refrained from interpreting his classification in any great detail. It is, nonetheless, easy to expose the lack of discrimination in this arrangement. And when I cite Lagneau's theory of division, it is only to show just how complicated the terminology has become in our effort to define the Jews as a race.

#### 1. *The Jews as an Aggregate of Different Ethnic Elements*

New insights gained from ethnology have made the problem even more confused. The parameters of the previously mentioned schemas were not able to contain all possible varieties. The skull measurements and a series of other anthropological data only brought the absence of unity about racial type into stronger focus. Moreover, ethnology came along and introduced either new or recovered evidence, above all about the so-called exotic Jews. The Jews of Abyssinia, the Falashas, are a Volk characterized by powerful physiques, dark eyes and hair, and brown skin color.

On the eastern coast of Madagascar live those Jews who are the so-called Zafy-Ibrahim, that is, the descendants of Abraham. According to the report of the traveler Sibree (*The Great African Island*), it is difficult to distinguish these Jews from other social strata of the indigenous population.[27]

27. "... but could not detect any difference in color, feature, or dialect between them and the other people of the eastern coast" (*The Great African Island*). [The note is in English in the German text.]

In the account of the German expedition to the Loango Coast [central Africa], Bastian[28] mentions the inhabitants living in that region, the Mawambu, who adhere to the Jewish faith (*jüdischer Konfession*). They are said to be the descendants of those Jews who were driven out of Castile (1493) [1492] to St. Thomas Island; now, however, their countenance and skin color are similar to those of the Negroes (Andrée, 1881). On the Malabar Coast of Hindustan, near Bombay, mainly in Cochin and Travancore, "black" Jews have lived for a long time—the so-called *Kallah Israel*. The missionary Joseph Wolf, who visited Cochin in 1833, confirmed already at that time the significant similarity of the Jews with the local Hindus[29] (Nott, 1850; *The Church Missionary Atlas*, 1897).

An even more remarkable appearance is that of the so-called Chinese Jews. They constitute a quite particular colony in Kaï-fung-fu, in Hunan Province, and are said to have come to these places via Persia after the destruction of Jerusalem. Travelers note their yellow complexion, long pigtails, and physiognomic similarity to the Chinese (Cordier, 1891; Katz, 1900; etc.).

Identical reports come from researchers who examined the Daghestani Jews of the Caucasus. Here the mountain Jews possess both the same facial features and the same notably short heads as do the Chechens (Chantre, 1887; Erckert, 1881, 1883, 1885). At the same time, one can demonstrate the great similarity between the Jews of the Caucasus and the Kabardynier, Lezgins [Lesghier], Aranen, and so forth. One merely has to look at the photographs compiled by [Ernest] Chantre in his great four-volume work.[30]

The above-mentioned racial fragmentation should serve as proof of the Jewish ability to resemble the native-born population, even when it comes to their physical appearance; this, by the way, is supposedly also taking place, albeit to a lesser degree, in Europe—as some anthropologists would argue. Renan's far-reaching definition (1883)—"il n'y pas un type juif, il y a des types juifs" ["there is not one Jewish type, there are Jewish types"]—has become the working principle of many researchers. However, no one today would join Renan in claiming that "judaïsme est une religion, mais n'est pas un fait ethnologique, mais un type accidentel" ["Judaism is a religion, not an ethnological fact but an accidental type"].

28. *Die Deutsche Expedition an der Loangoküste* I. 43, 277.

29. "Their complexion is like that of Hindoos [*sic*], indeed, even at this time many of the Hindoos at Cochin become converts to Judaism" (*Die Aussage des Missionärs Wolf vom Jahre 1883*, cited in Andrée, 1881). [The quote is in English in the German text.]

30. [*Recherches anthropologique dans le Caucase* (Paris: C. Reinwald, 1885–85).]

No one today believes any longer that the Jews are a haphazard aggregate of different ethnic traits, with accidental characteristics. On the contrary, the reigning opinion is that there occurred intermixing in some countries, an intermixing that is said to have produced a certain similarity in physical appearance between the Jews and the local native populations among whom they have lived. As an example, let me quote Krzywicki [Krzywickis]: "Despite their fanatical separateness, the Jews actually have a good deal of non-Semitic blood in them. In India, on this side of the Ganges, they are black, in England blue-eyed and blond, in the western districts of Russia they have wide faces and 'Slavic' noses: they always evince the physical traits of the population surrounding them. According to the survey of German schools, 10.32 percent of Baden Jews were found to be of the pure blond type, 10.38 percent in Bavaria, 11.23 percent in Prussia, 11.77 percent in Hesse, and 13.53 percent in Braunschweig.[31] This is absolute proof of foreign admixture. Among the Polish Jews the foreign component is even more significant than among the German Jews. So one finds for instance among the Galician Jews that 14.1 percent are of the blond type. We arrived at the same sort of results concerning the distribution of short-headed types among them. Western Russian and Polish Jews often possess wide faces and noses, fair hair, and gray eyes—in a word, all those characteristics that make apparent that the Jewish racial traits are inhibited to a high degree by the blood flowing in the veins of the surrounding native populations. And if we hold on to the indexes of cranial measurements, it becomes evident that the aforementioned Jews possess more Polish and western Russian racial traits than genuine or ancient Hebrew ones" (*Die Völker*, pp. 210–41).

Alongside the results of anthropological research, various historical facts are put forth as evidence. Of course, we are speaking here only about the last two thousand years—that is, about the admixture of Aryan elements on the European terrain. The pre-Christian epoch has been ignored, apart from the comments of Flieger (1897), Alsberg (1891), Luschan (1892), and Jacques (1893) in regard to racial mixture during the period of Jewish national independence. In the opinion of a large number of researchers, the mixing of Jews with the native population is observable in almost every country; this occurs either through

31. [These numbers refer to the famous 1886 survey of German schoolchildren undertaken by the German physician and anthropologist Rudolf Virchow. See the discussion in John Efron, *Defenders of the Race: Jewish Doctors and Race Science in Fin-de-Siècle Europe* (New Haven: Yale University Press, 1994), 25–26.]

intermarriage or through conversion to Judaism. The marked racial mixing, which had reached a high level during the Hellenistic and Roman periods in the first century BC due to Jewish proselytism, had already begun to decline in the period immediately following; it begins to emerge again, according to Neubauer, in the era of Aryanism (fifth century) and during Moorish rule on the Iberian peninsula (from the eighth century on).

It is claimed that in this same period Gaul became a site of racial mixing for the Jews, indeed, to such a large extent that, according to Loeb [...] the majority of Gallic Jews at the time of Gontrand and Hilperic were descended from those heathens who had been converted to Judaism.

The same thing is said to be true for the Germanic and Slavic territories, and for southern and eastern Russia.

The Khazars, the Karaites , the sect of the so-called "Subotniki" were supposedly the most convincing proof for the above claims. There were so many intermarriages at the time that the clergy was forced to try to bring them to a halt through decrees passed by the various councils of Elvira, Chalcedon, Orleans, Toledo, and Rome. Moreover, even today, as some claim, so much intermarriage occurs in some countries that this must absolutely be seen as one of the factors modifying the particular physical elements of Jewry.

Although I will offer a detailed critique and analysis of this viewpoint in a later chapter, at this point I will only remark that the theory of the identification of the Jews with other ethnic groups has now become an accepted doctrine among many researchers. Let me only mention the name of [William] Ripley,[32] who in his splendid work (1900) shares and backs up the hypotheses of Loeb, Neubauer, and Krzywicki [Krzywickis].

As we can see from the above overview, in the field of the racial anthropology of the Jews there exist diametrically opposed views, and over and above this, between these oppositional approaches there is a whole range of different, intermediary theories.

In pursuit of a clearer orientation, I offer the following schema.

32. "The modern Jews are physically more Aryan than Semitic, after all. They have unconsciously taken on to a large extent the physical traits of the people among whom their lot has been thrown. In Algiers they have remained long-headed like their neighbors; for even if they intermarried, no tendency to deviation in head form would be provoked. If, on the other hand, they settled in Piedmont, Austria, or Russia, with their moderately round-headed populations, they became in time assimilated to the type of these neighbors as well" (*The Races of Europe* 1900, p. 390). [This note is in English in the German text.]

(1) The Jews as a pure, unified race:
   (a) the prototype—Jews from the time of Abraham (Nott);
   (b) the prototype—Jews from the Babylonian captivity (Graetz);
   (c) the prototype—Jews from the time of the Diaspora (Jacobs).

(2) The division of Jews into southern (Sephardim) and northern (Ashkenazim):
   (a) Vogt's theory: The Sephardim are Semites, the Ashkenazim are Aryans;
   (b) Broca's theory: The Ashkenazim are the result of the racial mixing of the Jews with the ancient Germans and Slavs.

(3) The division of the Jews into three groups:
   (a) Ikow's theory: The Southern, Western, and Eastern European Jews;
   (b) Lagneau's theory: The Jews of North Africa, Northern Europe, and Central Europe.

(4) The Jews as an aggregate of different ethnic elements:
   (a) The Jews are the result of their mixing with the native populations of those countries in which they settled in their exile (Renan, Krzywicki, Ripley);
   (b) The Jews are a race that succumbed to intermixing in exile and during the time of political independence (Flieger, Alsberg, Buschan, Jacques).

The goal of this essay, then, should be perfectly clear: an exposition and critique of the dominant theories, by means of an analysis of the anthropological results and the relevant historical facts, so that in the end we might offer an answer to the question: What would it mean for the Jews to be a pure race?

# 9 | The Brain Weight of Jews

## Richard Weinberg

"Das Hirngewicht der Juden," *Zeitschrift für Demographie und Statistik der Juden* 1, no. 3 (1905): 5–10.

Richard Weinberg was a *privatdocent* (a formal academic title indicating that the individual had a doctorate and holds an academic position somewhat akin to lecturer in the US system) at the University of Dorpat—known today as the University of Tartu—in Estonia. Sander Gilman identifies Weinberg as a physician (*Smart Jews: The Construction of the Image of Jewish Superior Intelligence* [Lincoln: University of Nebraska Press, 1996], 52). Whether or not Weinberg was Jewish is unclear, though it is highly unlikely. At the time, the university town of Dorpat (Tartu) was relatively tolerant of Jews, and there was a significant Jewish student presence at the university. However, according to Tonu Parming ("The Jewish Community and Inter-Ethnic Relations in Estonia, 1918–1940," *Journal of Baltic Studies* 10, no. 3 [1979]:250), "The University of Tartu had no Jewish faculty members until 1934." (I thank Rachel Rothstein for this reference.) I have nonetheless included Weinberg's article here because of the material discussed and because the piece appeared in a "Jewish" journal—that is, a journal funded by the Jewish community and created and run by Jews, with the explicit purpose of influencing Jewish public opinion. Whether or not the editors agreed with every detail of Weinberg's argument, it seems safe to say that they believed the general topic of the essay was a legitimate one.

It is known that numerous researchers have dealt with the national and racial traits of the Jews from a variety of perspectives. Physical anthropology, too, has frequently sought to get a grip on this object of study. Since Blumenbach, Pruner Bey, and H. Welcker,[33] who gathered the first real facts in this area, observers have been arming themselves with calipers and tape measures, advancing ever deeper into the racial body of the Jewish Volk. A great number of facts and findings have been accumulated, which will hopefully yield rich results once researchers succeed in differentiating between the essential and nonessential,

33. [Hermann Welcker (1822–97) was a German physical anthropologist.]

and once a presentation thereof becomes feasible on the basis of a well-founded methodology and unified principles. We already possess several statistical surveys from the East and Southeast of Europe—and now recently from America as well—which aim for a systematic inquiry into general anatomy, head form, pigmentation, and proportions of limbs, and even cover the consideration of certain physiological and pathological conditions.

At any rate, it must be admitted that the research done up until now has made its way only to the threshold in terms of exploring the racial organism. Its inner spaces, that holy of holies, the sinuous paths of the brain's convolutions, the wonderfully delicate structure of the nervous system, the labyrinthine systems and components of the cells and fibers, encompassing the most sublime riddles of the human spirit—at no time have these been opened up and illuminated. Even enthusiastic and intrepid researchers have not dared to approach and then knock on this door. And yet it remains true that nowhere else than in the brain can the "birthplace" of human history be located, the cradle of art and that mysterious bridal chamber in which body and soul—the gods of light and the children of nature—celebrate orgies (Reil); that it is not merely the fate of individuals, but just as much the past and future of entire races and organic communities that have been decided by a rather small amount of brain matter, which, with its precious particles and atoms, hides itself from us in its marble vault.

I will make an attempt here to contribute some material to the problem at hand and to explain its relevance for the racial theory about the brain.

## I

The observation has been made in some countries that the Jews already differ from the surrounding populations in terms of head size, and in particular the formation of the cranium. Lombroso,[34] for instance, noticed that the Semitic elements within the Turin population possess a somewhat smaller cranial capacity than the other inhabitants of this region,[35] and this was attributed to the fact

34. [Cesare Lombroso (1835–1909) was an Italian Jewish anthropologist and medical researcher who is considered one of the founders of modern criminology. He is best known for his theory of the "born criminal," which posited that criminality was an inherited trait and that criminals could be identified, even before they committed a crime, by their particular physiognomic features.]

35. C. Lombroso, *Der Antisemitismus und die Juden im Lichte der modernen Wissenschaft*, German translation by Dr. H. Kurella (Leipzig, G. H. Wigand, 1894). [. . .] The larger average

that, relatively speaking, one seldom meets with very large crania among Jews, whereas middle-sized and long cranial shapes predominate.

The smaller cranial development might in this case have led to a certain underdevelopment of brain mass.

This question, which of course is of no minor importance for the anthropological status of a race, thus has to be tackled first. That is to say it has, on the one hand, to be considered whether or not this phenomenon is more generally observable and also to what extent it accords preliminarily with the results of firsthand examinations of the brain.

[...]

## II

Seeing as the direct, though of course still insufficient, investigations into the crania and brains appear to corroborate, to a certain degree, the aforementioned assumption of a quantitative underdevelopment of the brains of Jews, it has to be asked, in order to establish a solid foundation for the matter: what can we learn, in this regard, from measurements taken of living individuals, which numerically appear to be relatively uncontestable as objects for our method? And might these, in turn, serve as a control [a control group] for those direct weightings and cubings, or even as a framework for anatomical comparisons of the races?

In order to determine this in the most direct way, I will take as my departure point the horizontal circumference of the head as the means by which to measure brain size. This [circumference] generally, and particularly within one distinct cranial type, stands in a more or less constant and direct relation to the volume of the cranium.[36]

---

of the measure of cranial capacity among the non-Jews of Turin is conditioned in part by the greater frequency of individuals of larger stature, in part by the greater number of those who are trocho- and hydrocephalic; in addition, other anomalies that produce larger crania volume. According to Lombroso, small crania often appear among Jews and non-Jews alike in Turin.

36. A detailed analysis of skull diameter and circumference in relation to the internal volume of the cranium, as it has been made possible now by the method of Manouviers and especially due to the recent suggestions of Beddoe (*L'Anthropologie* XIV, 267, 1903), has been intentionally omitted here since the fundamentals of these methods cannot be given in a few lines within the limited space of an essay.

Rather uniform results regarding the dimensions of the cranial circumferences of Jews emerge out of the anthropological surveys undertaken in various regions of the Russian Empire. The table found below [not included in this book], based on the efforts of Weissenberg (southern Russia, 1897), Jakowenko (White Russia, 1898), Talko-Hrynewicz [Talko-Gritschewitsch] (Kleinrussland, 1892), and Elkind (Poland, 1903), includes the measurements of approximately 1,000 adult males of Jewish nationality. It shows the largest average horizontal circumference (565 mm) in White Russia, and a somewhat smaller (550–53 mm) circumference among the southern and western Jews of the empire. Within the Slavic environment, the Russian Jews appear, when it comes to cranial circumference, to be absolutely superior to Poles and White Russians, to whom we can make comparisons thanks to the previously mentioned work of Elkind and Talko; the average measure among Poles and White Russian Jews is 550 mm, and among Russian Jews roughly 554 mm.[37] They have the same advantage when, instead of absolute brain size, one takes into consideration comparative percentages in relation to body size. It then also becomes evident that while the Jewish elements in Russia show on average 35 percent head circumference, their Slavic compatriots demonstrate only 33.4 percent. The difference in the numbers, as should be readily acknowledged, is not really as insignificant as one might think at first glance.

Seemingly unfavorable for the Jews are the conclusions of a general comparison of head circumference between the Jews and their racial neighbors—that is, the actual Poles of the Vistula region. [A chart not included in this book shows: Polish Jews: 1,610 kg; Polish Slavs: 1,640 kg. Polish Jews: 1,249 mm; Polish Slavs: 1,255 mm.] These totals—1,255 and 1,249—at least show there is some difference, though [the Jews' number] is hardly significantly less than that of the Slavs (the other tribal groups [*Stämme*] could not be compared, since for them the survey did not concern itself with matters of cranial circumference measurements). One should not forget, however, the role played here by the differences in height. The Polish Slavs are on average a total of 30 mm taller than their Jewish compatriots.

37. One finds analogous results among Venetians. Lombroso (op. cit., 1893) identified there [in Venice] among five Jews an average cranial circumference of 580 mm, while among 10 non-Jews 569 mm. The same was true for the cranial capacity calculated from external head masses, which among the former [the Jews] is 1664 cbcm [cubic centimeters] while among the latter only 1561 cbcm. Lombroso freely admits, and rightfully so, that his sample is small and that it is hardly conclusive given the much more abundant material from Turin, measurements which produce different results.

If, for example, one equalizes the ratio or proportion with regard to stature, then for a 1,000 mm height, one finds an average of 765.2 mm head circumference among Poles, and 775.7 among Jews—as the numbers above will easily show. It has already been remarked about many races that small individuals have larger heads in relation to their body size than do larger individuals.

As far as I can see, the available surveys thus do not seem to support the contention that there is a quantitative underdevelopment of the cranium among those of the Jewish race (*Volksstamm*); the results from Russia in fact rather contradict that contention. The evidence from direct measurements of skulls—which, on account of the meager amount of firsthand material on which such evidence rests, does not elicit a great deal of confidence in the first place—gets completely drowned out by what comprehensive studies of living material tell us. The same probably holds true for the results of brain weight, which undoubtedly will have to be corrected in the future. For if these results were correct, then we would be left with the option of assuming that, since the underdevelopment of cranial capacity among the Jews cannot be demonstrated, Jewish brains of the same size are *lighter* than those of other races—that is, that they are lacking in specific brain mass. As far as current research goes, it is not completely improbable that notable differences and fluctuations in specific brain weights are connected to race and individuality, perhaps as well to gender and particular health conditions.[38] But more certain proof concerning the connection to race has not been brought forth, and the materials at hand still appear too indeterminate and uncertain to find a practical utilization in comparative racial science.

In comparison to the research into the development of brain mass, one might emphasize the conclusion that, as Galen said, it is not the quantity (how much) but the quality (the how) of a thing that determines its real value. As the oft-used analogy has it, a church clock is not necessarily more precise than a pocket watch. The first steps in the investigation into the morphological racial particularity of Jewish brains have already been taken. Its success appears in many respects remarkable and signifies the need for further inquiry into this difficult subject. Space forbids any further discussion here; this has been dealt with already elsewhere.[39]

38. L. Bolk, *Beziehungen zwischen Hirnvolum und Schädelkapazität nebst Bemerkungen über das Hirngewicht der Holländer*, Petrus Camper, 1904.

39. R. Weinberg, "Das Gehirn der Juden Russ.," *Zeitschrift für Anthropologie*, 1902; ibid., "Über einige ungewöhnliche Befunde an Judenhirnen," *Biologisches Centralblatt*, vol. XXIII, 1903.

# 10 | The Jewish Racial Problem

## Samuel Weissenberg

"Das jüdische Rassenproblem," *Zeitschrift für Demographie und Statistik der Juden* 1, no. 5 (1905): 4–8.

Samuel Weissenberg (1867–1928) was born in Elizabethgrad, in the Ukraine. He was a celebrated physician and anthropologist, whose research on the physical measurement of Jews in southern Russia was awarded a gold medal by the Moscow Society for Natural Sciences. In addition to anthropological work on the Jews, Weissenberg published essays on Jewish folklore, proverbs, and music. His major work was *Wachstum des Menschen nach Alter, Geschlecht und Rasse* (Human growth as related to age, sex, and race), 1911. See the entry in the *Encyclopedia Judaica*, 16:417–18. Also see John Efron, *Defenders of the Race: Jewish Doctors and Race Science in Fin-de-Siècle Europe* (New Haven: Yale University Press, 1994), chapter 5.

Ten years ago I concluded my work on the Jews of southern Russia with the following words: "At any rate, it will not be possible to offer a definitive answer to the question of the anthropological status of the Jews until research on the Jews in Western Europe, Asia, and Africa has been done. Such important research, undertaken following unified principles, will allow, it is to be hoped, a primordial type (*Urtypus*) of Jew to be discovered; with such a standard in hand, we can then more easily appraise the anthropological status of individual groups as well as their relation to the whole. The gain [in knowledge] to be had from this investigation will be my greatest reward."

Since then I have waited in vain for such a reward, and my wish for such an anthropological investigation into non-European Jewry has remained just that: a wish. How much we nonetheless still need such research I will show in what follows. Over the past decade there have, it is true, appeared numerous works specifically devoted to the anthropology of the Jews; yet only one among them has been devoted to Sephardic Jews. And so I believe I am justified in repeating my plea more urgently.

What makes the Jewish racial problem particularly interesting is the curious result that follows from all of the anthropological studies: the Jews, though known as Semites, have nothing in common with the latter. We are mainly referring here to the shape of the head: Semites possess long, dolichocephalic skulls; Jews short and brachycephalic ones.

My research had led me to the following conclusion, which the subsequent work of other authors only confirmed: although the Jews represent a conglomerate of different types, nonetheless we can see one type emerge, which generally dominates and which allows all of Eastern European Jewry to be considered, anthropologically, as more or less a unified mass. This type can be described in the following way: The southern Russian Jews (like all Eastern European Jews in general) are, when they are evaluated along the lines of their most predominant type, of average size and of the brunet color type; their head form is sub-brachycephalic; the face is more oval, in its lower part somewhat tapered in shape, chameprosopic. They have a rather flat forehead, often relatively prominent cheekbones and straight jaws. The eyes are level; the nose is leptorhine,[40] more narrow above than below, generally somewhat large and rather prominent; its shape is predominantly straight. The lips are regular; the mouth relatively wide, the ears of average size. This type is fundamentally different from the true Semitic type, the Arab, in its chief characteristics—the head form and facial features. In order to make this quite apparent, allow me to reproduce here Topinard's description of the Arab type:

> The Arab type is one of the most beautiful in the world, said Larrey. His skull, seen as a whole, forms a perfectly regular oval. His complexion remains perfectly white when it has not been subjected to the effects of the atmosphere, but bronzes easily, his hair and his beard are smooth and jet black, the limits of his hairline are distinctly defined; his eyes are black; his palpebral [eyelid] openings elongated, almond-shaped, and bordered by long black eyelashes; his forehead is slightly elevated; the curve of his nose and his receding chin, however, lend his profile a shape more rounded than straight. His superciliary [eyebrow] arches as well as his glabella [area between eyebrows] are not very developed; the root of his nose is not very indented, in such a way that the forehead and the edge of the nose follow one another in an almost straight line. His nose is aquiline, and the tip is detached from the nostrils and descends below them hooking like an eagle's beak. The cheekbones do not jut out; the mouth is small; the teeth are white and vertical; the ears well made, rather small, and close to the head.

40. [Leptorhine means having a narrow nose.]

> His height is a little below the average in Arabia and a little below in Algeria. He is lean, sinewy, loose-necked, and small-boned. He is subdolichocephalic (index of 76.3 on the living individual, 74.0 on the skull), a moderate leptorhine (45.5) and mesoseme (88.6).[41]

Even the first researchers in this area noticed the fundamental differences between the two types, as well as the total transformation and distancing of the Jewish from the Semitic type. One attempt to explain this fact was to propose that within Jewry there actually existed two types, one next to the other: the first was the primordial, genuine, Semitic type, represented by the numerically quite small group of Southern European and African Jews—the Sephardim; the second, meanwhile, was represented by a nongenuine, highly [racially] intermixed Eastern European Jewry (Vogt, Weisbach, Blechman, Stieda, Hovelacque, Andree).

However, the measurements done by [Joseph] Jacobs on several Sephardic Jews in England yielded the unexpected fact that they, too, were short-headed.

Convinced of the invariability of the Jewish type from ancient times until the present, and thoroughly obsessed with the idea of Jewish short-headedness, a number of other authors (Alsberg, von Luschan, Jacques) on the other hand have tried to use these as proof of a strong intermixture of foreign blood even in ancient Palestine. This view has found its clearest expression and scientific explanation in the work of von Luschan. His conclusion is as follows: "The modern Jews are an amalgamation: in the first place, of the Aryan Amorites, second of genuine Semites, and third and foremost of the descendants of the ancient Hittites. Next to these three most important elements of Jewishness (*Judentums*), other intermixings—which were at least possible and certainly did occur in the course of several thousand years of Diaspora—are negligible."

Von Luschan's position is shared in general by Judt, who strove in his recently published book to bring everything that has been published on the Jewish racial question under one roof. Unfortunately, the entire book is marred by a certain bias toward historical data, which is also reflected in the rather superficial treatment and arbitrary interpretation of the anthropometrical materials.

Just how deeply the prejudice regarding the short-headedness of Jews has penetrated the minds [of researchers] can be seen in the fact that [Maurice] Fishberg has attributed the long-headedness of African Jews to their exclusion from the original short-headed [Jewish] type.

41. [Mesoseme means having a medium orbital index. The extract is in French in the German text; the translation here is by Shaina Hammerman.]

Is the general short-headedness of the Jews an actual, well-established fact?

As I have already remarked, we are unfortunately lacking in ample examinations of the so-called Sephardic Jews; yet even the few studies we do possess illustrate clearly enough that the [racial] composition of the latter is quite different.

[. . .]

In any case, Judt's bold claim that there is no difference to be observed in the structure of the heads between Ashkenazim and Sepharidm is not in the least true.

This becomes even clearer when we look at the few Jewish skulls we have, which are furthermore scattered across many museums, which makes studying them all the more difficult.

In Table II I have gathered together all the material I had access to, and I do not believe I have failed to consider anything of true significance.[42] I have myself researched and measured the skulls from Sliwno and Yamboli (Turkey) that are found in the anthropological museum in Moscow, and I can only confirm what Ikow has already proposed—that they are dolichocephalic. In order to highlight what is most significant, I have brought together in Table III [not included in this book] the data on these same skulls according to age and land of origin, and divided them into two larger groups by allowing myself to add, considering the general short-headedness of the Jews, the number of the medium-headed to that of the long-headed.

From these two tables we can draw the following two conclusions, which are highly significant for the Jewish racial problem: (1) The skulls from antiquity are almost all dolichocephalic, while three-quarters of those from the Middle Ages are brachycephalic. A complete reformation [of the skull] shape occurred, whose cause surely must be sought in intermixtures that took place on a wide scale. (2) Sephardic skulls evince a remarkable uniformity of type, and are almost without exception dolichocephalic, while half of the skulls of Eastern European Jews are brachycephalic. This brachycephalicity must have some connection to that of the medieval skulls. The only Caucasian skull is brachycephalic.

These two conclusions mandate a third: The ancient Israelites, who were most likely long-headed—just as all Semites are—came into contact, in the Diaspora,

42. [Table II, which is not included in this book, contains comparative information on cranial measurements, organized around the following categories: country of origin; gender; total number; percentage of dolichocephalic, mesocephalic, and brachycephalic; average size; and the scholarly source of the information.]

first with the short-headed Caucasians and Alpine Europeans, and second with the long-headed [populations] of the Mediterranean. Although the first group was transformed, the second maintained the ancient type.

Further research is necessary, however, to determine whether these conclusions can be confirmed or rebutted. Without such research, all further work in this area would be a wasted effort.

# 11 | Anthropological Research on the Russian-Polish Jews, and the Value of This Research for the Anthropology of the Jews in General

## Arkadius Elkind

"Anthropologische Untersuchungen über die russisch-polnischen Juden und der Wert dieser Untersuchungen für die Anthropologie der Juden im allgemeinen," *Zeitschrift für Demographie und Statistik der Juden* 2, no. 4 (1906): 49–54, and no. 5 (1906): 65–69.

Arkadi Danilowich Elkind (1869–?), who wrote under the name of Arkadius Elkind, was a Russian physician and anthropologist. He received a medical degree from Moscow University in 1893. Elkind was the author of a number of works on physical anthropology, including *An Anthropological Study Based Mainly on Observations of Polish Jews*, *An Investigation into Anthropological Parallels between Jews and Non-Jews*, and *The Jews*. The last book, published in 1903, was described by Maurice Fishberg as "the largest and most comprehensive work ever published on the anthropology of any section of the Jews" ("Elkind, Arkadi Danilowich," in *The Jewish Encyclopedia*, 5:140). See the entries on Elkind in *The Universal Jewish Encyclopedia* 4:83, and the *Encyclopedia Judaica*, 6:678.

The geographical distribution of the Jews, their dispersal over so many countries of the world, makes the task of an anthropological investigation of this nation quite difficult. Different sorts of social and climatic conditions and different standards of living obscure their external or physical character and make it necessary, before one can possibly speak about any sort of general anthropological type of Jew, to investigate the particular components of the Jewish population living throughout the most disparate regions of the Old and New Worlds, especially Europe. Along these lines, very little is known even at present about the many Jews living within the borders of the former Kingdom of Poland, nowadays known as the Vistula region. Crowded together in dense areas of settlement, their lives are completely separate [from those of their non-Jewish neighbors], a situation arising out of a myriad distinct or peculiar historical conditions. They [the Jews] remained true to their ancient and medieval ancestors and customs; and since they are highly resistant to external influences, Polish Jews—as Baer[43] testifies—have changed very little with regard to their Semitic type. This opinion is not peculiar to this well-known naturalist of the nineteenth century. Quite a few equally significant anthropologists have put forth analogous opinions. On the other hand, equally renowned scholars have denied not only that the Jews of today belong to the Semitic race, but that there exists any autonomous or distinct type of Jew at all. Without going into any detailed analysis of this question (since I have done this already elsewhere[44]), what I wish to do in the following pages is to address the question, by means of a comparative anthropological analysis, to what extent the above-mentioned Polish Jews are in accord with one or the other of these opinions on the anthropological typology of the Jewish nation. In the hierarchy of descriptive traits, hair and eyes play the major role, particularly when it comes to the Jews. With great probability one can claim that their ancient forebears were distinguished by dark coloring. The Jews who wandered out of Egypt were characterized by dark hair and by a variety of shades of dark skin. Even in later times we see many travel accounts and ethnographical works describing the Jews as, for the most part, possessing dark eyes and hair, the latter usually curly, and often red. Firsthand observation confirms this view, and shows that among the Jews dark hair and eye color prevail significantly over light ones.

## HAIR COLOR

When we compile the results on adult Jews living in various regions within Russia, and even in some parts of the rest of Europe, and compare these with our observations on Polish Jews, we can see that blond hair in general appears rarely among Jews. Among the Polish [Jews] blond hair is rarely found; in other cases, one has observed it in 1.4 percent of Lithuanian Jews and up to 12 percent among those in Riga. Admittedly, Mayer and Kopernizki have found even higher numbers among the Jews of Galicia: 14 percent, 16 percent, even 23.2 percent with blond hair. Yet one must note that these Krakow researchers have often

43. [Karl Ernst von Baer (1792–1876), an Estonian biologist, is considered to be the founder of modern embryology.]

44. Die Juden. *Mitteilungen der kaiserlichen Gesellschaft der Freunde der Naturwissenschaft der Anthropologie und Ethnographie*, vol. 104, Moscow, 1903 (Russian). All the material and literary data for the current article is contained in this work.

counted dark blond—what ought more likely to be called light brown—as blond hair—and that this [dark blond hair] constitutes the highest percentage of Jews with lighter colored hair in general. Yet even if one were to adhere to this method of registry, Polish Jews would still occupy last place, as there was just one individual with dark blond hair found among them. Accordingly, blond hair—both light and dark blond hair—is in no way consistently widespread among the Jews. As is evident from Table I,[45] the numbers fluctuate between 0.5 percent among Polish Jews and 32 percent among Jews of Riga; the overall average among all the Jewish groups, excluding those in the Caucasus,[46] is 18.46 percent. If we include them, the average drops to 17.09 percent.

We understand dark hair to mean black, dark, and light brown. Black hair in general is met with less frequently than dark brown hair. The Jews of the Caucasus are an exception to that. Pantjuchoff has found among them 84.1 percent with black hair and only 12 percent with dark brown. In all other cases, black hair is met with significantly less often, the percentages fluctuating between 54 percent among Jews in southern Russia, 52.9 percent in Italy, to 4–15 percent among Spanish, Galician, Lithuanian, Ukrainian, and Riga Jews. The Polish Jews, with an average approaching 30 percent, are in the middle. On the other hand, dark brown hair is found more frequently among Polish, Galician, and Ukrainian Jews. The total percentage of dark-haired Jews reaches 77.64 percent if one excludes the Jews of the Caucasus; when they are included, the number reaches 79.17 percent.

After dark hair, scholars agree that red hair is most widely distributed among Jews; it is of interest, then, to set forth the relevant observations on this matter of different researchers. The majority of writers find from 1.8 percent (Spanish) to 4.3 percent (Galician and Ukrainian Jews) redheaded individuals among the Jews; according to our observations, there are to be found up to 2.66 percent redheads among the Jews of Poland. The average percentage of redheaded individuals among the total number of Jews found in Table I is 3.31 percent.

45. [Table I, which is not included in this book, divides its Jewish subjects into ten geographic areas and gives numbers of individuals from each area, then percentages of those with dark, blond, and red hair; dark and light eyes; dark, light, and mixed types referring, it seems, to skin color; and then the scholarly source of each statistic.]

46. [Table I contains Caucasian Jews as a category, but there is no total number of individuals provided. Thus Elkind treats their percentages differently.]

## EYE COLOR

In the case of Polish Jews, the dominance of dark over light is far less significant when it comes to the color of the iris than when it comes to the color of the hair. In comparison to the 39.5 percent of gray and blue eyes (Table I), we find merely 49.5 percent brown and black. The remaining 10 percent among those counted fall in the category of so-called mixed eye-color; that is, those whose iris, whether gray or blue, contains radial streaks of yellow or brown. According to the results of other researchers, this appears among all other Jews in the same proportions. Taking the two main categories—dark and light eye color—into consideration, we find the following: The maximum [percentage] of dominant dark eye color is found among the Jews of the Caucasus, since among them one observes something close to nine times more cases of dark eyes than light. In other places, the comparative numbers never reach this high: [in] Italy, in the Rogachev region, as well as in the Mohilev region,[47] there are only twice as many dark-eyed individuals as light. Within this parameter also fall the Spanish, Lithuanian, and Ukrainian Jews. The smallest percentages in favor of dark eyes can be found among the Polish Jews (10 percent) and the Galicians (7.7 percent). The mean for dark eyes among Jews (58.1 percent, excluding the Jews of the Caucasus) is close to one-and-a-half times as large as for those with light eyes. If one wishes to include the Jews of the Caucasus in this equation, then both ends of the ratio (60.2 percent and 39.8 percent) increase somewhat, though neither reaches the same levels as the percentages of hair color.

## TYPES

All of this leads to the conclusion that, considering hair and eyes together, Polish Jews most frequently have the combination of dark eyes with dark hair; this will become apparent from the following facts. Among 183 Polish Jews investigated, there are: 106 individuals (57.92 percent) who fall under the category of dark type; 1 (0.55 percent) the light type; 76 (41.53 percent) mixed. Therefore, almost three-quarters of those Jews observed were dark, while the remaining—with the exception of one alone—are of the mixed type.

Similar results have been reported for other Jews. The dark type is distributed

47. [The Rogachev region (*Rogatschauer Kreise*) was an administrative district in Belarus. Mohilev, a city in eastern Belarus, is on the Dnieper River.]

among the south Russian Jews to an almost equal degree; it is even more strongly marked among Italian Jews and those in the Rogachev region, while it is weaker among those Jews in the Ukraine, Lithuania, and Riga. The number of light types among the Jews, according to results from all authors, is significantly higher than that found among Polish Jews; thus, the number of light individuals fluctuates between 9.4 percent in the Rogachev region to 18 percent in Riga. Finally, various other writers have offered figures related to the mixed type that are lower than those given by me; the lowest number of mixed type is to be found among the Jews of the Rogachev region. With regard to all the Jews found in Table I, including the Polish Jews but excluding the Italians, I have calculated the overall mean attained by each type. According to this method, I have found among 1,715 Jews, analyzed by Talko-Gritschewitsch, Weissenberg, Blechmann, Jakowekno, and myself: 55 percent dark, 13 percent blond, and 32 percent mixed individuals.[48]

[. . .]

## HISTORICAL MATTERS

To return again to the Polish Jews, we see that with regard to both head size and cranial index they occupy a middle position among the various groups within the Jewish nation being compared, since they constitute the most widely distributed type. If one also considers the data about body size, which is characterized by small values, the small number of blonds among them, and finally the highly distinctive dark color of their hair and eyes, one can then claim with some certainty that the Polish Jews have preserved particularly well those anthropological traits that distinguish their nation as a whole.

The fine maintenance of the characteristic traits of their physical type might be traceable back to the external historical conditions of their settlement and to the way of life in the regions of the Vistula. The date of their first appearance in this region cannot be determined with certainty. Just as the history of German settlement relies to a large degree on conjecture and murky traditions, so too does the question of the earliest Jewish settlements in Polish lands. When dealing with this question, it is necessary to bear in mind extant opinions about the emigration of the Jews from their original homeland in the Near East to

48. [Elkind next offers a detailed analysis of body sizes and cranial measurements along lines similar to what he has done above. He then offers a summary and a historical view.]

the various parts of Europe. We can identify three distinct routes. The first led through the Caucusus, the second to the banks of the Black Sea and the Sea of Azov, and the last—the best researched and the most credible, and the one that attracted the largest group of Jews before the beginning of their dispersion—encompasses the numerous lands on the coast of the Mediterranean.

Recent works by Professors Miller, Harkavy, Chachanoff, and Pogodin have shed a great deal of light on the first two routes, and sought to clarify the connection between the different migrations of the Jews to south and southeastern Russia. If the conclusions of these researchers yet require reanalysis and investigation in order to ground them more firmly, it nonetheless remains certain that the above-mentioned shores served as the points of departure for the eventual Jewish colonies in Southern, Western, Central and in parts of Eastern Europe; and this must also include the Baltic regions. Ripley, one of today's most outstanding anthropologists, holds that the settlement of the Polish Jews proceeded from all directions. It is possible that this claim is partly accurate, since the Jews were already living in Kiev in the tenth century, from which they then would have been able to enter Poland. Our knowledge of this, however, is rather sparse and disjointed. Far more certain is the evidence about the immigration of the Jews into Poland from the West. Jews already had trade relations with the Slavic lands in the time of Charlemagne. Since they must have traveled to neighboring Poland for this purpose, it seems likely that they set up permanent residences there. From the end of the eleventh century on, when the persecution of the Jews began under the influence of the Crusades, their movement toward the Polish borders was heightened and took on even greater magnitude in the coming centuries. Moreover, many Polish princes and kings, recognizing the usefulness of the [economic] activity of Jews, lured many of them through the granting of different privileges and rights, thus creating an advantageous situation for the Jews. In this way the Jews over time came to constitute a considerable portion of the population of this land; despite this, they remained outsiders and remained thoroughly separate from the general population, which became particularly evident in the wake of the rising power of the church and the concomitant growth of religious intolerance. These factors helped to create the isolated condition of the Polish Jews. Completely autonomous in their internal existence, the Jews preserved themselves according to their religious and social traditions from any intimate interaction with the general populace, and in particular from the practice of intermarriage. Through this way of life, the Polish Jews have been able to maintain not only their traditions, but also the purity of their anthropological type.

# 12 | Are the Jews a Race?

## Sigmund Feist

"Sind die Juden eine Rasse?" *Zeitschrift für Demographie und Statistik der Juden*, new series, 4, nos. 1–2 (1927): 6–11.

Sigmund Feist (1865–1943) was born in Mainz, Germany. Trained as a philologist with a specialty in Indo-Germanic languages, Feist also worked in the field of anthropology. He published numerous books on general philology and also wrote about the Jews in the light of anthropological and ethnological research. His *Stammeskunde der Juden* (The ethnology of the Jews) appeared in 1925. In addition to his scholarly career, Feist served as the director of the Reichenheim Orphanage, a Jewish institution in Berlin, until 1935. See the entry in *The Universal Jewish Encyclopedia*, 4:269. See also Ruth Roemer, "Sigmund Feist: Deutscher—Germanist—Jude," *Muttersprache* 91 (1981): 249–308.

This old and contentious question has now been discussed anew by Professor Hans Friedenthal in issues 1–3 and 4–6 of the 1926 volume of this journal,[49] and immediately the answer is given along the lines of what has been proposed by Maurice Fishberg, in his 1913 work *Die Rassenmerkmale der Juden*,[50] and by others, claiming that the Jews represent a religious community (*Religionsgemeinschaft*) and that there was never a time, even when they still constituted a Volk, when one could speak of a Jewish race, as science would call it today. Even the concepts of family and race diverge, so even if the Jewish Volk, in primordial times, emerged in part out of one family (Abraham and his lineage), the descendants by no means necessarily constitute individuals linked "racially" (that is, by precisely defined inherited traits shared by each), bearing Gregor Mendel's laws of inheritance in mind. Pure lines [of descent] exist only on paper and conceptually, not in reality and not in nature. Certain individuals can perhaps by chance appear as racially pure representatives of the original [biblical] patriarchic couple (if

49. [Hans Friedenthal, "Zur Anthropologie der Juden," *Zeitschrift für Demographie und Statistik der Juden*, new series, 3, Part 1, nos. 4–6 (1926): 45–48; Part 2, nos. 1–3, 86–91. Hans Friedenthal (1870–1943) was an anthropologist and physiologist who taught at the University of Berlin.]

50. Munich: Ernst Reinhardt, 1913.

they themselves were even racially homogenous); still, the probability of such a chance occurrence is as good as nil.

Now, there are accounts (for example, in Günther's *Rassenkunde des Deutschen Volkes*)[51] in which the Jews are conceived of as a "second order" race—that is, a race that emerged through inbreeding from an original mixture of many races.

Professor Friedenthal would like to negate even this "modest" view of the "racialness" of the Jewish Volk on the basis of an anthropological evaluation of the Jews living today. The European Jews are as different one from another as Central Europeans are more generally. However, they [the Jews] do belong as a whole to the white race, and only some contemporary Jews possess those traits that are usually taken as racial characteristics of Semites.

Furthermore, Friedenthal discusses the constituent components of the Jewish Volk in antiquity: Semites, Hittites, and Amorites (according to Felix von Luschan's theory of 1892, later abandoned). This discussion in itself actually contradicts his [Friedenthal's] assertion at the outset that there never existed a Jewish race. For if that were indeed the case [that the Jews were never a race], then there would be no point in inquiring into its components. Moreover, Friedenthal does not repudiate the idea of the "Aryan" Amorites with quite enough decisiveness. They were actually a pure invention, conjured up to explain the light-skinned element among today's European Jews. This is to assume that blond and blue-eyed Jews had to have already existed in ancient Palestine. About this, however, we know nothing. We do know very well, however, that the Amorites were a Volk who spoke a Semitic language, just like the Phoenicians, the Moabites, the Edomites, Canaanites, and others. Like the Hebrews, the Amorites were an older immigrant class or group. The physical representations of Amorites that one finds on Egyptian reliefs—for instance, in Medinat Habu one finds an Amorite next to a Hittite[52]—show in an exact way the Semitic type, akin to other inhabitants of Syria and Palestine. The assumption that the Egyptians had represented the Amorites as blue-eyed and blond can be traced back to the inexact observations of previous scientific illustrators. Dr. Max Burchardt, the leader of the expedition mentioned in footnote 1 [52], wrote the following to me shortly after his return from Egypt:

51. [Hans F. K. Günther (1891–1968) was a German anthropologist and race scientist. He was a strong advocate of Nordic superiority, and his writings were highly popular with Nazis.]

52. Eduard Meyer, *Bericht über eine Expedition nach Aegypten zur Erforschung der Darstellungen der Fremdvölker*. Sitzungsber. Berl. Akad. Der Wiss., 1913, p. 793 (Nr. 300).

> I have been working for years on a cultural history of the Semites according to Egyptian sources. The old publications of Champollion, Rosellini, [and] even one work by von Lepsius present Semites with blue eyes. I paid particular attention during my work over the past winter to this phenomenon and determined that all these blue-eyed Semites, insofar as I could still gain access to the originals, are the result of errors made by these older illustrators! The eyes are light brown to the darkest brown. At the same time, the hair of the Semites was never blond, but always black or dark brown, and the same held true for the beards. And the beard occasionally had a streak of red. The fantasy or fairy tale about blond Semites can be traced back to inexact observation. Many Egyptian artists used yellow together with black as a foundation or primer. The yellow, however, would cause the color painted on or over it to flake off. And if in some of the tombs one finds Semites with yellow-blond or ash-blond hair, one cannot find a well-preserved black-haired figure in the sepulchers' pictorial representations! Even the Egyptians are blond there!

There never were "Aryan" Amorites in Canaan, and no one can ever know in any case if the "Aryans" (that is, the hypothetical Indo-Germanic primordial Volk) were blond and blue-eyed. It is not even likely [that this was the case], but I cannot go into this at length here. It is true that in the middle of the second millennium "Aryans" came to Palestine, as the names of the municipal rulers found in the Tel-Amarna letters (from the archive of Pharaohs Amenhopis III and IV) demonstrate; but we do not know if these dynasties in fact even brought with them greater numbers of "Aryans," who would have exerted a racial influence on the inhabitants of Canaan. And then, as we have already stressed, these need not have been blond and blue-eyed.

There is nothing at all to the notion of the "Aryan" Amorites then; nor can one speak of partial Aryans, as Professor Friedenthal admits. Like all the other historical inhabitants of Syria and Palestine, the Volk of the Amorites spoke a Semitic dialect; as far as the Egyptian representations allow us to judge this, they were not racially different from those other groups.

Those blond and blue-eyed Jews that one encounters today in greater numbers in Eastern and Central Europe, although only sporadically elsewhere, do thus not descend from the primordial period of the Jewish Volk; like many other racial types, they mixed with them later. From what source? One cannot say for certain. Presumably from those very populations, in the aforementioned countries, that evince similar anatomical traits [that are blond and blue-eyed].

Professor Friedenthal is also correct when he declares: "There is no European trait that the Jews lack, and no trait that can be said to be characteristic of the Jews (for example, the crooked nose)."

Likewise, we must agree with him when he repudiates the insistence on a fixed cranial index for the Jews. Among the Jewish population around the world, head shapes range from an extreme dolichocephalism to an extreme brachycephalism; nor is there any clear connection or relationship in this regard between the Jews and the other populations in whose midst they live. One does encounter individual cases of similitude, but this does not allow us to draw any conclusions. The size of the Jewish body, just like the shape of the head, varies quite significantly, and this among Jews living in the same country. In addition to hereditary factors, social conditions play a considerable role, as do certain other environmental influences, which are difficult to grasp scientifically. Anyone can observe at present in many Jewish families that the children grow up to be taller than their parents. This is due not only to better nutrition and more athletic activity, since we encounter this phenomenon even when either one or both of these factors are absent.

Within this category also belong those frequently encountered examples of children whose parents are typically Jewish looking, but who themselves display this characteristic in only a very weak way. Cases such as these are also easily verifiable by everyday observation.

And with this we arrive at a matter that Professor Friedenthal's otherwise admirable presentation deals with in too cursory a manner: the *facies judaica* (the Jewish face). It is this more than anything else by which the Jewish race is thought to be identifiable. The development of the soft or malleable parts of the face, however, depends neither on heredity alone nor on the skeletal structure or musculature; rather, it develops in its own way. In it are reflected influences of environment and mental processes that are independent of the abovementioned factors. The facial features of a European scholar, for instance, have greater similarity to a Japanese of equal status than to a lower-class individual[53] of his own race and language. In the same way, a Jewish mentality will imprint itself upon the Jewish face. We ought to ignore those external features such as beard and hairstyle (side locks), although these contribute in no small way to the characterization of the Jewish face. The public naturally uses the "Jewish face" to make judgments about whether or not some people belong to the Jewish "race," and

53. [*Lastträger*—literally, a porter or servant.]

many naive observers are almost indignant when told that no such thing as a distinctive Jewish race exists, for [to these observers] the racial quality of being Jewish is so apparent when "just looking at them."

Now the Jew certainly does differ from the Northern European not only with regard to the face but also in discernible anatomical differences. The Jew often, though not as a rule, has a long and stocky upper body with short limbs, while the typical Northern European has a short and slender or narrow upper body with long limbs. This difference occurs only in Northern Europe, not in Southern Europe or in the Orient; in these places, the same sort of stocky type [as the Jews] is frequently found. This, therefore, is a trait that is not specifically Jewish, but nevertheless becomes distinct in a racially different environment. I assign little importance to the posture of many Jews: the crooked backs, the rocking back and forth of the upper body, the frequency of bowleggedness. These are not racial traits, but rather characteristics that have been acquired due to external conditions (sitting in a stooped position for long periods of time, traditional habits of prayer, rachitis [inflammation of the spine] due to deficient diet, and so forth); these will immediately vanish with a change in adolescent habits or behaviors.

Professor Friedenthal is thus quite right in claiming that there are no Jewish racial traits; rather, distinct individual Jewish populations display common or average physical and mental abilities and disabilities. These include the following: the shape of the nose—there are just as many Jews with straight noses as there are with crooked noses, it is just that we pay less attention to the former; the shape of the cranium—whether long-, middle-, or round-headed, all variations are represented among the Jews; [and] body size, which varies as much among Jews as it does among the European population in general. Remarkable to me is Friedenthal's claim that studying is more conducive to greater height than is agricultural labor. One should assume the contrary, if the latter occurs in absence of undernourishment or negative hereditary conditions. In fact, those Jews who have earned their living through manual labor for generations are the ones who are taller and stronger than those Jews who have predominantly engaged in mental labor. One thinks of the Lithuanian wagon drivers; the porters in Salonika, Constantinople, Cyprus, and elsewhere; the numerous Jews engaged in sports (boxing and so on). Where is one to find intellectual laborers characterized by noteworthy physical size? As in all professions, I am aware of only isolated individuals, not an enormous number, of advanced students who exceed the average when it comes to anatomical development.

I have serious doubts as to whether one can deny, as Friedenthal does, the claims about Jews with regard to one of the surest anthropological characteristics—namely, the hair. In Central Europe as in Russia, the curly-headed Jew is a type so often encountered in literature that this could only be a product of real-life experience. In my experience, the Jewish head of hair is specifically distinct from that of the average Northern and Eastern European population; it is more similar to the Southern European type, which displays curly hair more frequently in both males and females. Do we have here a Negroid influence (*negritischer Einschlag*) that traces back to the primal period of European humanity?

Friedenthal furthermore argues that the racially based talent of the Jews does not deviate in any significant way from that of the general population. If one is going to stress that the great majority of mankind's geniuses have been non-Jews, then this merely corresponds to the statistical probability, as the Jews have always been a tiny minority. Friedenthal also denies that the Jews possess a special aptitude for intellectual vocations. Is he not in this case proceeding a little too schematically? There must indeed be some advantageous effect of the superior and much older tradition of intellectual training among the Jews in contrast to the European population. This must be true to the same extent that one would acknowledge discernible differences along these lines within the European population itself. Should one really place the average Frenchman on the same intellectual level as the average Russian? In France we have had (Celtic-Roman-French) culture for at least 2,500 years; in Russia, for the most part, culture was introduced only during the reign of Peter the Great, 250 years ago, and it still has not penetrated into all segments of that society as it has in Western Europe. And this is how it stands with the Jews vis-à-vis most of the other European peoples (Germans, Poles, Hungarians, Russians, and so on). Jews on average, for historical reasons, must necessarily stand on higher intellectual ground than the average above-mentioned peoples. Of course, Professor Friedenthal is correct when he writes that this enormous intellectual talent must not be seen as an anthropological—that is, racial—trait. Rather, this gift is a historical outcome that any race could have attained if it had enjoyed a similar continuity in the level of intellectual engagement as had the Jews.

When Professor Friedenthal opposes the notion, at the end of his presentation, that the Jews, as West Asians, constitute an entity foreign to Europe, one must agree with him insofar as fundamental differences with regard to race do not exist between Europe, particularly Southern Europe, and Western Asia. What attracts our attention about the Jews in Central and Northern Europe, however, is the distinctive mixing of their "representative population average," as Friedenthal puts it. This is the immediate result of the widespread inbreeding that the Jewish Volk has been engaging in for a very long time. A result of this is the (unintended) cultivation of particular types that are conspicuous within the particular population, and that may in part have their origins in primordial elements of the Jewish Volk. This is the only way that one can account for a uniformity of type that exists among Jewish individuals, and not only among those groups or social strata that live in close proximity but also among those that are geographically widely dispersed. Certainly, if one considers the notion of "race" in the narrow definition given to it by Professor Friedenthal, then indeed a pure race could never have continued to exist in the civilized regions of Europe or Asia, for such races—which might at some time in the distant past have been pure or unified—would have been dominated by foreign elements through immigration and conquest. Yet in many cases we can still recognize the geographically determined type, and it is also from this type from which some Jewish groups differ so distinctly by virtue of a different mixture of [racial] features in those groups. This is what one would commonly refer to as the "Jewish race." Though one might not take this as scientifically tenable, we must nonetheless recognize common or popular opinion (*Volksbewusstein*) as a reality and integrate it into our considerations.

# III | Medicine and Biology

Inquiries into Jewish racial identity and difference consisted of much more than questions of origins and development, and of physical attributes. The idea of a distinct Jewish racial identity or nature also raised questions related to health and disease. And statistics played a crucial role in this discussion. Working with numbers generated largely by official governmental agencies, racial and social scientists compared Jewish and non-Jewish rates of birth, death, infant mortality, and affliction by a host of diseases—and then sought to explain the differences.

Thus, if Jews seemed to suffer in appreciably lower numbers from tuberculosis or certain forms of cancer, or in higher numbers from diabetes or mental disorders, was this due to their racial nature or to some social or environmental set of factors? Were Jews racially immune to certain diseases and susceptible to others? What impact did Jewish religious law and ritual have on Jewish health and disease? What were the consequences of the abandonment of religious observance by many Jews in the wake of civic, social, and cultural emancipation? What impact did the Jews' physical isolation in ghettos have on their immunity or susceptibility to illness? What was the result of the end of this isolation and the subsequent integration or assimilation of the Jews into the surrounding populations? Were Jews strengthened or weakened physically by assimilation? These issues bore directly on debates between Jews and antisemites, but also between Jewish integrationists and Jewish nationalists.

# 13 | The Comparative Pathology of the Jews

## Maurice Fishberg

"The Comparative Pathology of the Jews," *New York Medical Journal* 73 (1901): 537–43 and 576–82.

For biographical information on Maurice Fishberg, see the note at the beginning of selection 3.

The influence of race and nationality on the susceptibility and comparative (because we know of no absolute) immunity to the various diseases that afflict mankind is at present well recognized by the medical profession. The physicians of the United States have especially studied the comparative pathology of the Negro race, owing to the fact that these people are to be found in relatively great numbers, particularly in the southern states. The total number of Jews in the United States at present is estimated to be 1,058,135;[1] and it is quite surprising that, on consulting the most important medical journals published in the United States, I have been unable to find any article on the comparative pathology of these people, excepting a few scattered notes and remarks. The literature on this subject in Europe is also very meager, and many difficulties have been met with while collecting the materials for the following paper.

All over Europe, wherever tested, the Jews have been found, in spite of their frail physical aspect, to live longer than the Christians. Thus we find that in Budapest, Hungary, the average duration of life of the Christian population in the city is twenty-six years; that of the Jews, thirty-seven years. The Christians between the ages of one and fifty have a death rate of 14 percent, the Jews one of only 10 percent. Among the Christian population, 50 percent of all newborn children will reach the age of thirty years; from the Jewish population, 50 percent will reach the age of fifty years. Eight percent of Jews reach the age of from eighty-five to ninety years, while only 2.4 percent of the Christians reach this age. Twelve percent of the Jewish population have reached the age of from sixty to seventy years, while only 9.8 percent of Christians have reached this age.[2]

1. *American Jewish Year-book*, 1900.

2. C. Lombroso. *Der Antisemitismus und die Juden*, Leipzig, 1894, p. 95.

In Prussia, according to Mulhall,[3] the death rate has been found to be, yearly per 1,000 population:

TABLE 13.1

| | Christians | | Jews | |
|---|---|---|---|---|
| Years | Males | Females | Males | Females |
| 1822–22 | 28.7 | 27.0 | 22.1 | 19.1 |
| 1841–66 | 30.2 | 28.2 | 19.8 | 17.9 |

In Austria the number of births among the Jews has been calculated to exceed that of the deaths in 30.80 percent, and among the rest of the population as only 28.30 percent.[4]

In Amsterdam the mortality of children under five years of age has been found to be: among Christians, 11.52 percent; among Jews, only 8.85 percent. The death rate of adults, of the ages between twenty and fifty years, [is] for Christians, 5.98 percent; for Jews, only 3.06 percent.[5]

Table II [13.2] shows the relation of births and deaths among Jews. In Algiers we find that in 1856 there were:[6]

TABLE 13.2

| | Europeans | Mussulmans | Jews |
|---|---|---|---|
| Births | 1.234 | 331 | 211 |
| Deaths | 1.553 | 514 | 187 |

The excess of births over deaths among the Jews is quite evident.

In Rumania, where the Jews are found to be in numbers almost equal to that of the Christians, we find that[7] during three years the births and deaths were as in Table III [13.3]:

3. Mulhall. *Dictionary of Statistics*, London, 1899, p. 185.
4. G. A. Schimmer. *Statistik des Judenthums*, Wien, 1873.
5. Lombroso. Loc. cit., p. 94.
6. G. F. Kalb. *Handbuch der vergleichende Statistik*, Leipzig, 1868, p. 574.
7. Leroy-Beaulieu. *Israel among the Nations*, New York, 1895, p. 154.

TABLE 13.3

| Years | Births: Jews | Births: Orthodox | Deaths: Jews | Deaths: Orthodox |
|---|---|---|---|---|
| 1884 | 9,729 | 185,000 | 4,626 | 114,300 |
| 1885 | 9,542 | 197,000 | 5,036 | 114,000 |
| 1886 | 9,458 | 196,000 | 5,194 | 124,500 |

We see from these figures that in 1884 the proportion of births among the Jews was 2.10 to one death, while the births among Christians were only 1.62 to one death. Almost a similar proportion can be reduced from the other figures given above.

We thus see that, almost all over Europe, the Jews enjoy an unprecedented tenacity of life, showing a lower death rate and an excess of the number of births over deaths. Another important fact is that, almost everywhere, the Jews, at present, show a proportionately smaller marriage rate, and produce relatively a less number of children to each marriage than Christians. This fact goes to prove that it is his longevity that gives the Jew his unprecedented tenacity of life over that of the Christians, and not the number of marriages and births. Thus, in Prussia, the Jewish population, from 1822 to 1840, increased 34.5 percent, while, in the same lapse of time, the Christians augmented only 28 percent, increase by immigration being about the same [among Jews and Christians]. There was one birth to every twenty-eight Jews, one to every twenty-five Christians; one marriage among every 139 Jews, one among 112 Christians; one death among forty Jews, one in thirty-four Christians.[8]

[. . .]

On carefully considering the above facts and figures, we are forced to agree with W. L. Ripley that the Jews show an "unprecedented tenacity of life." This is more forcibly depicted by Dr. John S. Billings in his "Report on the Vital Statistics of the Jews in the United States"[9] by a table of the expectation of life of the

8. John S. Hough. "Longevity and other Biostatic Peculiarities of the Jewish Race." *Medical Record*, 1873, pp. 241–244.

9. *Census Bulletin* No. 19, p. 12.

Jews in the United States, as compared with that for England and the average American population of Massachusetts. From that table we find that a young Jewish child of five years would have, on an average, about sixty-two years more to live; the average Americans of Massachusetts, only fifty-three years; a Jew at the age of twenty-five would have, on an average, forty-five more years to live; an American, only thirty-nine years; etc.

The experience of European observers about the low death rate of the Jews, as compared with that of non-Jews, is thus fairly well sustained by the United States census. It is only surprising that very few physicians of those who practice among these people [the Jews] are aware of this fact.

Dr. Glatter,[10] the director of the statistical bureau of Vienna, gives the following table [13.7] illustrating the relative frequency of disease among different races in the same locality:

TABLE 13.7

| Inhabitants | Number ill | Number to 1,000 |
|---|---|---|
| Magyars | 6,034 | 534 |
| Germans | 3,806 | 223 |
| Slavonians | 1,522 | 182 |
| Servians [*sic*] | 252 | 28 |
| Jews | 1,540 | 32 |

These figures show that the Jews are relatively less liable to be attacked by disease.

When we turn again to the causes of death among the Jews, we find that the most dangerous diseases, as tuberculosis, pneumonia, nephritis, typhoid, malaria, etc. (except diabetes), claim a proportionately smaller number of victims from among the Jews than from among non-Jews. The testimony of many European physicians proves, also, that most of the epidemic diseases kill, proportionately, a smaller number of Jews than of non-Jews. Thus the mortality of children from small-pox in Posen during twenty-six years was: Catholics, 3.13 percent; Protestants, 2.26 percent; Jews, only 0.9 percent.[11]

10. *Das Rassenmoment in seinen Einfluss auf Erkrankungen*. Caspers Vjsch., 1864, Vol. xxv, pp. 32–45. Quoted from Hough, loc. cit.

11. Virchow's *Jahresbericht*, Vol. i, 1869, p. 284.

This may be due to the fact that the Jews submit more readily to vaccination than non-Jews (as can be readily seen even in New York, where they flock to the health board for that purpose proportionately more frequently than Christians); but on consulting the reports of epidemics of other diseases we arrive to almost the same results. For instance, Tschudi, in speaking of the plague in 1346, says that this disease did not affect the Jews of any country. Fracastor mentions the fact that the Jews escaped completely the epidemic of typhus of 1505. Rau mentions the same immunity from typhus observed at Langeons in 1824. Ramazzini insisted on the immunity of Jews from the intermittent fevers observed in Rome in 1691. Degner says that the Jews escaped, in 1736, the epidemic of dysentery of Nimegue. Michael Levy remarks that this immunity was manifest at the same time in the French and in the Israelites.[12]

During the epidemic of cholera in Budapest, in 1851, there was a mortality of 1.85 percent among the Christian population, while the Jews succumbed only to the extent of 0.257 percent—i.e., seven times less;[13] a writer in the *Revue scientifique*[14] states that during the epidemic of cholera in London, in the seventies, the Jews remained almost not at all affected. Again, in Algiers, notwithstanding the fact that the Jews are crowded in small and dark dwellings, often in basements, they still are more resistant to the effects of contagious diseases than non-Jews, as can be seen from the following figures.[15] During the epidemic of cholera the mortality was found to be as in Table VIII [13.8]:

TABLE 13.8

MORTALITY PER 1,000 POPULATION DURING THE CHOLERA EPIDEMIC IN ALGIERS

| | 1844 | 1845 |
|---|---|---|
| Europeans | 42.9 | 45.5 |
| Mussulmans | 32.4 | 40.8 |
| Jews | 21.6 | 36.1 |

This peculiar resistance of the Jews to the noxious effects of contagious disease has been noted already in the Middle Ages, especially during the great epidemics

12. Quoted from Hough, *Longevity*, etc., loc. cit.

13. Tormay. *Lebens und Sterblichkeitsverhältnisse der Stadt*, Pest, 1866.

14. 1881, Vol. i, p. 825.

15. Boudin. *Géographie médicale*, Paris, 1857, Vol. ii, p. 216.

in Europe of the plague known then as the "Black Death." At that time they suffered severely, because of the fact that they were affected by the pestilence to a less degree and had a proportionately smaller mortality than the Christians. The Jews were accused of being the special emissaries of Satan in causing the plague; it was said that their immunity was due to a special protection by Satan as a compensation for the services they rendered him by their wholesale poisoning of the wells; the use of poisoned water was thought the cause of the Christians being attacked by plague. By torturing and murdering the Jews, and especially by confiscating their property, it was thought that the Almighty might be propitiated, the terrible scourge driven from good Christian countries, and Satan thwarted. As a result of this, hundreds of thousands of Jews were burned or otherwise killed. The plague disappeared in due time—of course only after killing 25,000,000, a quarter of the population of Europe at that period.

Such immunity of the Jews to contagious diseases is not observed at the present time; during the late epidemic of cholera in 1892–94, in Russia, it has been observed that the Jews were no more spared by the pestilence than their non-Jewish neighbors, and that in some cities the Jews were even more affected than the Christians. But the percentage of deaths from a given number of cases has, as a rule, been smaller among the Jews than among non-Jews. Thus, Dr. Barazhnikoff reported to the St. Petersburg Medical Society in 1894 that, during the epidemic of cholera in the government Mogileff [the city of Mogilev], the morbidity among the Jews was greater, and the disease, as a rule, ran a severer course, than among the Christians. But the percentage of mortality was smaller among the Jews. He adds that the fact must not be forgotten that the Jews in that locality are more intelligent than the Christians and take more care of their health, although they are generally poorer.[16]

[...]

The various other acute infectious diseases, diseases of the respiratory and urinary systems, of the liver, and nervous system, according to the *Report on Vital Statistics of the Eleventh Census of the United States,* claim a proportionately smaller number of deaths from among the Jews than from among the non-Jews. And, according to Dr. John S. Billings' "Report on the Vital Statistics of the Jews in the United States," we find that "the Jews have suffered a relatively greater loss than their neighbors, by deaths from diphtheria, diarrheal diseases, diseases of the nervous system (and especially diseases of the spinal cord), of the circulatory

16. *Proceedings of the St. Petersburg Medical Society,* 1895, p. 206.

system, bones and joints, and of the skin, while their mortality has been relatively less from the tubercular diseases, including consumption, scrofula, tabes, and hydrocephalus, than the other people with whom they are compared."

Alcoholism and syphilis are diseases that are very rare among Jews. During the six years ending May 31, 1890, alcoholism caused in each 100,000 persons, of each race in New York, 31 deaths annually among the Irish, 10 among the Germans, 9 among the Americans, 6 among the Negroes, 3 among the Italians, and only 1 among the Russian and Polish (Jews). This may give us a clue to the reason why the Jews suffered such a small loss through nephritis, as the following figures show: during the same six years nephritis caused in each 100,000 persons, of each race in New York, 142 deaths among the Irish, 67 among the Germans, 54 among the Americans, 27 among the Italians, and 18 among the Russian and Polish (Jews).

That syphilis is relatively infrequent among the Jews has been observed almost all over Europe. Thus, according to Mr. Jonathan Hutchinson, syphilis is less common among Jews than among Christians; at the Metropolitan Free Hospital, in the Jews' quarter of London, in 1854, the proportion of Jews to Christians among the outpatients was nearly one to three, yet the ratio of cases of syphilis in the former to those in the latter was only one to fifteen, and that this difference was not due to their superior chastity was evident from the fact that the Jews furnished nearly one-half of the cases of gonorrhea that were treated during the same period.[17]

Dr. A. Cohen, late senior house surgeon of the Metropolitan Free Hospital in London, has, at the request of Mr. Joseph Jacobs, collected the statistics of venereal diseases that came to this hospital during his service in 1882–83, and has found that the proportion of Christian to Jewish patients affected with syphilis has been as three to one.[18]

We have not exact statistics as to the frequency of syphilis among the Jews in the United States, but the testimony of physicians practicing among this people goes to show that, while among the Jews syphilis is often met with, it is not so frequently encountered as among non-Jews.

The fact that the Jews are not very often attacked by alcoholism and syphilis has a very important bearing upon the comparative pathology of their people.

17. Bumstead. *Venereal Diseases.*

18. Joseph Jacobs. "On the Racial Characteristics of Modern Jews," *Journal of the Anthropological Institute*, xv, pp. 23–62.

Besides the fact that this is one of the reasons that nephritis and diseases of the liver (especially cirrhosis) are less commonly met with, the varieties of nervous diseases to which the Jews are most liable are also determined by these factors, as we shall see later in this paper.

A disease from which the Jews suffer more than any other nationality is diabetes. It is extremely frequent among the Jews in large cities, according to Bordier;[19] out of 400 patients suffering from diabetes, Frerichs found that 100 were Jews—i.e., 25 percent. Osler,[20] Strümpell,[21] Naunyn,[22] Saundby,[23] and most other observers say that the Jews are especially prone to this disease.

Dr. Heinrich Stern,[24] in an exhaustive analysis of the mortality from diabetes in the city of New York in 1899, states that "the Hebrews, no doubt, are more commonly affected with chronic glycosuria than natives among whom they dwell. Out of the total of 202 deaths (from diabetes in New York City in 1899), fifty-four—that is, 25 percent—occurred in Jews. Of these, twenty-one were males, and thirty-three females." Dr. Stern further intimates that while "mental exertion, the characteristic modes of living, gluttony, alcoholic intoxication, etc., might be considered predisposing factors in the production of the diabetic state," it is his opinion that "the cardinal predisposing cause is the breeding in and in to which, in a very pronounced measure, the Jewish, as well as the Irish, race still adheres."

Dr. R. Saundby, again, states that the frequency of diabetes among the Jews is to be ascribed to the following cause: "The Jew raises himself easily, by his superior mental ability, to a comfortable social position, and notoriously avoids all kinds of bodily exercises."[25] This cause cannot hold good for the mortality from diabetes of the Jews in New York. As Dr. H. Stern has shown, 25 percent of the deaths from diabetes in New York are found to be in Jews; and, examining the original death certificates in New York City for 1899, "almost 70 percent of deaths occurred in tenement houses, 15 percent occurred in hospital practice and

19. Bordier. *Pathologie comparée,* Paris, 1889, p. 154.

20. Osler. *Practice of Medicine,* p. 320.

21. A. Strümpell. *Specielle Pathologie u. Therapie,* Leipzig, 1885, Vol. ii, p. 240.

22. B. Naunyn. "Der Diabetes Mellitus"; *Nothnagel's Specielle Pathologie u. Therapie,* Wien, 1898, p. 124.

23. R. Saundby. *Allbutt's System of Medicine,* Vol. iii, p. 197.

24. Heinrich Stern. "The Mortality from Diabetes Mellitus in the City of New York, 1899"; *Medical Record,* November 17, 1900.

25. Saundby, loc. cit.

coroner's cases, and only 15 percent in private houses. This tends to show that the malady has virtually little to do with high living."[26] Furthermore, the New York Jews living in tenements are hard-working people—working long hours in sweatshops, having a sufficient amount of bodily exercise, so that the cause that Saundby assigns for the prevalence of diabetes is not operative among them.

C. Van Noorden, in a recent paper on diabetes,[27] states that it is his belief that the cause of the frequency of diabetes among Jews is the close intermarriage among them. Consanguineous marriages are really more frequent among Jews than among Christians,[28] and this fact has been very much exploited by medical writers, who have attributed to it all the ills the Jews are liable to. We shall return to this question later in this article.

As to the other diseases to which the Jews are more or less predisposed, the various nervous and mental diseases stand out preeminently; after these come the diseases of metabolism, called by French authors arthritism and herpetism—for instance, gout, gallstones and nephrolithiasis, chronic rheumatism, some forms of neuralgia and migraine, asthma, pulmonary emphysema, varicose veins, and especially hemorrhoids, arteriosclerosis, and some diseases of the skin. Finally, some authors state that blindness, colorblindness, myopia, trachoma, glaucoma, and almost all the skin diseases are more frequent among the Jews than among the non-Jews.

Concerning the frequency of nervous and mental diseases among the Jews, the evidence is overwhelmingly abundant. It appears that the ancient Hebrews were already great sufferers of hysteria and insanity, as can be seen by many statements in the Bible, particularly in the New Testament, where it is mentioned that numbers of people "possessed with devils," lunatics, "men with unclean spirits," etc., called upon Christ for relief and that He cured them (see particularly Matthew 8:16, 9:32, 12:22, 17:15; Mark 5:2; Luke 8:27, 13:11; and in many other places).

In modern times Charcot, Lancereaux, Oppenheim, Erb, Strümpel, Jolly, Möbius, Krafft-Ebing, Löwenfeld, Müller, Binswanger, Putnam, Collins, and many others have observed this fact and speak of it in their textbooks and monographs. Neurasthenia and hysteria are mostly found among the Jews. Some authors have even stated that the majority of the Jews are neurasthenics and that most of the [Jewish] women are hysterical. Thus Raymond[29] states that hysteria is frequent

26. *Journal of the American Medical Association*, January 26, 1901.

27. *Berliner klinische Wochenschrift*, December 3, 1900.

28. Joseph Jacobs. *Studies in Jewish Statistics*, London, 1891.

29. Raymond. *L'etude des maladies des systéme nerveux en Russia*, Paris, 1889, p. 71.

among both men and women in Warsaw (Poland). The Jewish population of that city alone is almost exclusively the inexhaustible source for the supply of hysterical males for the whole continent. "Among the European nations," says Dr. Binswanger,[30] "the Jews supply, relatively, the largest contingent of neurasthenics"; according to Dr. Jolly,[31] "the Jews have a hysterical and especially nervous disposition to an overwhelming degree." "Nervous diseases, especially neurasthenia," says Krafft-Ebing,[32] "affect the Jews with exceptional severity."

Dr. James J. Putnam[33] states that "the psychoneuroses in general are particularly common in the Latin and Hebrew races." Dr. Joseph Collins and Dr. C. Philips,[34] analyzing 333 cases of neurasthenia which came under their observation, have found that more than 40 percent of the patients were of the Jewish race, although "their *clientèle* was not conspicuously foreign."

Mental diseases occur more frequently among the Jews than among non-Jews. It has been asserted by many competent and reliable observers that the Jews supply proportionately from two to five times more mental defectives than the Christians. Thus Lombroso[35] shows that the Jews in Italy had, in 1869, one lunatic to 391 of their people—that is, almost four times more [a rate four times higher] than the Catholics in that country. Verga confirmed this in 1879, and stated that there were:

| | |
|---|---|
| One lunatic to | 1,775 Catholics; |
| | 1,725 Protestants; |
| | 385 Jews. |

[. . .]

All the statistics show plainly the frightful disposition of the Jews to insanity and idiocy. We shall speak of the causes of this peculiarity of the Jews hereafter in this paper, when discussing the causes of the comparative pathology of the Jews in general.

[. . .]

The frequency of functional nervous diseases in the Jew, as we have seen be-

30. Otto Binswanger. *Die Pathologie u. Therapie d. Neurasthenia*, Jena, 1896, p. 46.

31. F. Jolly. *Handbuch der practischen Medicin*, Ebstein and Schwalbe, Stuttgart, 1900, Vol. iii, p. 755.

32. Von Krafft-Ebing. *Nervosität u. neurasthenische Zustände*, Wien, 1895, p. 54.

33. J. J. Putnam in Loomis and Thompson's *System of Medicine*, Vol. iv, p. 553.

34. *Medical Record*, March 25, 1899.

35. C. Lombroso. *Génie und Irrsinn*, Leipzig, 1887, pp. 70–71.

fore, is attested by most of the observers on both continents. He is most liable to the diseases of our age—neurasthenia and hysteria; he has the distinction of having his nervous system predominating over his muscular. The Jews are far less muscular than nervous, probably because they are the most brainy, having lived for centuries only on the products of their brains; and, therefore, having for two thousand years overstrained their nervous system, they very easily become disordered, "out of gear," and even collapse entirely; a fatigued organ is easily disturbed in its function.

"The nervous derangements which are the effect of psychic trauma," says H. Oppenheim,[36] "explain to some extent the reason why the Jewish race—after being persecuted and oppressed, mostly only tolerated among the nations, living in peace for short times only, and then again tormented—is suffering in such immense numbers from the neuroses and psychoses, and particularly hysteria."

[...]

Of the great number of other diseases which were, at one time or another, supposed to have been of more frequent occurrence among Jews than among Christians, we will but name gout and chronic rheumatism, and also various eruptions on the skin, especially psoriasis. French authors, as Charcot, Lancereaux, Féré, and many others, find a close connection between the neuroses and what they call "arthritisms" and "herpetisms," including under these names a number of diseases and conditions, as gout, lithemia, chronic rheumatism, psoriasis, diabetes, gallstones, nephrolithiasis, etc., all of which occur in people of a nervous diathesis. They describe all these afflictions as occurring very often among the Jews. "The pathological history of the Jewish race," says Charles Féré,[37] "is particularly favorable for the observation of the following fact: nowhere else do we see so clearly the close connection which exists between the neuroses and the arthritisms, which are especially represented by gout and diabetes and the nervous diseases. Neurasthenia manifests itself in the Jews in its most complex forms."

Physicians who practice extensively among the Jews do not generally notice that the Jews are more prone to herpetism, gout, etc., than Christians. The case is, as we have seen, different with the functional neuroses and diabetes.

Varicose veins, and particularly hemorrhoids, occur very frequently among

36. H. Oppenheim. *Lehrbuch der Nervenkrankheiten*, Berlin, 1894, p. 636.
37. Charles Féré. *La famille neuropathique*, Paris, 1894, p. 105.

the Jews, probably more often than among Christians. It is a fact that can be attested by most of the physicians practicing among these people, that a very great proportion of Jews who have passed the fourth decade [of life] have their hemorrhoidal veins more or less enlarged. The various forms of visceral hernias appear also to be very frequent among the Jews.

According to Dr. Hardy[38] and many others, Jews are more often affected by eczema than non-Jews; but dermatologists with extensive practices among Jews and Christians inform me that the Jews in the United States are not any more liable than any other nationality to this disease.

Of the afflictions of the eyes, the Jews are said to be more liable to blindness, colorblindness, astigmatism, trachoma, glaucoma, and, according to M. Hervé,[39] there is a frequency of lacrymal tumors among the Jews, due to the narrowness of their nasal canal.

Concerning blindness, Dr. Herman Cohen[40] brings the following statistics for Bavaria:

| | *Percent* |
|---|---|
| Among 10,000 Protestants | 7.2 blind |
| 10,000 Catholics | 8.2 |
| 10,000 Jews | 13.8 |

and for Prussia, in 1880:

| | *Percent* |
|---|---|
| Among 10,000 Protestants | 8.2 blind |
| 10,000 Catholics | 8.4 |
| 10,000 Jews | 11.0 |

There are similar statistics showing the frequent occurrence of blindness among the Jews in the various other European countries.

According to the "Report of the Committee on Colorblindness" of the Ophthalmological Society of London,[41] the Jews are more subject than the ordinary population to colorblindness. Among 730 Jewish women examined, 3.1 percent were found affected; and among 949 Jewish males, 4.9 percent. The report adds that the Jews were, on the whole, of a poor condition of life, and their defects were

38. *Medical Bulletin*, September 16, 1891.

39. *Précis d'anthropologie*, p. 309, 1887.

40. *Real Encyclop. d. gesamt. Heilkunde*, Vol. iii, p. 139.

41. *Transactions of the Ophthalmological Society*, London, 1881.

of pronounced character. Jacobs and Spielman[42] found no less than 12.7 percent of London Jews to be colorblind. Fuchs and many others mention that trachoma and glaucoma are very often met with among Jews. "In many countries the Jews are special sufferers from trachoma," says Fuchs,[43] and he ascribes it to the fact that they live in crowded houses and are uncleanly. About glaucoma, the same opthalmologist says that "among Jews inflammatory glaucoma is more frequent than among Christians."[44]

Of the many other diseases considered to be more common among Jews than non-Jews we will not speak here, because the writers who have described these peculiarities either have not substantiated their statements with facts, or their evidence is inadequate and is not borne out by experience among the Jews.

The causes of the peculiarities of the comparative pathology of the Jews have at different times received different interpretations. Some have attributed the fact that the Jews have a longer duration of life, a lower mortality, etc., and also their greater liability to be affected with nervous diseases than non-Jews, to indolence of the Jew, to his lack of exercise, to the rich, highly-seasoned food that the Jews are supposed to eat. Some have even gone so far as to say that the Jews consume very many sweets, and that on this account they are more liable to diabetes than Christians. That "the Jews are obliged to keep two Sundays in a week, besides Jewish, Christian, and political holidays, or two out of every seven days being lost to business, gives them, by necessity, about twice as many days of leisure as Christians"[45] is another argument. But all these reasons do not hold good at present, particularly with our American Jews, as almost everybody who comes in contact with modern Jews will testify.

Others have tried to explain the comparative pathology of the Jews as consisting of "biostatic" differences of the physiological organization of the Jews as compared with non-Jews. But there are no proofs that the Jews possess peculiar racial characteristics of a purely physiological or anatomical nature. The so-called biostatic differences of the Jews can be easily explained by their past history; the differences in customs in relation to the customs of non-Jews; to the devotion of the Jews as husbands, as wives, and as parents—to the family spirit of the Jews, the *sentiment de la famille*, as M. Legoyt[46] calls it, which is

42. *Journal of the Anthropological Institute*, August, 1889.

43. E. Fuchs. *Text-book of Ophthalmology*, Second edition, p. 873.

44. Ibid, p. 371.

45. Hough. Loc. cit.

46. [Alfred Legoyt (1815–88) was an eminent French statistician and civil servant.]

more developed in them than in Christians, and which ensures to their children, to their aged and infirm parents, a solicitude more active; to the newborn, the mother's breast; to the poor and afflicted, a more efficacious assistance. As a result of the pure, chaste, married life which the majority of the Jews lead, we find that alcoholism and syphilis are very rare among them, and, with this, a number of diseases the etiology of which in a great measure depends on these two virulent poisons, as nephritis, arteriosclerosis, tabes, etc. The result is that the Jew has that "unprecedented tenacity of life" which the above statistics have proved.

The custom of ritual circumcision practiced by the Jews on every newborn male infant has been given by many authors[47] as a cause for the longevity of the Jews and their comparative immunity to certain diseases. Others have attributed the tenacity of life of the Jews to their excellent system of meat inspection, by which all those animals that are found to be suffering from disease, particularly pulmonary afflictions, are not allowed to be consumed by the Jews. Circumcision has probably a great deal to do with the fact that syphilis is uncommon among the Jews; it has hardly any influence on their susceptibility to gonorrhea, excepting, of course, some of its complications, as balanitis, phimosis, and paraphimosis, which are unknown among Jews. But, excepting syphilis, in the opinion of the writer, circumcision has no influence whatever on the comparative pathology of the Jews. The "Kosher" meat, which the Jews almost invariably eat, may be a factor in the infrequency of tuberculosis among them, but outside of this we do not think that it prolongs their lives.

The past history of the Jew explains to us the reason why he has such a wretched aspect. Persecuted and abused for two thousand years, the Jew of today has comparatively less physical strength and muscular power, his blood is more diluted, his stature smaller, his chest and shoulders narrower, than those of his non-Jewish neighbors. But notwithstanding all these physical infirmities, the Jew resists misfortune, disease, and even death, as we have seen above, better than almost any other race. The reason for this apparent contradiction is not far to seek: the modern Jew is, physically and mentally, a product of natural selection, of a process of survival of the fittest which has been going on for two thousand years.

Being persecuted, oppressed, and tormented for centuries, only those who

47. P. C. Remondino. *The History of Circumcision*, Philadelphia, 1891. In this book can be found an excellent bibliography on the subject of circumcision.

were the most stubborn, the most callous, the most energetic, could venture to remain Jews. All those who were too weak, sickly, and infirm, bodily and spiritually, were eliminated from the race either by death or baptism. The modern Jews are, therefore, possessed of a great "tenacity of life."

Another important point in the comparative pathology of the Jews is the fact that they are predisposed, in such a high degree, to the diseases of modern life—to hysteria, neurasthenia, most of the functional neuroses, and diabetes, as we have seen in the course of this paper. The Jew has been for centuries an urban resident, only rarely living in the country and engaged in agricultural pursuits. The diseases of the city population are therefore accentuated on his body and mind. We know that with the majority of the Gentiles the case is different. It has been shown by Mr. Cantlie, in his book *Degeneration amongst Londoners,* that the London poor do not survive beyond three, or at most four, generations; the same has been proved to be the fate of the poor inhabitants of Paris. It is, indeed, rare to find among the poor in modern large cities families which could trace their ancestors back for five or six generations as city dwellers. The population of the cities is kept up by the constant influx of good, pure, fresh blood from the country, which counteracts the deteriorating influences of the busy, enervating city life.

The Jews have not had this advantage, and all the evil effects of the strained, nerve-shattering city life have consequently been transmitted to their offspring. With each new generation the nervous vitality of the Jewish race has lessened, and, as a result, we find that most of the diseases that increase with the advance of civilization, particularly the neuroses and psychoses, are relatively more frequent among the Jews than non-Jews.

"The Jew," says Leroy-Beaulieu,[48] "is the most nervous, and, in so far, the most modern of men. He is by the very nature of his diseases the forerunner, as it were, of his contemporaries, preceding them on that perilous path upon which society is urged by the excesses of its intellectual and emotional life, and by the increasing spur of competition. The noisy army of psychopaths and neuropaths is gaining so many recruits among us that it will not take the Christians long to catch up with the Jews in this respect. Here, again, there are no ethnic forces in operation."[49]

The frequency of diabetes among the Jews is another confirmation of this

48. [Anatole Leroy-Beaulieu (1842–1912) was a French writer and historian.]

49. Leroy-Beaulieu. Loc. cit., p. 169.

contention. Diabetes is very much on the increase in all civilized countries, particularly in large cities. Some are even inclined to place it on the list of diseases of modern life. The Jews, as we have just shown, being hard sufferers of most of the diseases of modern life, could, of course, not escape it. The relation of diabetes to lesions of the nervous system has long since been observed, particularly by Claude Bernard.[50] The Jews, suffering very much from nervous diseases, are, therefore, to a large extent liable to diabetes.

As has been shown recently by Dickinson,[51] the most common variety of diabetes is associated with diseases of the nervous system; pancreatic diabetes is uncommon. "Grief, anxiety, terror, may all be followed by diabetes so closely that there is no room for doubt as to their having occasioned it . . . It is well known as a result of commercial disaster, and it may be said truly that every panic on the stock exchange produces its results in diabetes. It has recently come to light that engine drivers are especially subject to this disease, presumably from the anxious nature of their occupation." Diabetes is twice as common among engine drivers as in the ordinary population.

According to competent observers in England and America, Dr. Dickinson further points out some cases of insanity are accompanied by diabetes, and, while the pathology of both remains largely a problem for the future, the association between the two conditions seems conclusive to Dickinson. This view of diabetes explains best the reason why the Jews are such great sufferers from this condition: being the most nervous of the European and American races, they show the largest percentage of insanity in their ranks, and they consequently have the largest proportion of diabetics in their midst.

Before we dismiss the subject, we want to state that it has been observed in Europe that the tenacity of life of the Jew and his resistance to certain diseases, as tuberculosis, syphilis, alcoholism, etc., diminish gradually as we proceed from East to West, from the countries where the Jew lives isolated, pursuing his life in his own fashion, adhering to the customs of his forefathers, to those countries where the Jew commingles and assimilates with the non-Jewish inhabitants, adopting their modes of life and habits. This has also been observed to be the case in the United States. Thus Dr. Billings has pointed out that "those (Jewish)

50. [Claude Bernard (1813–78) was a French physiologist, acclaimed as one of the most important medical researchers of the nineteenth century.]

51. "The Baillie Lectures. Considerations Touching the Pathology and Relations on Diabetes." By W. H. Dickinson. *Lancet*, February 2, 1901.

mothers who were born in the United States average only 3.56 children each, as against 5.24 for those born in Germany, 5.63 for those born in Russia and Poland, 5.27 for those born in Hungary, and 5.44 for those born in Bohemia, indicating a diminished fertility in those women born in this country."[52]

In another place Dr. Billings shows that "the death rate among the Jews in this country is decidedly increasing," and that "the death rate among the native-born (Jews) of native-born parents was 9.16, and among the foreign-born 7.61."

It has also been observed by physicians that syphilis and alcoholism are decidedly increasing among those Jews living, for a longer or shorter time, in the United States. If this is actually the case, then we may expect that all those "biostatic" or "ethnic" differences of the American Jews will soon disappear.

## SUMMARY

(1) The death rates of the Jews, at all ages, are relatively and absolutely lower than those of the people among whom they live.

(2) The marriage rates and birth rates of the Jews are smaller than those of the Christians; the Jews increase in number more rapidly than non-Jews, because they lose by death relatively fewer children and bring more to maturity.

(3) The Jews die less often than their neighbors from many of the infectious diseases, particularly epidemic cholera, smallpox, and tuberculosis.

(4) Syphilis and alcoholism, and also diseases due in great measure to their poisons, are comparatively rare among the Jews.

(5) Diabetes is very frequent among the Jews. Most observers have recorded that almost 25 percent of all the cases of diabetes occur in Jews.

(6) All the functional neuroses and psychoses, particularly neurasthenia and hysteria, occur more frequently among Jews than among non-Jews; while all the organic nervous diseases, as tabes, general paralysis, etc., are less frequent, commensurate with the infrequency of syphilis and alcoholism, among them. The great majority of cases of amaurotic idiocy occur in Jewish children, and insanity is met with among Jews between two and five times more often than among Christians.

(7) Blindness, colorblindness, trachoma, and glaucoma, and also varicose veins—particularly hemorrhoids and hernias—are very frequent among Jews.

(8) All these peculiarities in the comparative pathology of the Jews are not

52. *Census Bulletin* No. 19, 1890, p. 9.

due to any ethnic, "biostatic," or racial characteristics of a purely anatomical or physiological nature in relation to non-Jews. They have their origin in the past history of the Jews, in their habits of life, and in the fact that syphilis and alcoholism have but rarely been seen among them.

(9) Where the Jew is commingling with his Christian neighbors and adopts their customs and habits of life, he sooner or later loses his "racial characteristics," and his comparative pathology presents no special peculiarities.

# 14 | Contributions to the Jewish Racial Question

## Felix Theilhaber

"Beiträge zur jüdischen Rassenfrage," *Zeitschrift für Demographie und Statistik der Juden* 6, no. 3 (1910): 40–44.

Felix Theilhaber (1884–1956) was a German Jewish physician, sexologist, racial scientist, and Zionist activist. He was born in Bamberg, Germany, and raised in Munich. He published works on health and medicine, sexual politics and social reform, and Jewish politics. In 1911 he published his best-known work, *Der Untergang der deutschen Juden* (The decline of German Jewry), in which he employed statistical evidence to prove that German Jewry would eventually disappear unless Jews embraced Jewish nationalism and reversed the process of assimilation. The work generated a great deal of public attention and controversy. See John Efron, *Defenders of the Race: Jewish Doctors and Race Science in Fin-de-Siècle Europe* (New Haven: Yale University Press, 1994), 142–45; and Mitchell B. Hart, *Social Science and the Politics of Modern Jewish Identity* (Stanford: Stanford University Press, 2000), 84–87.

The question as to whether the Jews constitute a distinct race is so interesting that researchers are continually inquiring into it. In some Jewish circles the question has been quickly solved, according to the subjective position of a given Jewish individual to the Jewish Question. Not so in science. Here the controversy still rages. Therefore the following research results dealing with the Jewish race question, results that heretofore have not been dealt with, should be of interest. First, however, allow me to set forth a few general remarks.

The Jewish race cannot be proven to be distinct or particular by referring to the fact that Jews suffer in smaller numbers statistically from certain known infectious—that is, communicable—diseases. We know that the Jews often suffer less from infectious illness because of their different social conditions and their better hygienic habits (where the religious laws are no longer a factor, a higher material standard of living often accounts for this). These circumstances are in no way conditioned by racial disposition. At most, one might ask whether their race offers a specific protection when they are exposed to infection under external living conditions analogous or similar [to those of non-Jews].

Here, for instance, it would be both interesting and important to undertake a scientific inquiry into whether those Germans settled in Palestine actually suffer from malaria to a greater degree and whether, as is claimed, they tend toward sterility, while such phenomena are encountered to a far smaller degree in those Jews recently settled there. Although those Russian farmers who converted to Judaism, the *Gerim*, and those who have settled at Jemma in the Galilee, were so afflicted with malaria that they were forced to abandon their small portion of land, Jews are now settled in that same area.[53]

However, here as well, we are not necessarily dealing with some specific traits of the Jewish race that have been guarded over the centuries. As Dr. L. Sofer[54] has set forth elsewhere, a selection process had occurred earlier in those areas where malaria raged, producing a formidable antidote against the disease. Those elements highly susceptible to malaria died out. Today's Jews would thus be the descendants of those settlers who came to terms with malaria. Their grandchildren therefore can nowadays overcome this illness more easily than do the Nordic immigrants.

One can see how interesting the question is, but we have neglected one point. Might there not be something else? The *Gerim* were drinkers of hard liquor who, as is sometimes said, somewhat weakened their cells through alcohol and poisoned themselves, thus making themselves abnormally weak and susceptible to malaria. How are the Germans presently settled in Palestine faring?

Infectious diseases are largely the product of purely external conditions, so that the search for racial characteristics can only consider them last of all.

Rather, we must explore the realms of hereditary and congenital illnesses. According to what von Lubarsch has recently set forth in what can now be virtually considered a classic study,[55] something inherited can only be what was already apparent in the individual lives of the ancestors; a disposition to disease, then, can only be designated as heritable when it is already present within one's ancestral line. "If, however, a deterioration of the germ plasm of the ancestors, emerging as a consequence of an arbitrary illness or the introduction of poisons, creates a new disposition to disease within the germ cells of the descendants, then this obviously cannot be considered as a hereditary process, but rather as

53. Felix Theilhaber, "Die Gerim," *Die Welt*, 1907.

54. Dr. L. Sofer, *Zeitschrift Palästina*, vol. 4, no. 2, 1910. [For information about Leo Sofer, see the headnote for selection 28.]

55. *Jahreskurse für ärztliche Fortbildung*, vol. 1, no. 5, 15. [Otto von Lubarsch (1860–1933) was a renowned German pathologist and professor of medicine.]

a trait acquired by the poisoning of germ cells." So, for instance, what originally was social or religious-hygienic practice could very well cause acquired traits to become part of the racial disposition. A specific engram is being generated in the germ cells of many ancestors and primal ancestors, which, in the descendant, causes a hereditary predisposition, for instance, toward a certain illness. The essence of heredity resides, then, in the complete absorption of the acquired traits, without the possibility to lose them in the following generations, through special processes (for example, according to Mendelian laws).

If we thus apparently have to differentiate carefully between acquired and inherited traits, we shall have to stick to the scheme [for doing that] offered to us by the new research in this area. I should begin by saying that these works will certainly not be the last word on the subject; their categories finally allow us, however, a positive undergirding for our research. Two books are of relevance here: Ebstein, *Vererbare zelluläre Stoffwechselkrankheiten*,[56] and Fr. Martius, *Das pathologische Vererbungsproblem*.[57]

Investigations into the Jews, which until now have been exclusively focused on head shape and hair and eye color, are now finally supposed to take other questions into consideration.

Martius offers the following categorization:

(1) Innate anatomical positive variations, conditional on the appearance of additional determinants.

An example: Polydactylism (six toes, the formation of surplus fingers, and so on).

(2) Innate anatomical negative variations, produced by the lack of certain physiological determinants.

An example: colorblindness.

(3) Racially aberrant traits.

An example: hemophilia (the so-called bleeder sickness).

(4) Inheritances that as aberrations or deviations first appear after birth [literally, post-uterine]; these often have the tendency to emerge during certain phases of development. Examples include chlorosis (paleness), myopia (shortsightedness), and osteosclerosis.

(5) Inherited tissue and organ weaknesses, of a kind that result in a

56. Published by F. Enke, Stuttgart, 1907.

57. F. Deuticke, Leipzig, 1909.

negative life force (*Lebensenergie*) and weaken one's resistance to external or environmental threats.

> Examples: spastic spinal paralysis (convulsive spinal cord paralysis),[58] muscular dystrophy (progressive muscle degeneration), constitutional albuminuria [albumin in the urine].

The last two groups must naturally evince their heritability—that is, must appear as weaknesses in entire families or sexes. Otherwise, it could be easily disputed that these are "inherited" faults.

Qualitative research on the Jews regarding these questions is almost entirely lacking. We still lack up-to-date work on mental illnesses of the Jews, on diseases of the blood, inheritance of albuminia, and hypophalangism among Jews. There remains as well a need to investigate the predisposition of Jews in individual countries to multiple births and so forth.

In what follows I seek to touch on a number of the issues briefly. Some individual results can be found in studies already published.[59]

Among Jewish women, menstruation occurs earlier than among women in the general population. [Samuel] Weissenberg[60] has published, independently from my own research, similar results and found what I have confirmed in the German case—that Jewish women in Russia menstruate earlier than do Christian women. My investigations reveal that women in the German rural population begin to menstruate at age sixteen; the urban population, depending on level of prosperity, at fourteen to fifteen years of age. Jewish women, however, both rural and urban dwellers, begin to menstruate at twelve and a half to fourteen years of age.

It would be important to verify this phenomenon in other places, since menstruation—as we shall later see—is an event not insignificant for the health of an individual.

However, it is not only that the onset of menstruation (what is called menarche) is too early, but also that its cessation [menopause] occurs later. Jewish women in Germany experience menopause (the end of menstruation) on average later than do women of the same social standing, or average German women overall.

58. Translations into lay terms have been done following Schreiber, *Med. Taschenwörterbuch*, 1900.

59. *Hofrat* Dr. A. Theilhaber, *Münch. Mediz. Woschenschrift*, 1909, no. 25; *Zeitschrift f. Krebsforschung*, 1910; Dr. Felix Theilhaber, *Zeitschrift f. Krebsforschung*, 1910.

60. *Centralblatt für Geburtshilfe und Gynäk[ologie]*.

And something else is of interest here. The beginning of menstruation is hereditary. According to our surveys, which we naturally had to conduct in the most discrete fashion, we have ascertained that mothers and daughters began to menstruate at precisely the same point in their lives. We can thus speak of particular menstrual conditions of Jewish women that, on the basis of our discussions and investigations, we can claim to be hereditary traits.

Statistics from *Hofrat*[61] A. Theilhaber's clinic yield further results. Myome (benign growths in the uterus) affected 40 percent of the Jewish women, while cancer of the cervix was discovered in only 0.75 percent of Jewish women examined. We repeatedly sought to explain such statistics by reference to external factors. We did not succeed. Jewish women who become ill with cancer surely do not die without having consulted a physician. Should we imagine that only those women with benign tumors visited the clinic, while others with malignant tumors were treated by other physicians?

We have examined the death registers of the Jewish communities. H. Kirschner kindly allowed me to extract the following material from an as yet unpublished work.

In Munich, 185 Jews died of cancer between 1876 and 1908. Of these, 98 were women. Of these, 6 suffered from uterine cancer. (One case proved to be a false identification.)

In Nuremberg over the past decade, 77 deaths from cancer were recorded, only one from uterine cancer.[62]

[. . .]

I owe these statistics to the official statistical yearbooks of the city of Budapest.[63]

[. . .]

Although uterine cancer commonly makes up approximately 35 percent of the cases of cancer among women, and almost never falls below 25 percent, one finds that among Jewish women the figure is 10 percent at the highest. Cancer of the cervix, which is so common among women in the general population, is rarely encountered in Jewish women.

61. [Adolf Theilhaber, Felix's father, was a well-known researcher specializing in gynecology. *Hofrat* was an official honorary title in the Austro-Hungarian Empire.]

62. [There follows a table giving comparative statistics for Budapest from 1902 to 1906, on overall deaths and deaths from cancer of Jews and the general population.]

63. [There follows another table for the same years, giving comparative statistics on uterine cancer deaths.]

This striking phenomenon, which was first discovered and publicized by A. Theilhaber and which has aroused great interest in cancer research circles, has recently been repeatedly confirmed—admittedly, chiefly through private means alone for now. It would be important, however, to secure evidence from wider Jewish circles.

The questions for science resulting from these facts cannot be addressed here. It ought only to be briefly mentioned that the development of cancer is connected with localized inadequate blood supply, and that Jewish women have always had particularly stronger blood circulation in the genitals, as do all those who stem from southern tribes or nations (*Völkerstämme*).

Another type of illness, which on the contrary Jews do seem to be frequently afflicted by, is peripheral vascular disease (presenile gangrene caused by arteritis obliterans) [Buerger's disease].

This disorder is characterized by convulsive pains in the foot or in the calves that develop after a time while walking, and that induce limping, or alternatively force one to stand still; for years [symptoms] consist of a frozen sensation in and a paleness of the foot; a coolness, and sometimes a loss of sensation in the affected limb; and a tendency to suppurating inflammation. Young men are especially affected, women more rarely.

Schümann, especially, has earned recognition for his research into this disease.[64]

"In the case of this disease, heredity is not without influence" (Schümann). Weiss and Sternberg have each treated, among others, two siblings suffering from this seldom-seen illness.

The oldest of recorded cases concerns a Jew (Burow). Erb published (in 1904) forty-five cases, of which fourteen concerned Jews. Borchard, Michels, and Weber have published similar statistical results. Idelsohn[65] identifies twelve Jews among his twenty-four cases, and Higiers, in his research in Warsaw, identifies twenty-two Jews out of the twenty-three individuals in total.

The cause of this disease still awaits explanation. Given the fact, however, that so many Jews are affected, and that external dangers or damaging forces such as the influence of syphilis, alcohol, or nicotine must be discounted as negligible, one can conclude that we are dealing here mainly with a constitutional malady.

64. *Münch. Med. Wochenschrift*, 1909, no. 39.

65. "Zur Kasuistik und Aetiologie der intermit. Hinkens," *Zeitschrift für Nervenheilkunde*, vol. 24, p. 285.

Thus, the question regarding a Jewish racial disposition opens up a vast field of inquiry. This question ought not to be solved or clarified in some one-sided way. The fact is that cervical cancer, which is the most common form of cancer among women and yet the least common found among Jews, has provided quite an important foundation for cancer research. Hence, the study of Jewish traits that are inherited or acquired is a question of general scientific implications, and we hope that an understanding of this point might finally break through to wider circles.

What has been achieved until now in the realm of knowledge about Jewish diseases is insufficient and, for the most part, out of date; moreover, it is false to imagine that head measurements and other related sorts of anthropological investigations can completely illuminate questions of race. Whether the Jews represent today a singular entity [racially] in some sense will not be determined as much by anthropology as by pathology or, as we might also put it, nosology—knowledge of diseases. We must finally commit ourselves to the effective paths [of investigation] delineated here, and if I were to suggest a motto, it would not be "let us free ourselves from anthropology," which has up until now been predominant. Rather, I should merely like to call for the founding of another scientific discipline that I would like to designate Jewish pathology.

# 15 | Heredity and the Jew

## Redcliffe N. Salaman

"Heredity and the Jew," *Journal of Genetics* 1, no. 3 (1911): 273–92.

Redcliffe Salaman (1874–1955) was an English pathologist and geneticist, and an activist on behalf of the Anglo-Jewish community and Zionism. He is best known for his research into the history and influence of the potato. He also published a number of works related to Jews and race, Jews and medicine, and Palestine. See Todd Endelman, "Anglo-Jewish Scientists and the Science of Race," *Jewish Social Studies* 11, no. 1 (2004): 52–92.

[...]

Ethnologists may be said to agree that the Jew is not racially pure, but on the other hand they have to admit that the Jews constitute a definite people in something more than a political sense, and that they possess though not a uniform, still a distinguishing, type.

Nothing is more confusing than the varied accounts of the shapes of head, nose, eyes, and color of the hair of Jews in different countries, and if one's only acquaintance with Jews were through the literature of anthropology one would be inclined to think that the "chosen people" had no existence apart from books, and the imagination of the anti-Semites. It is with no small degree of comfort therefore, that one finds Ripley[66] making the following statement: "Who has not, on the other hand, acquired a distinct concept of a Jewish face and of a distinctly Jewish type? Could such a patent fact escape observation for a minute?" Again, Weissenberg[67] says: "The Jew in an anthropological sense forms no specific type, but the facial expression is absolutely characteristic." Fischberg [*sic*] is not so wholehearted as to [wholeheartedly convinced of] the general occurrence of this characteristic facial expression but he does recognize it and considers it not strictly a physical trait but rather an expression of the soul. Others will tell us that this Jewish expression, so impossible to define, is merely an emblem of the ceaseless wanderings and the countless agonies of the Jew—of the *tausend-*

66. William Z. Ripley. *The Races of Europe*. New York, 1889, p. 383.
67. *Census Bulletin*. No. 19, 1890, p. 10.

*jährigen Schmerz,* as Heine calls it. Others again tell us it exists because the Jew is landless, and if only he were once more back in his native land, the facial type would vanish. All, however, practically agree that whether blond or dark, tall or short, long-headed or round-headed, the Jew is a Jew because he looks like one. The peculiar facial expression is at least not the outcome of recent times. We have evidence of the greatest antiquity. In the Assyrian sculptures, 800 [BCE], are depicted Jewish prisoners who are thoroughly Jewish, and Petrie[68] has brought home from Memphis terra-cotta heads dating [from] 500 [BCE] of Jews at once recognizable by their Jewishness. On a forest roll of the pre-expulsion times in England is a pen-and-ink sketch, or one might rather say a caricature of a certain Aaron, "Son of the Devil," dated 1277, which, crude though it is, hits off [depicts] a distinctly Jewish type. The great master Rembrandt has given us numerous drawings of Jews. He was mainly attracted by the Sephardic Jews, but whatever the shape of their face may be, the curious expression that we recognize as Jewish never escaped the artist. More interesting than the examples given of the persistence of this facial expression is the fact that the Samaritans of today who live in the land of their forefathers, have an unmistakable Jewish expression, and this though their heads are dolichocephalic and those of the majority of Jews brachycephalic.

At this point one might with advantage consider the relation that the existence of the *Kohanim* has to the question of Jewish type. The *Kohanim* are the traditional descendants of the tribe of Aaron. There is, of course, no written record of such descent, but the hallmark, as a rule, is shown by the name of Cohen or some modification of it. It is not at all unusual, however, to find people not possessed of the name of Cohen who are still *Kohanim.* It is most improbable that anyone could, and much less would, assume the title of *Kohen* without having a right by birth because it conveys neither social distinction nor advantage, while on the other hand, it brings in its train some undoubted disabilities, the chief of which directly concerns us, and is that no *Kohen,* according to Jewish law, can marry a stranger, a proselyte or the daughter of a proselyte, or a divorcée: so that we have a sect whose descent may be regarded as strictly Jewish. If now we review the physiognomies of the various *Kohanim,* it will be found that they exhibit no type in any way distinct from that of other Jews. Every phase of Jewish bodily form will find its representative among the *Kohanim,* so that one is inclined very much to the view that whatever value may be ascribed—and I personally think

68. [Flinders Petrie, "Palace of Apries Memphis, vol. II, plate XXVIII, *British School of Archaeology, in Egypt,* 1909, p. 155.]

a very high one may be—to the purity of descent of the *Kohanim* during the last 2,000 years, practically the same value may be ascribed to their brethren among whom they live.

What the elements are that go to make up the expression of a face that is at once so elusive of description and yet so characteristic, it is difficult to say. The nose is often peculiar, not because of its length or even its convexity, which may be often outdone in non-Jews, but by the heavy development of the nostrils. Jacobs has described this "nostrility" and has most aptly compared the Jewish nose to the figure six with a long tail. Remove the tail, he says, and the Jewishness will disappear. The eyes are generally elongated, and a fairly characteristic feature is the length of the upper eyelid. The face that exhibits the expression of Jewishness is never of the angular type with square jaw, a type that is indeed extremely rare among Jews. Far more usual is it to find rounded features, long sloping jaw, fairly developed chin that is round and not square, a good-size forehead devoid of that angularity in the region of the temples that is not uncommon among Teutonic people. However it may be brought about, there is no doubt that the character of Jewishness is a real one. Weissenberg[69] relates that he put several hundred photographs of Russians and Russian Jews without peculiar dress or other distinguishing feature before two scientific friends, one a Jew, the other a native Russian. His Jewish friend picked out 70 percent of the Jewish subjects correctly and the Russian 50 percent. If so high a percentage of Jews could be identified by their looks alone in a photograph, it is not surprising that the opinion is current that the Jew may be recognized wherever he goes. Notwithstanding the fact that the great majority of Jews look Jewish, it cannot be denied that one meets, not rarely, individuals, perhaps more often men than women, who do not exhibit this type and who are either indistinguishable or at least practically indistinguishable from North Europeans. It is relying on these apparently non-Jewish faces that Fischberg [*sic*] and others have rashly assumed that they are the direct results of mixture with the surrounding people. I think I shall be able to offer some evidence that will show that this view is untenable.

Impressed with the great frequency and the distinctiveness of the Jewish type of face, it occurred to me that this character might form excellent material for research on Mendelian lines. Intermarriage today with the English is very common in Anglo-Jewry, and one had only to follow out such cases of mixed marriage to obtain results comparable to those the genetic student has been obtaining in

69. *Census Bulletin*. No. 19, p. 12.

TABLE 15.1

FIRST GENERATION

| Number of Families | Father | Mother | Children: Gentile | Children: Jew | Children: Intermediate |
|---|---|---|---|---|---|
| 50 | Gentile | Jewess | 88 | 15 | 4 |
| 86 | Jew | Gentile | 240 | 11 | 4 |
| Total 136 | | | 328 | 26 | 8 |

plants and animals. My method has been to collect personally, as far as possible, all cases of mixed marriage and to obtain the assistance of those on whom I could rely, and whose duty it was merely to state whether they considered the children of the mixed marriages of their acquaintance as Jewish or gentile in appearance. Most of my observers were quite ignorant of the purpose of my examination and of the results I expected, while none were conversant with Mendelian or other theories of heredity. All who have assisted me have been themselves Jews, and I have noted a distinct tendency on their part to claim, wherever possible, a Jewish type of face for the children they have examined, and although, as I shall show, the results are entirely in the opposite direction, yet what error there is, is distinctly toward increasing the number of supposed Jewish faces in the offspring of mixed marriage. Wherever possible, I have seen the children myself or have obtained photographs, but in at least half of them, I have had to rely on others. In doing so I have been rather encouraged than otherwise by finding that the bias of my assistants has been always against the results that they, to their own surprise, have found. In all cases the Jew is of the Ashkenazi section and the gentile is either a native of England or Northern Europe.

Briefly, the results of the intermarriage of Jew and Gentile may be stated thus [see table 15.1].

In fifty families where the father was gentile and the mother a Jewess, there were 88 Gentile-looking children, 15 Jewish, and 4 intermediate in type. In eighty-six families where the father was Jewish and the mother gentile, there were 240 Gentile-looking children, 11 Jewish, and 4 intermediate. In both cases the intermediates are practically gentile-looking. Adding the two classes together, we find that there are 336 gentile children to 26 Jewish—that is 13 gentile to 1 Jewish.

The result is a surprise to both the anthropologist and to the Mendelian. To the former who looks for blending, we have the fact that, so far from blending, we have no less than 93 percent of the mixed bred offspring resembling one parent only. To the Mendelian some surprise must occur [at the fact] that the dominance is not absolute, but this is, to a slight extent, due to the Jewish bias in the observations and, to a much greater extent, to a Jewish permeation of the English people in certain localized districts that is much more prevalent than is generally suspected. I have, while making these observations, come across certain cases where I was assured that in a certain family the father was a Jew, the mother a gentile. In one such [family], I examined the children carefully and found that two were without doubt gentile in appearance while one was equally without doubt Jewish. I then discussed the family history with the parents, and I was able to obtain the pedigree shown in Figure 1, which at once explains the occurrence of the Jewish child. In another case I found a very similar state of affairs, but I was unable to trace it further as the non-Jewish parent objected [declined] to elucidate the Jewish blood in her grandparent, which she, however, admitted. In a third and fourth case where complete dominance was expected but not obtained, I have reason to believe that it will be discovered that the gentile parent has Jewish ancestors. In determining the nature of so complex a character as the facial expression, the personal equation of the observer must play an important part. I have in some cases found that observers not specially acquainted with the subject, although agreeing that a given individual of the first generation is of gentile appearance, have yet felt that there was somewhere lurking in the face an expression that suggested "Jewishness," and there is very little doubt that such opinion may often be well founded. I have myself come across a few cases where without doubt the recessive Jewish facial expression has come to the surface as the individual grew older. One case was particularly apparent. The parents were characteristically Jewish and non-Jewish respectively; there was a large family, of which I saw one personally and the remainder in photographs. Most of them were, to my mind, not Jewish at all, but the one whom I was interviewing, though not in any way strikingly Jewish, would probably have been recognized by many people as such. His age was about forty-five, and he assured me, and his assurance was confirmed by his wife, that when he was a young man he was never by any chance recognized as a Jew in public. This same individual has married a gentile and has three children who are, I think, without doubt totally non-Jewish in appearance. It is not without surprise that one finds that very many of the leading families of this country, as given in Burke [*Burke's Peerage and Baronetage*],

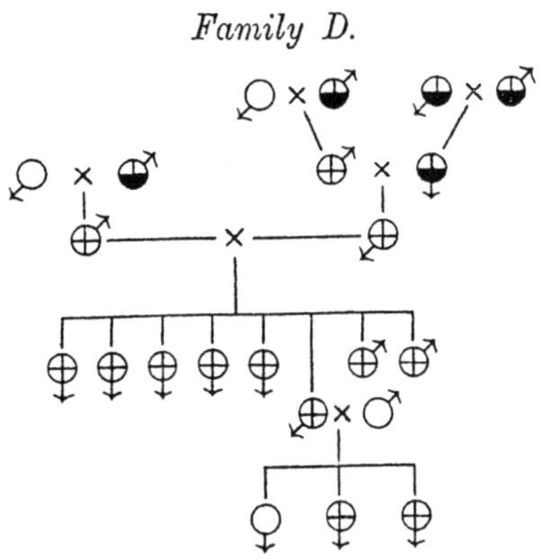


○ = Jewish appearance.
⊕ = Gentile appearance.
◒ = Gentile appearance and birth.

FIGURE 15.1

contain Jewish blood, and I know of at least one case where two parents, neither Jewish in appearance, have a daughter who is typically Jewish. A reference to Burke showed that in the family tree of both parents was Jewish blood.

To obtain portraits of families for the purpose of exhibition has been a most difficult matter, but I am able to show in Plates XXXVIII and XXXIX a few examples [the plates are not included in this book].

To the student of heredity, the phenomenon of dominance is, after all, a matter of secondary importance. The vital question that he has to deal with is, whether the character in question is one that segregates or not—that is, when in an individual the character and its opposite are both present, are these two opposite characters represented together in the sex cells or gametes, or does one go to one gamete and the other to another? Two methods are open to us in testing this question, one to observe the matings of the hybrid individual with those possessing recessive character only, the other to observe the matings of such hybrid individuals with each other. Of the matings of hybrid with hybrid I have not found a single example. This is hardly surprising when one considers the vastly greater choice the hybrid has of finding his mate either in the Jewish community or in the outside world. Of matings between hybrid and Jew I have nine families where the Jew is the father and the hybrid the mother, giving rise to twenty-five children, thirteen of whom are undoubtedly gentile and twelve are unequivocally Jewish. Four families where the father is hybrid and the mother

TABLE 15.2

HYBRID AND JEW

| Number of Families | | Father | Mother | Children | |
|---|---|---|---|---|---|
| | | | | Gentile | Jew |
| | | Jew | Hybrid | | |
| | 9 | Jew | Hybrid | 13 | 12 |
| | 4 | Hybrid | Jew | 2 | 5 |
| Total | 13 | | | 15 | 17 |

TABLE 15.3

SECOND GENERATION

| Number of Families | | Father | Mother | Children | |
|---|---|---|---|---|---|
| | | | | Gentile | Jew |
| | | Gentile | Hybrid | | |
| | 1 | Gentile | Hybrid | 3 | — |
| | 4 | Hybrid | Gentile | 8 | — |
| Total | 5 | | | 11 | — |

Jewish contain seven children, of which two are gentile and five are Jewish. Taking the families together, their offspring consist of fifteen gentile and seventeen Jewish children, the Mendelian expectation being equality. Besides these matings, I have been able to collect a certain number of families where a hybrid has married a gentile. In four the father is hybrid, the mother gentile, with eight offspring, all gentile in appearance. In one the mother is hybrid and father gentile, with three gentile offspring (cf. Table[15.3]). I have indirect knowledge of several other families comprising a large number of children, all of whom are said to be gentile in appearance, but I have not included them as the observations were not sufficiently reliable.

In Figures 2, 3, 4, and 5 are given further pedigrees showing the results of the matings of hybrid individuals with Jews and gentiles, respectively.

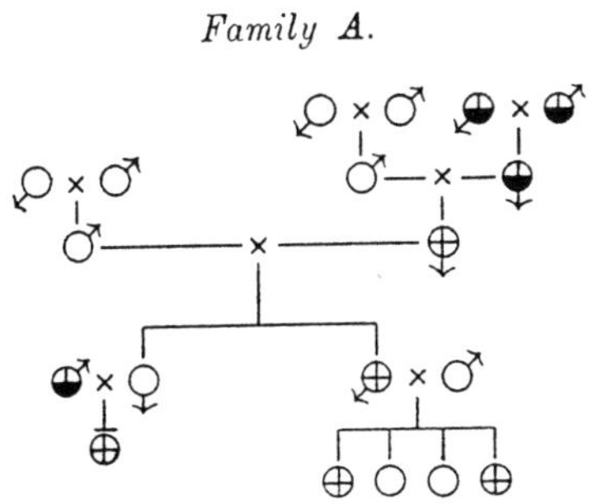


FIGURE 15.2

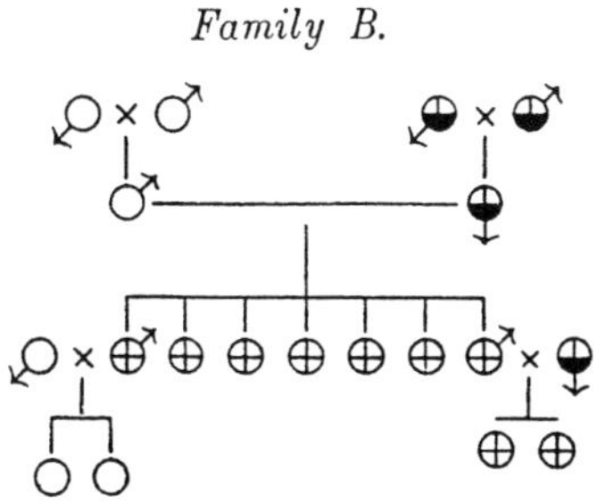


FIGURE 15.3

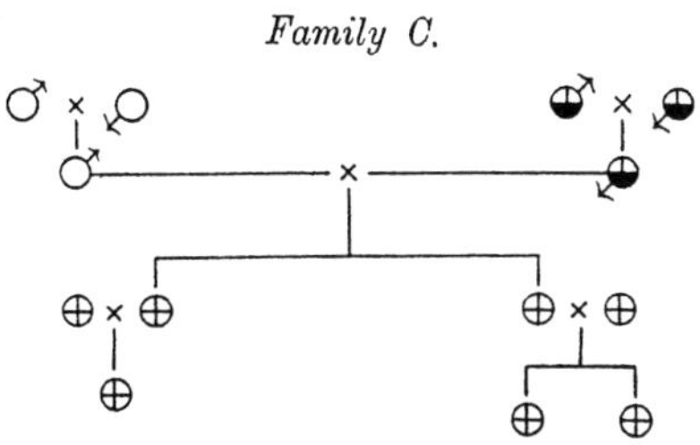


FIGURE 15.4

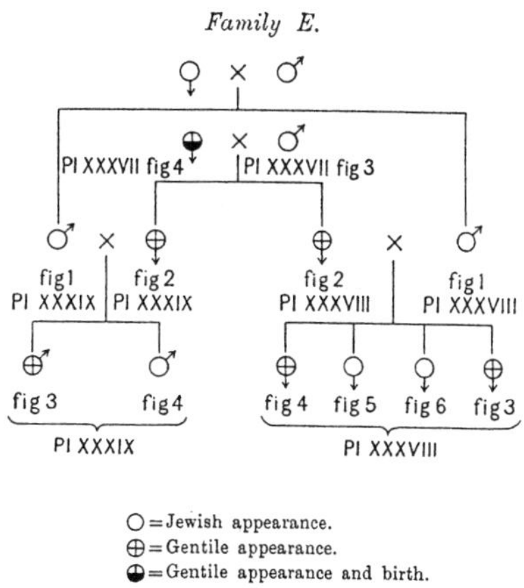


FIGURE 15.5

The conclusion to which these results inevitably lead is that the Jewish facial type, whether it be considered to rest on a gross anatomical basis or whether it be regarded as the reflection in which facial musculature of a peculiar psychical state, is a character that is subject to the Mendelian law of heredity.

# 16 | The "Nervousness" of the Jew

## Abraham Myerson

"The 'Nervousness' of the Jew," *Mental Hygiene* 4 (1920):65–72.

Abraham Myerson (1881–1948) was a highly regarded authority on nervous and mental disorders. He was born in Yanova, Lithuania, but emigrated with his family to the United States when he was four years old. He attended Tufts Medical School, where he later taught, holding a chair in neurology. He was also a professor of clinical psychiatry at Harvard Medical School and chief of neuropsychiatry at Beth Israel Hospital. He authored several books on the nature of the human personality and on mental disorders. See Andrew Heinze, *Jews and the American Soul: Human Nature in the Twentieth Century* (Princeton: Princeton University Press, 2004), 116–18.

The subject of racial disease has the added fascination that history, biology, and sociology lend to medicine. On a broad canvas pathology can more easily be traced than on a minute one, for individual and minute variations thus tend to standardize themselves. How much of history is written in racial diseases can easily be summarized by those who know how profoundly malaria, yellow fever, hookworm disease, gonorrhea, and syphilis have influenced the world. Conversely, and this is the theme that I wish to develop, we may read something of the history of a race in the symptoms of the patient that stands before us.

Now there need be no difference of opinion about the liability of the Jews to psychoneuroses. Step into any clinic for nervous diseases in any large city in Europe or America, and the Jew is unduly represented among the patients. Figures similar to those I have collected in the Psychopathic Outpatient Department of the Boston State Hospital can be shown to be true for any clinic in Boston or if we follow the neurologist and psychiatrist into his private office. It is easy to dismiss the subject by saying that there is a predisposition in the race that accounts for this undue occurrence of mental disease, but I contend that this is a cheap solution in that it ascribes causation to a totally unknown factor, heredity, whereas environment and history can easily be examined and analyzed as to causative influences. Analysis of the life conditions of the Jews in the present day and historically needs to be made and perhaps is best made by a Jew familiar with the intimate life and history of his people.

The thesis that I wish to develop essentially is this: *as important for practical purpose as biological heredity, and often mistaken for it, is what we may term social heredity.* By this is meant that groups of life factors may be handed down for generations and may influence the life of every individual in the race as potently as if a change had occurred in the stock.

It is idle, of course, to deny that the Jew has an innate character, different from that of other races, which perhaps predisposes him to psychoneuroses and other mental diseases. Unquestionably deeply emotional, clinging to belief and opinion with a tenacity unparalleled in the history of the world, extremely active mentally, and in point of intellectual achievement to be compared only with the great races of the world, he is curiously passive in his resistance and curiously indomitable in his hold on life and success. Accused of materialism and yet furnishing proportionately more social reformers than any other race; accused of materialism and yet responsible for the two most ethical religions in the world; said to be dominated by love of gain, but the birthplace of the ethics that govern his accusers, the Western peoples; a race of contradictions, inconsistencies, strongly individualistic and extraordinarily social, it may well be that such a soil would produce great failure as well as great success, psychoneurosis as well as genius.

But even racial character may be a matter of social heredity. In the face of what we know about the life factors of the Jew, and of the extraordinary changes that have taken place in his character in the last generation, no surmises as to an innate character are permissible. Let us, then, examine these life factors, governed by the thesis that social heredity has been established through these factors. *First,* we may state that the main factor and the one out of which the others arose has been the persecution of the Jew. Because he felt his religion to be superior to those of the nations with whom he came in contact, and because he refused in any way to acknowledge the potency or the reality of the gods of the people among whom he lodged, he was looked upon as unsociable, different, and because of this a sinister person, one to be restricted and guarded against. *The basis of dislike is normally unlikeness.* The restrictions prior to the Christian era are of no importance to us, but with the rise of Christianity, a competing religion, what was the mother religion became a thing to be proscribed and harried. Through the pagans the Jew suffered no serious misfortunes; with the rise of the Christian church the blackest chapter in Jewish history begins. The Christian church fell into a state of ambivalence. In its attitude toward the Jews as Christ killers and as refusing to acknowledge his Messianic character, it looked upon them as subjects for persecution and extermination; but it adopted a curious restricting attitude in addition—that the Jews, having been witnesses of the Passion, must also witness the Triumph. Therefore, they were to be kept alive, but to be made miserable, kept from real living. To the religious basis for persecution we add this—that with the downfall of the Roman Empire, the Jews and Arabs alone kept the torch of culture and science lit. In other words, the Jew was easily superior in these matters to his uncouth, warriorlike hosts. This superiority brought about a jealousy, a fear of the ability of the Jew; a fear that has never been stilled, though the culture of the Western races has reached a very high plane; a fear that yet actuates most of the hostile feeling of neighboring races.

Now the restrictions that arose from this hostile attitude gradually increased in number and gradually narrowed the activities of the Jew. For many centuries, and especially in those countries where Christianity was late in coming, as in Russia, many fields of activity were open to him. He was a handicraftsman, an agriculturist, as well as a merchant, a peddler, and so forth. But with the rise of guilds, with the rise of shopkeeping classes among the Gentiles, and especially with the amalgamation of church and state after the Crusades, the Jew became excluded from the soil, in which condition he remained down to our own day, and still remains in such countries as Russia, Poland, and Rumania, where the bulk of the Jews live. He was forbidden to become a handicraftsman, though, previous to his exclusion, in such countries as Italy he was the main handicraftsman of the country. *In other words, he was excluded from all occupations in the pursuit of which the manual motor side of his nature might find expression.*

Because of the fact that he spoke many languages, because the Jews were scattered in small colonies, and because the Gentile looked down upon mercantile life as a sort of usury, the Jew shifted to mercantile life, and if not the greatest factor in establishing international banking, was at least exceedingly prominent. As time went on, with the rise of the kings into power and the crumbling of the feudal system, the Jews became the tax collectors of Europe, and thus, while exceedingly useful to the kings, became their scapegoats. What I wish to emphasize in this is that here was a factor that tended to make a race of inferior physique, in that all those occupations that tend to develop strength of body and hardihood were forbidden. The Jew became a sort of sedentary adventurer, living by his wits. Having a full share of brains, he was quick to see his advantage and to form a dislike for the occupations from which he was excluded.

This brought about another factor in the life history of the race, and that is its urban character. Until the nineteenth century became distinguished by the great urban movement, all of the races of Europe have been largely rural—agriculturists and peasants. The cities were small and inconspicuous, comparatively speaking, and the vast bulk of the people lived on the land. That urban life develops neurasthenia and the like conditions is an old story. Any nervous organization that stands country life may go to pieces when assailed by the extraordinary stimuli of the city. Now the Jews became exclusively an urban people. They lived in small towns, perhaps, but in crowded, dirty, disagreeable towns. In this urban life, not only was a sedentary life necessary, but the race developed a curious antipathy to exercise and even to play. For centuries the Jews were a race that despised sports and discountenanced play. The importance of the basal movements—that is, the large movements of sports and play—has been wonderfully emphasized by Stanley Hall.[70] They form an incomparable avenue of discharge for nervous tension. They breed confidence in oneself. Being extensor in their character, they allow for the rise of pride and courage. Circumstances excluded the Jew from their wholesome influence, and the children of the race grew up to be very serious, very earnest, too early devoted to mature efforts, excessively cerebral in their activities, and not sufficiently strenuous physically. *In other words, the Jew, through his restrictions, was cheated out of childhood.*

This urban, sedentary trend would in itself have sufficed to change the character of the Jew. In addition, because of their exclusion from friendly and wholesome contact with other races, the Jews became more clannish. The ghetto life was not only unwholesome physically, but unwholesome mentally, emotionally, and spiritually. Living in constant dread of massacre, exposed to ridicule, degradation, and more serious disaster, the race developed an apprehensiveness and acquired a lowered threshold for fear stimuli. The ghetto life developed an overintimate and close family life. On its plus side, this family life was characterized by devotion and purity, and on its minus side was a reverberating emotionality which intensified the neurasthenic trend of the Jewish child. There was little rest or quiet in the small dwelling crowded with children watched over by apprehensive parents—guarded so well, indeed, that the Jewish infant and child death rate for centuries has been the lowest of any race, but with the evil result that this intense care and solicitude increased the fear attitude of the Jew. Thus

70. [G. Stanley Hall (1844–1924) was an American psychologist and educator, and the first president of Clark University.]

we may add to the urban, sedentary, cerebral character of the Jew an apprehensiveness and an emotionality that arose from the conditions of life to which his Christian neighbors subjected him.

I need not go into detail concerning the persecution of the Jew. Every untoward event that occurred in the town or country in which he dwelled was in part ascribed to him, often directly to his evil and even magical efforts, indirectly because God was angry that Christ killers lived and were prosperous. For example, the black plague was a pestilence that occurred as the result of their evil tendencies, and they were accused of starting the great London fire. The most disastrous accusation of all was the infamous blood-ritual accusation. Some day historians will follow the lead of the anthropologists such as Frazier [Frazer][71] and correctly ascribe to superstition the leading place in the development of ideas. That historian will trace a good deal of the character of the Jew and much of his unhappiness to this superstition of his neighbors that the Jews required the blood of a Christian child to celebrate the Passover ritual.

In addition, of course, to the persecution that was expressed in massacre and insult and restriction of occupation, there was the liability to expulsion from the land of his birth at any moment. The Jews were successively expelled from England, France, and Spain in the years 1190, 1291, and 1391 [*sic*], and they were expelled from various cities in Italy at different times. Gold, cash, became the only stable good of the world to the Jew because he had no other property that he could be sure of. The hate of his Gentile neighbor for the Jew was fully returned. He did not wish to be like him in any way. He rejected his learning, his art, and his sports together with his food and his religion.

But the feeling of hate and contempt was not the main emotional trait that arose from the centuries of persecution. Apprehensiveness I have already spoken of, but in addition there was a melancholy which expressed itself in motto, in song, and in the Jewish literature. *Der Yid hat kein masel* (the Jew has no luck) was the opinion of the Jew of himself. Despite an occasional ephemeral prosperity, the bulk of the race was undernourished, underdeveloped, and overstimulated mentally and emotionally. Here it is well to emphasize what is well known, yet commonly overlooked. Emotion is not a matter of mind; it is something that concerns the whole body. It is an intense display of somatic activity, in which blood vessels, glands, great viscera, and skeletal muscles all take part. An emo-

71. [James George Frazer (1854–1941), a British anthropologist, was the author of an extremely influential work, *The Golden Bough: A Study in Magic and Religion.*]

tion may disturb the functions of the organism, or perhaps it had better be stated that a pathological emotion *is* a pathological function—*is* a loss of appetite, a spasm of intestine or bladder, a drying up of milk ducts, and so forth. Fear emotions especially bring about disorders in function of a persistent type, such as those seen in the psychoneuroses, and may, so far as we know, produce little by little permanent structural changes in the organism. That the liability to arteriosclerosis and diabetes that exists among the Jew can be related to his unfavorable emotion-engendering environment may be a far-fetched assumption which I believe, nevertheless, to be true.

Now every race—all human beings, in fact—may be classified roughly into two groups—the extrospective and the introspective, the objectively minded and the subjectively minded. It is conceded on all sides that to be objectively minded is healthier from the psychological standpoint, though this life is not, perhaps, so rich in genius, in artistic and creative ability. Whatever introspective tendency existed in the Jewish race as a whole and in its individuals was exaggerated by the exclusion from play, sports, [and] military life, and from occupations such as the handicrafts. He who tended to be introspective became deeply so, and this introspection was deeply apprehensive and melancholy. An intensity of character developed, an extraordinary eagerness and overseriousness of purpose which led in two directions insofar as the fate of each individual was concerned. It led to great success, and I need not point out how marvelously successful in many directions the Jew has been. In our own profession, since the Jew has been allowed to participate in it within the last hundred years, there have arisen the commanding figures of Henle, Cohnheim, Weigert, Ehrlich, Freud, and Barany, to say nothing of the Rombergs, Flexners, Loebs, and the innumerable lesser lights without whom no medical account of the nineteenth and twentieth centuries would be complete. But while this intensity led to great success, it also led to *poignant failure*. The Jew who has not succeeded or who is struggling feels his situation the more keenly because of the intensity of purpose that has been frustrated.

How quickly racial characters can be changed under a fostering environment may be exemplified by the development of the last generation in Jewish life in the free countries of Europe and America. Intermarriage, especially in Germany, Scandinavia, and France, are [*sic*] so extraordinarily prevalent that, unless checked, the Jew will disappear in these countries, to be merged into the general population. The intensely religious character of the Jew disappears in America in one generation. He gives up his kosher, his Sabbath, his traditional religion in general, as if by magic. *What persecution could not do throughout the centuries, toleration does in a generation.* The alleged stinginess and miserliness of the immigrant Jew can certainly not be charged against his children. Of all the prodigal spenders in America, the American Jew stands foremost. Nothing is too good for him or his, and he is a sport of the first water, totally and completely different from his father. The dislike of the Jew for athletics and especially for all combatant forms has been supplanted by the surprising phenomenon of the Jewish prizefighter, who in the weights, from the lowest up to the light heavyweight, outclasses proportionately to his numbers any race. The race that produces so many Phi Beta Kappa scholars likewise produces the champion prizefighter. Nor can any lack of gameness be charged to these representatives of Israel. Shrewd, scientific, and powerful, the yellow streak is surprisingly uncommon among the boxers of the race that once wore the yellow gabardine.[72]

This dissolution of Jewish life that has taken place in America is also responsible in part for the psychoneuroses that we witness among the American Jews of the first generation. A surprising change in ideals and in life-governing notions works havoc with the less stable of the race. But the second generation, brought up in American methods, learning early to fight physically, taking part in athletics in ever-increasing numbers, discarding the intensely communal life of the past, coming into contact with the less emotional, more controlled life of the neighboring Gentile, is being changed in character, has much less liability to the psychoneuroses. A lover of his race will counsel control of emotion in the family and the bringing of discipline into the home, participation in sports, less intensity upon scholarly and financial success, more handicraftsmanship, and more manual motor effort. The urban life of the race is now fostered by the urban trend of the entire world, and it would be impossible to make the Jew into a rural dweller except, perhaps, in his own homeland. But it seems to me possible, as well as eminently desirable, that the steps which I have outlined above will bring about a new social heredity for the Jew, one that will not rob him of his great virtues, but will lessen his liability to the psychoneuroses.

72. [Myerson is most likely referring to the decree (Canon 68) passed by the Fourth Lateran Council in 1215 that commanded Jews to sew a piece of cloth on their outer garments so as to visually identify themselves as Jews. The decree did not originally mandate the color yellow, though over time this color did become associated with the patch or badge. By the late thirteenth century the color yellow was legally mandated in some places, such as England and Spain.]

# 17 | The Problem of Tuberculosis among the Jews: A Racial and Socio-Pathological Study

**Noel Haltrecht**

"Das Tuberculoseproblem bei den Juden: Eine Rassen- und Sozialenpathologische Studie," *Zeitschrift für die Demographie und Statistik der Juden*, new series, 2, no. 2 (1925): 28–33.

I have been unable to find any biographical information on Noel Haltrecht. The article is included not only for the material in it, but because it appeared in this particular journal in the form it did, with the imprimatur of the editors, and because it provides a good sense of the professional, scientific views of the period on the topic. This article is a summary by the editors of an original article by Haltrecht. In a footnote, the editors note that the article from which this summary is derived was published as "Das Tuberkuloseproblem bei den Juden," *Beiträge zur Klinik der Tuberkulose* 62, nos. 3–4 (1925): 442–80. For a discussion of Haltrecht's arguments, see Sander L. Gilman, *Franz Kafka, the Jewish Patient* (New York: Routledge, 1995), 225–27.

The bulk of the Jewish masses work in those professions that produce the highest mortality rates from pulmonary tuberculosis: peddler, baker, furrier, tailor, shoemaker, and so forth. This Jewish proletariat, in Warsaw, Lodz, New York, and elsewhere, usually lives in small and overcrowded apartments, where the tuberculosis bacillus loves to dwell. As a result of such occupational and living conditions, physical weakness is very widespread among the Jews. Their chests are commonly tight, narrow, and flat; the shoulder-blades protrude at the back, the breastbone is concave; they show all signs of *habitus phthisicus* [predisposition to pulmonary tuberculosis]. Investigations conducted on underage workers in Odessa between 1920 and 1923 yielded the following results: average chest circumference and lung capacity among underage Jewish and non-Jewish workers in Odessa.

Jews, then, should necessarily be expected to suffer from tuberculosis in greater numbers than other inhabitants; however, according to research conducted by numerous physicians in London, New York, Vienna, Warsaw, and elsewhere, this is not the case. On the contrary, according to the indisputable

TABLE 17.1

(A) FIRST INVESTIGATION (1920)

| | Chest Circumference (cm) | Lung Capacity (ccm) |
|---|---|---|
| Jews | | |
| Male | 72.15 | 2578 |
| Female | 77.91 | 2261 |
| Non-Jews | | |
| Male | 74.99 | 2890 |
| Female | 78.89 | 2429 |

TABLE 17.2

(B) SECOND INVESTIGATION (1923)

| Males | | | Female | | |
|---|---|---|---|---|---|
| | Chest circumference in cm. | | | Chest circumference in cm. | |
| Age | Jews | Non-Jews | Age | Jews | Non-Jews |
| 14 | 69.6 | 72.1 | | — | — |
| 15 | 71.7 | 75.5 | | — | — |
| 16 | 75.0 | 76.6 | 16 | 76.5 | 76.6 |
| 17 | 77.6 | 80.4 | 17 | 78.5 | 77.8 |
| 18 | 80.6 | 82.7 | 18 | 79.3 | 81.3 |

results of this research, Jews suffer numerically to a lesser degree from pulmonary tuberculosis.

[. . .]

In this regard Haltrecht discusses two questions concerned with tuberculosis-related morbidity: To what extent are tuberculosis-related illnesses distributed among Jews? Which clinical forms [of tuberculosis] are prevalent among Jews? Nowadays the construct of the so-called "pathological racial constitution" is being advanced as a causal explanation for the Jew's peculiar situation in regard to tuberculosis. Buschan[73] goes even further. He is not only convinced of a specific disposition and resistance to the disease on the part of the Jews but is also able to derive from this the notion of the ethnological purity of the Jewish race. He writes, among other things: "Lately it has been denied that the Jews nowadays are still what we call a race, or that they constitute a distinct type. For my part, and despite the argument put forth in support of it, I cannot agree with this position. I have always had the impression that the Jew substantially differs both physically and psychologically from the European Aryan. Racial pathology confirms such a view. We see that the Jewish race, in contrast to the Aryan race, displays a heightened disposition, on the one hand, and a heightened resistance, on the other hand, to the influences of certain pathological phenomena." Buschan disputes most vehemently the notion that other factors, such as social and sanitary conditions, can have an influence on morbidity and mortality.

Other researchers trace the relatively small number of Jewish victims of tuberculosis back to the influence of their religion. Many authors put an especially high emphasis on the dietary laws, that is, the ritual examination of meat (*bedika* = examination of the lungs of the slaughtered animal), which serves at the same time as a sanitary measure against tubercular infection. At this point Haltrecht goes into detail about Fishberg's well-known theory[74] that the Jews, while living in the ghetto, underwent a selection process (*Ausleseprozess*) in which those elements [within the Jewish population] that were not immune to infection from tuberculosis were killed off and thus could not reproduce. "Those elements that could not endure this atmosphere [of the ghetto] . . . were killed off by tuberculosis, and they had no opportunity to reproduce." Fishberg's hypothesis has enjoyed especially wide dissemination and is generally taken today as the explanation for the low level of tuberculosis among Jews. Fishberg's hypothesis is based on the following principles: (1) that there exists such a thing as an inherited constitution predisposing a person to phthisis; and (2) that this type now exists to a far lesser degree among Jews than among other peoples. In order to establish the validity of the Fishberg hypothesis, the author examined in great detail the validity of these two principles; we will omit the particulars here. Let us quote Haltrecht's conclusion verbatim:

73. [Georg Buschan (1863–1942) was a German physician and anthropologist.]

74. [Maurice Fishberg's theory on Jews and tuberculosis can be found in "The Relative Infrequency of Tuberculosis among Jews," *American Medicine* 2 (1901):695–99; and "Tuberculosis among the Jews," *Medical Record* 74 (1908):1077–81.]

As the chief cause of the low mortality from tuberculosis, and the tendency to a benign, chronic progression, we cannot posit an inherited but rather an acquired immunity in Jews. Moreover, the Jews are acclimated to city life, while the Christian population—a significant portion of which originally come from rural lands—is weakened by the new [urban] living conditions. The influence of such changes in dwelling and way of life manifested itself very clearly among the colored peoples [lit., the colored] who have been the subject of Ziemann's research.[75] Those Negro tribes, who abandoned their free, primitive dwellings and were herded together in urban dwellings, quickly fell victim to tuberculosis.

Furthermore, the rarity of alcoholism and syphilis among the Jews also helps account for the low death rates from tuberculosis. It has been demonstrated both clinically and statistically that consumption preys more easily on bodies debilitated by alcohol or syphilis. In Paris tuberculosis mortality among male adults (30–49 years old) amounts to 36.1 percent, while among saloonkeepers it reaches 46.9 percent. In England, among every thousand deaths from tuberculosis, 384 are workers and 607 are waiters. In India, the [TB-related] mortality rate for those who abstain from drink is 72 percent; among those who do not abstain, 95 percent.

Among the Jews, however, alcoholism is a rare thing. Fishberg, who as resident physician of the United Hebrew Charities in New York examines each year thousands of Jews seeking assistance, might have seen over the course of twelve years barely a dozen Jews sunk into poverty through alcoholism. Among other peoples, the rate of pauperism on account of alcoholism amounts to between 25 and 60 percent. According to the statistics offered by John Billings, in New York (1858–1890), 31 percent of the Irish died of alcoholism, while the figure for Jews was 1 percent.

What may also be considered as an important factor is the exemplary concern [that Jews demonstrate] for sick family members, consulting a physician in time, and the solicitude in the treatment and care of the Jew suffering from consumption.

The main causes of the low numbers of death and morbidity from tuberculosis among Jews are to be sought in social and cultural hygiene as well as the

75. [Hans Ziemann (1865–1939) was a German physician and a professor of medicine at the University of Berlin. His research focused on tropical and colonial diseases and medicine.]

immuno-biological condition of this people. The religious family life of the Jews, their morality and temperance, in addition to the immunity acquired in childhood, are all factors that contribute to the low numbers of deaths among Jews from tuberculosis.

Concerning the World War and its influence on the outbreak of tuberculosis among the Jews, it did initiate among the Jews, just as among the general population, a strong increase in the number of diseased.[76]

[. . .]

The fight against consumption can be undertaken only by an organization founded specially for this purpose. As never before, the establishment of a League for the Struggle against Tuberculosis among the Jews is a necessity. Such an organization alone would be able to take on itself the solution to the problem of tuberculosis among the Jews.

Should my presentation arouse a practical interest among the professional classes for the founding of such an organization, I would consider this the best compensation for my work.

76. [There follow statistical tables showing the number of Jews who suffered from tuberculosis in Berlin, Vilna, Bialystock, Petersburg, Warsaw, Elizabethgrad, and Odessa during the first two decades of the twentieth century. The article then summarizes Haltrecht's pessimistic appraisal of Jewish resistance to tuberculosis after World War I, including his belief that the disease will be a serious problem for Jewish communities "for decades to come." The article ends with the editors quoting Haltrecht's urgent call for an organized, institutional struggle for prevention.]

# IV | Society and Economy

The same overarching ideas and assumptions that produced questions about Jewish health and disease also produced debates over Jewish social and economic patterns. Did a connection exist between race and crime? Were Jews predisposed to certain types of criminal behavior? As with health and disease, statistics seemed to indicate a difference between the sorts of crimes Jews committed (or at least were charged with) and those committed by non-Jews. Jews, it seems, were more likely to commit white-collar crimes—crimes such as embezzlement and fraud that involved "intelligence"—than "physical" or violent crimes such as rape and murder. What accounted for this difference—biology, or history and environment?

Similarly, what explained Jewish occupational patterns? Jews in Christian Europe, it was widely acknowledged, had by the late Middle Ages been confined to certain professions having to do with money lending and minor forms of commerce. Was this due to fairly clear historical reasons, in particular state and church laws that banned Jews from owning land and forced them into narrower ways of making a living? Or was there something more? Were Jews racially predisposed to certain livelihoods? More specifically, did Jews posses a biological or racial affinity for capitalism?

The theme of Jews and money, or Jews and commerce, had of course been a component of anti-Jewish imagery for centuries. One need only think of Shylock from *The Merchant of Venice*, or Fagin from *Oliver Twist*. The social and racial sciences made this issue a matter of empirical research and debate. The question of Jews and capitalism moved from the academic to the public realm in 1911, when the well-known German national economist Werner Sombart published *Die Juden und das Wirtschaftsleben* (published in English in 1913 as *The Jews and Modern Capitalism*). Much of the book was taken up with a history of the Jewish engagement with capitalism from a historical and social standpoint. Toward the end of the book, however, Sombart addressed "the race problem." After a prolonged discussion of anthropological issues, he invoked Arthur Ruppin, justifying a racial approach to the Jews on the ground that a Jewish authority (Ruppin) had already clearly demonstrated that the Jews were indeed a race. Given that, one also ought to grant that such a thing as a distinct Jewish spirit or genius (*Geist*) exists. Sombart argued that capitalism was and is an expression of this particular Jewish spirit. As such, Jewishness embodied a spirit that was opposite and hostile to the German or Teutonic spirit. As Sombart put it, the Jews were a "desert people" now living among a "forest people." Sombart's book received a great deal of attention within Jewish circles; it was received positively by some and attacked by others. In any case, the book gave vivid expression to the notion of a connection between race and economy.

# 18 | Is the Criminality of the Jews Racial Criminality?

## Rudolf Wassermann

"Ist die Kriminalität der Juden Rassenkriminalität?" *Zeitschrift für Demographie und Statistik der Juden* 7, no. 3 (1911): 36–39.

Rudolf Wassermann was a physician and social scientist who lived and worked in Munich. He was associated with the Bureau for Jewish Statistics in Munich and was an authority on crime and criminology.

Over and over again the question of the causes of the criminality of the Jews has stirred debate. Not one year passes that does not bring forth another new work! Most of the opinions revolve around the question whether the criminality of the Jews is predominantly due to occupation or race. Most of this research has already been discussed in this journal. In contrast, the work of the head of legal statistics in Amsterdam, J. R. B. de Roos, "On the Criminality of the Jews" (*Monatschrift für Kriminalpsychologie*, vol. 6, pp. 193f.) has remained undiscussed until now.

The work brings us new material related to the criminality of the Jews. For it provides us with what we heretofore possessed to an insufficient extent: a vivid image of the crimes of the Jews living in the Netherlands.

According to this, the criminality of the Jews has declined during the period of observation.[1]

[. . .]

In order to gain a more exact insight into the criminality of the Jews, de Roos then calculated their average participation in different crimes for the years from 1901 up until 1905. Unfortunately, he fails to present his results in the form of a statistical table. To the extent that he provides data, we shall attempt to reproduce it here. Thus, the following picture emerges:

1. [What follows is a chart that shows statistics from 1896 to 1906, divided into two main categories: the number of those convicted, and the number out of every 100,000 Jews. The author concludes: "These figures thus are essentially more favorable than those for Catholics and Protestants."]

| [Offense] | Christians sentenced (out of every 100,000) | Jews sentenced |
|---|---|---|
| Obstruction of justice[2] | 20.7 | 8.4 |
| Light bodily assault | 66.8 | 37.7 |
| Serious bodily assault | 1.7 | 0.5 |
| Willful damage to property | 15.3 | 3.6 |
| Libel | 5.2 | 15.1 |
| Larceny, petty | 33.3 | 17.5 |
| Larceny, grand | 16.8 | 12.4 |
| Poaching (forests and fields) | 12.8 | 0.7 |
| Embezzlement | 3.8 | 6.0 |
| Fraud | 2.1 | 3.1 |
| Receiving stolen property | 1.9 | 6.6 |
| Document forgery | 0.8 | 1.6 |
| Perjury | 0.5 | 1.1 |
| Disturbing the peace | 2.4 | 0.9 |
| Distribution of censored material | 0.05 | 2.2 |

One can see from these figures that the criminality of the Jews in the Netherlands is extraordinarily similar to that of the Jews in Germany and Austria. As Austria, where three-quarters of the Jews live in Orthodox and impoverished Galicia, represents East European Jewry, and as Germany and the Netherlands represent West European Jewry, we can then use de Roos to formulate and support a notion, already expressed by Ruppin and myself, that the liability of prosecution among Jews is rather consistent, despite numerical variations in frequency of commission, and despite the fact that they live under the most varied conditions in different countries.

Now what significance do these facts have for addressing the question: Is the criminality of the Jews to be conceived as a racial criminality or as the product of social conditions?

It is possible to be of different opinions on this question, and in fact notable researchers can be found on both sides: [Franz] v. Liszt on the one side, [Hugo] Högel and [Paul] Näcke on the other.[3] De Roos takes the middle ground. In his

2. [*Widerstand gegen Beamte*—literally, crimes against the civil service.]

3. [On the ideas of these three figures, and for a more general discussion of the history of criminology at the time, see Richard Wetzell, *Inventing the Criminal: A History of German Criminology, 1880–1945* (Chapel Hill: University of North Carolina Press, 2000).]

view, the criminality of the Jews is a product of a combination of the Jewish Volk's natural predisposition and the social and economic conditions in which they live at any given time.

De Roos invokes my own work to support his, in particular my article "Critical and Supplemental Remarks on the Latest Literature Related to the Criminality of the Jews," which appeared in volume 4 (p. 172f.) of this journal. De Roos is right in pointing to this work. There I did indeed explain that, despite the results I achieved through my methods, my position was never that the criminality of the Jews was the product of social conditions *alone*; but I did not provide there any basis for my position. So I would like to offer here those sections that I devoted to our problem, taken from my work *Begriff und Grenzen der Kriminalstatistik* [The concept and limits of criminal statistics] (Leipzig, 1909). I reproduce them here:

> In the realm of human behavior, no set of conditions could be declared to be necessary or sufficient to compel a particular type of human action or inaction. Through a sharper analysis of final causes one recognizes, though, that the numerically great mass of events ultimately depends on various conditions acting as motivating forces on individuals, which in turn are dependent upon a psycho-physical disposition.
>
> [...]
>
> We can put forth the following claim: the criminality of the Jews corresponds, insofar as the material at hand allows us to generalize, almost entirely to that sort of criminality that one would expect given their occupational position—that is, the criminality of the Jewish businessman in Germany is not essentially different from that of his Christian cohort—nonetheless, there remains a possible objection, which is undoubtedly justified to a degree. The parallel between A and B is explained by stating that B is the product of A or vice versa. It is, however, also possible that this parallel is the result of a third factor, C—or, translated into real-life terms: it is not impossible that in a great number of cases a choice of occupation can be traced back to a personal peculiarity, which later does in fact turn out to be the real causal agent for criminal activity, while social position actually has nothing to do with it. If, however, the correspondence between Jewish and Christian businessmen proves to be complete, then the supremacy of the social factor would have to be granted. The deficiency of such methods, which can never really be entirely denied or avoided, lies in this: that although those causes that have significance for criminality do appear in our results, it might appear to us, by virtue of having posed the wrong question, that certain

circumstantial motives or impulses were influential that in fact were almost completely meaningless. In addition to this, that which is absolutely individualistic cannot find [statistical] expression at all.

There are in these last sentences already an intimation of the reasons that induce me to embrace social causality as supreme, and there are further reasons for this choice, too.

De Roos even mentions one of these. It became evident that, in general, where the social standard of the Jews deviates from the norm, their criminality will also conform to this varied level. Thus, de Roos has established in the case of Amsterdam, where the Jews are chiefly engaged as laborers in the diamond industry, that the number of assault and battery cases (on average, between 1901 and 1905, 19 for every 100,000 Jews) nearly reached the same level as those for Christians (23), while those for fraud during the same timeframe was only half as many as for Christians (1.9 versus 3.8 out of 100,000 coreligionists).

I have identified a further argument in my work *Beruf, Konfession und Verbrechen* [Occupation, religion, and crime]. I said there: if one wishes to connect the criminality of the Jews with their status as pioneers of [a certain form of] economic life, then this will lead to an increasing similarity in the criminality of the Jews and Christians, to the degree that the specific capitalist traits of this economic way of life, which is particularly suitable to the Jewish character, spreads. This now is, as I have demonstrated in that work, indeed the case.

I derive further confirmation for my view from the results of research undertaken on other statistical issues concerning Jewish morality. I am thinking above all of the issues of suicide and population.

The statistics[4] show that the Jews, whose negligible tendency to suicide Durkheim[5] could still claim to be a "sociological law" at the beginning of the twentieth century, in hardly fifty years have attained suicide levels that significantly exceed those of the Christians.

Inversely, I have shown—as others have already in the *Zeitschrift für Sozialwissenschaft* (vol. 12, no. 11)—that the birth rate of the Jews, which in the middle of the [nineteenth] century was quite normal, today is only about half that of the Christians.

4. Compare vol. 6, p. 133 of this journal.

5. [Emile Durkheim (1858–1917) is considered to be the founding father of sociology in France, and one of the most influential figures in the development of sociology as a distinct discipline. His *Suicide: A Study in Sociology*, translated into English by John Spaulding and George Simpson (Glencoe, Ill.: Free Press, 1951), was first published in 1897.]

In both cases I believe I am justified in claiming that the causes of these phenomena can be located only in the fact that the tendency of the Jews to assimilate into their social milieu only significantly manifested itself when a wider sphere of Jews no longer felt themselves under the ban of religious laws.

When this time came, however, it became evident that this tendency was extraordinarily strong. Is not the conclusion quite obvious indeed that a national or racial body (*Volkskörper*), whose moral orientation with regard to two important questions appears to be decisively influenced by its social standards, will also show itself to be influenced by social conditions in other regards?

I am able, then, to summarize my views on the form and the causes of criminality among the Jews in the following way:

> (1) The criminality of the Jews expresses essentially the type of criminality associated with the general strata of the population to which the Jews belong socially.
>
> (2) Therefore, in all probability, it [criminality] is influenced by social class. A series of other considerations supports this.
>
> (3) It is by no means self-evident, however, that other factors—that is, one's racial makeup—are not involved in contributing to the criminal impulses of individuals; and there is also no denying that in the case of the Jews—and to whom does this not apply?—social conditions in part have to be traced back to racial characteristics.
>
> (4) It would be preferable if de Roos's statement that "the criminality of the Jews is generally a product of a combination of natural inclinations of the Jewish Volk and their social and economic conditions" had not been formulated in this manner. On the one hand, it does not allow us to recognize that in a particular case, individual causes are also always at work; and on the other hand, such a formulation places two very dissimilar factors on the same [explanatory] plane or level.

# 19 | Jews, Race, and Environment

**Maurice Fishberg**

Excerpt from *Jews, Race, and Environment* (1911; New Brunswick, N.J.: Transaction, 2006), 541–44.

For biographical information on Maurice Fishberg, see the note at the beginning of selection 3. On the history of European debates about the Jews and the economy, including the Jews and capitalism, see Derek Penslar, *Shylock's Children: Economics and Jewish Identity in Modern Europe* (Berkeley: University of California Press, 2001).

Certain peculiarities have been noted by many authors while speaking of the Jewish merchant and artisan. There appears to prevail a superstition that the Jew is superior to any merchant of other faith, as a trader. Some think he is more "smart," "clever," "calculating," and so forth. Ruppin thinks that all these and other terms are inadequate, and do not completely describe the Jewish superiority in this regard. He coins the word "*intellectualismus,*" and says that the superior intellectuality of the Jew explains his success in business. He [Ruppin] agrees, however, that the English are just as good as the Jews, while they are no match at all for the Americans, who are much better businessmen.[6] Both friends and enemies of the Jews thus often exaggerate the so-called Jewish commercial spirit, which on investigation proves to be a pure legend. There is no question that during the Middle Ages, when the higher classes of the European population looked down at commerce, the Jews, meeting with little or no competition, excelled as merchants. At the present, also, in Eastern Europe they excel because the bulk of the population is agricultural, while the cultured classes devote themselves mostly to military or professional pursuits. This is especially the case in Rumania, where the Christian natives sadly neglect mercantile pursuits; the [members of the] richer class live on the incomes from their estates, or pursue military or professional pursuits, while the common people are mostly peasants, and to a smaller degree artisans who are kept in ignorance, so that over 90 percent of the population is illiterate. Of course here the Jew excels in business, though

6. A. Ruppin, *Die Juden der Gegenwart*, pp. 176–178.

the Greeks in that country are at least as good, if not better, at commerce. For similar reasons the Jews succeed in other parts of Eastern Europe. But many of the Russian and Polish merchants are unquestionably shrewder and more successful in business than the Jews. A good public school system for the Christian population of Eastern Europe could within a few decades educate the common people so that they would rival the Jews in commerce. In addition it must be mentioned that most other religious minorities seem to develop good business capacity while living among a hostile majority. The Greeks and Armenians in Turkey are good examples. "The Armenian in a foreign land is an artisan, laborer, trader, merchant, banker, speculator, and so on, but never an agriculturist, as at home," says Rohrbach. It is particularly interesting to note that the Armenian merchants enjoy about the same evil reputation as the Jewish merchants in Eastern Europe. When inquiries are made in the Caucasus about the Armenians, a German, Georgian, Russian, or anybody else volunteers the information that they are despicable swindlers. It is well known that in the Orient three ascending degrees of fraudulent businessmen are proverbially known: one Greek is as bad as two Jews; one Armenian is as bad as two Greeks; and two Armenians are as bad as the devil. The opinion about the Armenian is not unanimously accepted. Sometimes it is said that two Greeks are as bad as the devil.[7] It is curious to note that Rohrbach's description of the condition of the Armenians in the Caucasus is exactly the same as that commonly given of the Jews in Eastern Europe. It appears that they are mainly the merchants and middlemen of that region. Anyone who wants to do any kind of business must come in contact with them. The result is that there is hardly an inhabitant of the Caucasus who has had no business transaction of any kind with an Armenian, and perhaps has even been cheated by him, which is almost inevitable, considering the bargaining and business methods of the East. The result is that nearly everybody bears testimony as to the unscrupulousness of the Armenian. The same is true about the Jews in Eastern Europe. The Russians, Poles, and others cannot successfully compete with the Jews, simply because the latter never drink to excess and assiduously attend to their affairs. When they meet, however, with Greeks, Armenians, and others who are equally sober and persevering, they do not excel at all; while with the Chinese they cannot even compare as traders, as has been repeatedly shown by many observers. Their poverty in Eastern Europe bears good testimony that

7. P. Rohrbach, *In Turan and Armenien*, pp. 214, 203. Quoted from Ruppin, *Zeitsch. Demographie und Statistik der Juden*, pp. 177–181; 1907.

they are not such good businessmen as they are reputed to be. To ascribe to them superior qualifications in this regard is absurd. Any other civilized people placed in the same position would be as successful in business as the Jews.

In a study of the Jewish spirit in modern commercial life, Sombart[8] brings forward considerable evidence to the effect that the Jews in Europe were the first to discard the ancient trade traditions which considered it unethical for a merchant to undersell another; to be satisfied with small profits on large and brisk sales; to occasionally sell at a loss when advisable to get rid of a certain line of goods or to push out a competitor; to sell on the installment plan; and above all, to advertise in newspapers and otherwise, and thus create a demand for their goods.[9] It is problematical whether they were alone in the field with these business methods during the seventeenth and eighteenth centuries. It seems to me that because they constituted the majority of the people engaged in commerce in those days, they were the most conspicuous, and for that reason Christian merchants of Germany, France, England, and so forth have complained that they are crowding them out, as Sombart shows. At any rate, at present they [the Jews] are not alone in this field. All successful business of today is conducted on these principles. To call this the "Jewish capitalistic method," as Sombart does, and ascribe it to race characteristics of the Jews is not justified. The most that can be said is that being the first merchants in Europe with international connections, brought about through historical vicissitudes, they were ahead of their time. Even at this game the English, and especially the Americans, have outdone them during the last fifty years.

8. [Werner Sombart (1863–1941) was a German sociologist and national economist. His well-known and controversial *Die Juden und das Wirtschaftsleben* (The Jews and modern capitalism) was published in 1911; it was translated into English by M. Epstein (New York: Collier, 1962).]

9. Werner Sombart, "Jüdischer Geist in modernen Wirtschaftsleben," *Die Neue Rundschau*, pp. 585–615, May 1910.

# 20 | Successes of the Jews in Capitalistic Enterprise

## Arthur Ruppin

Excerpt from *The Jews of Today*, translated by Margery Bentwich (New York: Holt, 1913).

For biographical information on Arthur Ruppin, see the note at the beginning of selection 5.

As merchants and entrepreneurs, the Jews were soon brilliantly successful, showing all that great business capacity which for 2,000 years had seemed to mark them out as predestined for commercial callings. It is a mistake to account for the fact that the majority of Jews are occupied in trade, by saying that the Christians of the Middle Ages shut them out from all other callings. It was not in Europe that the Jews first became traders; since the Babylonian exile, they had devoted themselves in ever-increasing numbers to trade in Syria, Egypt, Babylon, and so forth, while in Palestine itself, till the destruction of their nationality, they lived on the products of the land. In the Diaspora the Jews have never occupied themselves with agriculture to any extent.[10] The Middle Ages did not turn them into traders, but merely intensified and increased an aptitude that was already there. It may be taken as a general rule that legislation does not produce new conditions in domestic economy, it only legalizes existing conditions and thus secures them against changes. Laws would never have succeeded in confining the Jews to work as traders and peddlers if the Jews had not already come to Europe in these capacities. On the other hand, the Christians of the thirteenth and fourteenth centuries, when they took up commerce, and when all the great trades sprang up, did exclude Jews from their organizations, and thereby drove them from respectable and respected trades into the despised ones of peddling, pawnbroking, and usury.

It is commonly agreed that the Jews do not owe their commercial eminence to chance, but to an extraordinary inborn business capacity. "The Jewish race is—on one side of its character—the incarnation of the capitalistic business

10. The opposite is the view taken by Schipper (*Angänge des Kapitalismus bei den abendländischen Juden im früheren Mittelalter*).

spirit," says Sombart,[11] whose verdict will stand for that of others.[12] This means, in fact, that Jews, to a far greater extent than Christians, produce men who not only have energy and daring, but possess alert minds, with a special gift for swift comprehension and combination. It is this gift which makes the Jews the greatest chess players, excellent skilled workmen, technical inventors, and first-class businessmen.

It is only because this business capacity, from its great importance in industrial life, is so strikingly in evidence that we are apt to form the erroneous conclusion that the talents of the Jews are exclusively commercial.[13]

It is not unlikely that the Middle Ages helped to foster this natural inclination of the Jews; the continual persecutions and restrictions acted as a sort of natural selection by which the less cunning and resourceful Jews were removed, and only the very cleverest—those who could extricate themselves from the greatest difficulties—were able to survive. Similarly the smartness of the American is most simply explained by this theory of natural selection; that is to say, it was only the most energetic, adaptable, and courageous elements of Europe who risked the voyage over the ocean, and left these gifts as an inheritance to their descendants. The commercial ascendancy of the Jews must not be taken to mean that every Jew is *ipso facto* a good businessman, and that no Christian is his equal. There are and always were great businessmen among Christians. But the proportion is much greater among Jews than among Christians. The extraordinary part played by Jews in the building up of modern international trade and finance is proof of this. Jews have had no small share in inaugurat-

11. *Der moderne Kapitalismus*, vol. ii. p. 349 (Leipzig, 1902). Sombart has recently depicted in detail the eminent part played by Jews in the development of capitalism, in his book *Die Juden und das Wirtschaftsleben* (Leipzig, 1911).

12. Corroborations of this verdict can be found in Russell and Lewis, *The Jew in London*, p. 63; B. Webb, *The Jew of East London*, chap. ii.; Woltmann, *Politische Anthropologie*, p. 308; and so forth.

13. When we speak of the commercial superiority of the Jews, it is only in comparison with the European peoples among whom they live. Compared with some other peoples, particularly Indians, Greeks, Armenians and Chinese, this superiority is no longer apparent. In the East there is even a proverb to the effect that in business one Armenian is equal to three Greeks, and one Greek to three Jews. It is perhaps more than a coincidence that all these rivals of the Jews belong, like them, to the oldest civilizations, to nations who had reached a high state of culture at the time when the peoples of Central and Northern Europe were totally uncivilized. An ancient culture seems thus calculated to develop a predisposition to trade and commerce.

ing the present-day system of joint-stock enterprises and of banks, with their facilities for exchange, for the concentration of capital, for improvement in communications, for unbounded competition and wild speculation. In Germany the new kind of shop—the store—is entirely the creation of Jews, and the latest industrial combinations, trusts, syndicates, and so forth are, if not creations of Jews, at least used by them to the greatest advantage.

In the struggle for life, besides intellectual gifts, the industry, versatility, and powers of adaptation of the Jew stand him in good stead. The Jew does not despair if one of his enterprises fails; he begins again straight away with another. If he should be altogether unsuccessful in one calling, he is ready at once to take up another.[14] In this he is totally unlike the German Christian, for example, who is slow to change his vocation, but similar to the North American, who also changes his profession without the slightest hesitation. The adaptability of the Jew is shown also in another direction; he changes his manner of living according to circumstances, without being in the least upset by the change. Thus he can exist on less than the European Christian, and yet not be satisfied with the best that money can buy. This is due to the fact that the Jew, unlike, let us say, the German peasant, has no fixed standard of life: he is therefore always in a state of uncertain equilibrium, always pushing forward, never satisfied; whereas the Christian is usually content when he has arrived at the standard of his class.

14. That is, provided the calling is not held in contempt. For instance in Galicia, a Jew who had his firewood chopped by a Ruthenian told me in answer to my question [about] why a Jew was not employed for this work, that no Jew would undertake it for double the wage.

# V | "Racial Mixing"
## Intermarriage and Conversion

Much of the language of racial science and theory derived from the world of plant and animal husbandry. This legacy may be most obvious in the analyses produced by racial thinkers about "racial mixing," or miscegenation. Racial thinkers spoke about pure and hybrid races, about inbreeding and crossbreeding. A species was defined by natural science in terms of reproduction: members of the same species were capable of reproducing with one another. Though few seriously doubted that the races, no matter how different, could reproduce, many wondered if different races could breed together to any lasting effect. In other words, could different races produce offspring that would survive as hybrids over a generation or more? Moreover, could races that were significantly different from one another produce healthy offspring? Jewish and non-Jewish racial thinkers asked such questions about the Jews. Of course Jews could mate with Christians, but were such unions less fertile? Did they produce fewer offspring on average? And were these offspring less fit?

As we have seen, questions about Jewish racial purity and mixing constitute a crucial component of many—perhaps most—of the texts in this volume. Jewish thinkers engaged the issue by exploring the history of Jewish and non-Jewish encounters, beginning in the biblical period and moving into the present. To what extent did Jews mix their "blood" with foreigners? This question entails asking about sexual relations in many guises: intermarriage, but also extramarital relations, either freely entered into or not (as a result of conquest, enslavement, and so forth). It also includes conversion, particularly during those periods of Jewish history when gentiles converted in appreciable numbers to Judaism.

# 21 | The Jewish Racial Question

## Elias Auerbach

"Die jüdische Rassenfrage," *Archiv für Rassen- und Gesellschaftsbiologie* 4, no. 3 (1907): 332–61.

Elias Auerbach (1882–1971) was a physician, writer, and Zionist. He was born in an Orthodox Jewish home in Posen, Germany. He earned a medical degree in 1905 from the University of Berlin and emigrated to Palestine in 1909. Although he was trained as a physician, most of his written work deals with biblical studies and the history of the Jews. He also published a novel, *Prophecy*, in 1920. See the entry in the *Encyclopedia Judaica*, 2nd edition, 2:653–54. Also see John Efron, *Defenders of the Race: Jewish Doctors and Race Science in Fin-de-Siècle Europe* (New Haven: Yale University Press, 1994), 127–41.

The racial question is the question of the components of a racial mixture.[1] We call a race that which exhibits a certain indissoluble unity of significant uniformity [of traits]; when the object of our interest in this regard is to be found in a far-distant period of history, then we speak of a primordial race (*Urrasse*).

We must ask, then: What was the nature of the foundational stock of the Jewish race, and what types of intermixture have led to the partial transmutation of this foundational stock? The first question can essentially best be answered through an examination of the human (subject) matter existing today, and the second through a consideration of the fate of the race. History can offer us only a very unclear and murky notion of the nature of the race at the time when it emerged on the surface of human historical consciousness. And to draw conclusions from living human subjects about intermixtures that took place, without relying on history, remains a dangerous undertaking as long as the laws governing the mixture of human races are not more precisely understood than they are today.

1. Others understand by "the racial question" the question of the significance of the factor of race for historical development, or something of the sort. Practicability thus seems to demand that we either let this vague term go or specify it so as to render it unambiguous as a term.—A. Ploetz. [Alfred Ploetz (1860–1940) was a German physician and biologist, and a prominent figure in the early eugenicist and race-science movement in Germany.]

These two modes of consideration, the anthropological investigation of the living race and the historical assessment of its migrations and metamorphoses, must go hand in hand. We can arrive at a reasonably complete picture of a race only if both these paths can be traveled with some confidence. Certain ancient peoples (Völker) whose history, migrations, and intermixings we know about in great detail are still lost forever to racial research because these peoples are no longer available for measurement. Just the opposite holds true when it comes to modern peoples. Measurement is not a problem here; hundreds of thousands suggest themselves to the anthropologist, but in the majority of cases we cannot trace with desirable certainty the historical mixings and mergers of the historical race, cannot trace all the arteries of blood from which the wide—though often quite opaque—stream of contemporary peoples has been constituted.

For this reason, the Jews are a classic object of racial research, because we can work with both history and anthropometry better in their case than in that of other races. There is surely more that needs to be done here, but it can be done. Here we are presented with a race that throughout the time that we identify as historical almost never engaged in racial mixing.

The tribes of Canaan had virtually disappeared by the period for which the Bible offers historical and even contemporary historical (*zeitgeschichtlich*) documentation. [By this period] a unified nation of Israel already presents itself to the historian. The only influx of foreign blood imaginable would have to have occurred in that brief period from the immigration of the Jews (if this is the starting point from which we should view them as a primordial race, as the term is customarily understood) until their emergence into the clear light of history. Then, however, endogamy begins, which over the course of one hundred generations disperses and distributes the foreign blood equally within Jewry. These are conditions of intermixture, which not even an experiment could improve upon. And what are the results?

The Jewish race is very homogeneous around the world. It is not uniform, as no civilized race (*Kulturrasse*) is, but its variations do not differ fundamentally from one country to another. A different fate, a distinct environment, did not result in the blurring of a common and wholly durable type, and indeed the Jews demonstrate more clearly than any other race how overwhelming an influence heredity has, when compared to assimilation, in the matter of a race's fate.

In order to understand the Jews as a race, it is necessary for this study to clarify three points that have already been hinted at:

Were there indeed no noteworthy intermixings in the historical period?
Was there a notably higher degree of intermixture during the prehistorical period?
How should we envision the primordial Jewish race?

## RACIAL MIXING AMONG THE JEWS DURING THE DIASPORA

We shall proceed from the present to the past! Everyone is aware that today numerous mixings occur between Jews and other peoples in all civilized countries—far more frequently, in any case, than at any other time since the disappearance of the Jewish state. Nonetheless, a curious concatenation of factors, which the racial researcher has to be aware of, does not permit even now a thorough intermixture to occur.

In Germany at present (1903), the rate of Jewish intermarriage is approximately one-sixth that of pure (*rein*) Jewish marriages. This number is so large that one would be forced to derive from it a total and imminent dissolution of German Jewry. A *genuine intermixture, however, has only really taken place when the offspring of this intermarriage then introduce this foreign blood into the Jewish Volk.* Now the fact of the matter is that the overwhelming majority of these offspring of mixed marriages (*Mischlinge*) withdraw from Jewry both religiously and nationally, shutting themselves off thereby from any union through marriage with the Jewish nation (*Stamme der Juden*); thus, they remove themselves from the equation, for the most part, when it comes to [our analysis of] racial mixture. The Jewish human material (*Menschenmaterial*) that we are analyzing from an anthropological viewpoint and that is the foundation of the Jewish race in the progressive movement of history will consequently have altered very little and remains a homogeneous mass; they [the Jews] seldom lose elements to another people through dissolution. A careful and scrupulous authority on this issue, the statistician Arthur Ruppin,[2] estimates the number of offspring of mixed marriages who remain within Jewry to be only 10 percent of all offspring produced by the mixture of Jews and non-Jews in Germany. As to actual mixing of blood, we would thus have to figure that at only 1/60 of the racial stock of German Jews. However, even this small, though nevertheless not infinitesimal, number is valid only for Germany and a

2. Arthur Ruppin, *Die Juden der Gegenwart* (Berlin, 1904).

few other countries, in which altogether a very small percentage of the Jewish people [*Stamm*] live. If one goes back just a few decades, the number of Jewish intermarriages declines precipitously in relation to the number of the Jewish population overall. In Prussia, the number of Jewish mixed marriages declines by half, if one goes back twenty years; for the Jewish population in general this occurs only when one goes back sixty years. Before this period, around the turn of the nineteenth century, the intermixing of the Jews [with other peoples] in Europe dwindles almost to the vanishing point. For the entirety of the Middle Ages—and for Jewish racial history, the term "Middle Ages" is valid up until the French Revolution—the number of intermarriages was so minute as to be negligible, the more so as barely any offspring of such marriages mingled their blood with that of Jews.

The law of racial isolation of the Jews from the peoples around them in Europe held true for the entire Middle Ages. It would serve no purpose here to trace the two-thousand-year migration of Jews throughout all the countries of Europe; we find the same picture throughout. The Jews migrate to sparsely settled countries of low cultural levels, in most cases as welcome guests, sometimes having been called on or invited explicitly [by gentile authorities]. They introduce their more developed [mode of] economy to the country and form a middle class there. When the [host] nations then become sufficiently strong economically, so that they can do without the Jews, they are expelled as bothersome and dreaded competition or harshly oppressed through laws of exclusion. This sort of change occurred in France by the beginning of the seventh century, in Germany in the eleventh, in Poland in the thirteenth, [and] in Spain in the fifteenth. After this, one can no longer speak of racial mixing anyway;[3] yet even during the former periods of tolerance, we have no evidence for such mixing—save for a few instances that we must consider separately.

Intermixture between Jews and Arabs most certainly occurred in Spain during the period of Arabic rule. Of course we possess little documentary evidence for this. We can only assume that the undisturbed neighborly relations of the two peoples (*Stämme*), the lively participation of the Jews in public life, and their complete legal and economic equality made intermarriage possible. Nonetheless, an essential difference exists between this period and that of modern Jewish emancipation: the Jews [of Spain] were not inclined to surrender their

3. This is not the place to analyze in detail Fishberg's admirable work, and his thesis of a strong Slavic intermixture with the Jews (*Mem. of the anthrop. and ethnol. Soc. New York*, 1905). It is sufficient to say that we are not able to accept his numbers as an adequate proof of his thesis.

racial isolation. This example offers us a perfect opportunity to make the point vigorously that in general, over the course of the entire racial history of the Jews, the most rigorous opposition to racial mixing does not stem from other peoples but from the Jews themselves. It is only by knowing and taking into consideration this tendency that we are able to make anthropological use of the historical facts, for it is this tendency alone that allowed the Jews to remain unscathed [unaffected] by their long wanderings in exile, the enormity and length of which would have long since brought other races to the point of dissolution. The active reserve displayed by the Jews is, notably, taken to such lengths that it is forbidden for them to proselytize, because religious equality [between the Jews as a race and other races] would do away with the most powerful barrier against physical intermixing.

Quite frequently the well-known case of the conversion to Judaism of an entire tribe, the Khazars, is cited. Many researchers, Ikow chief among them,[4] viewed this as an opportunity for greater racial mixing. In fact, however, we know for certain only that the king of the Khazars, together with a number of elite Khazars, did convert to Judaism; whether or not the people in general followed is unknown, so we cannot estimate with any certainty the degree of contact [between Jews and Khazars]. Above all, it must be emphasized that in terms of any sort of substantial mixing with the Jews, a significant Jewish mass was lacking in these regions, and that everything the Khazars subsisted on after the destruction of their empire by the Russian principality of Kiev fell to the Karaites. Most of them [the Karaites], however, never mixed with the main body of Jewry, and therefore the Khazars are not a factor in Jewish racial research.

Finally, many—among them, Alsberg[5]—call attention to the fact that legislation forbidding marriage to a Jew was often enacted in the Middle Ages. According to Alsberg: "If King Ladislaus the Saint of Hungary forbade marriage between Christians and Jews through legislation passed in 1092, this sort of legal measure only makes sense insofar as such relationships actually occurred." It is obvious that this is a grave syllogism. Such a conclusion could be correct only if the prohibition sprang from a recognition that Jewish-Christian marriages were a [genuine source of] grievance. This, however, was certainly not the case. Such prohibitions were nothing more than one of many examples of a fanatic hatred

4. Ikow, *Archiv für Anthropologie*, vol. 15, 1884.

5. [Moritz] Alsberg, *Rassenmischungen im Judentum*, Virchow-Wattenbachs popularwissenschaftliche Vorträge, 116, Hamburg, 1891.

of the Jews. These prohibitions against intermarriage stood on the books for centuries in countries in which such marriages had ceased to occur long before, and they still exist today in the civilized country of Spain, where hardly any Jews live. This prohibition is merely the expression of the contempt of a putatively superior race for the persecuted Jewish race (*Stamm*), akin to the [ancient] Egyptian prohibition against marriage to swineherds. In any case, such prohibitions related to marriage cannot be taken as valid arguments for the miscegenation of the Jews (*Rassenmischung der Juden*).

To sum up, we can say that *during the entire Middle Ages and until the beginning of the nineteenth century, the Jews completely maintained their racial purity.*

For the Hellenistic and Roman periods, the matter presents itself differently. In any case, the preconditions for racial intermixing were present due to the existence of a strong proselytism. This phenomenon is usually underestimated. Yet all evidence from this period speaks to the fact that around the time of the birth of Christ, the Jews were economically and, above all, culturally a significant presence in the Roman Empire. We know of numerous conversions to Judaism; this reached into the highest circles [of Roman society], even into the ruling families. Non-Jews joined or affiliated themselves with numerous Jewish communities, and just as there existed a pagan Christianity during the early period of Christianity, so there existed a pagan Judaism during this period. Thus, we should not reject the idea that during this period, foreign blood entered the ancient Jewish race through conversions.

Certainly, this period came to a quick and sudden end. With the destruction of the Jewish state by Titus, the aforementioned struggle for the self-preservation of the Jewish race began—the principal means of which was the preservation of racial purity, and consequently the abandonment of proselytizing efforts. Tacitus already mentions this exclusive attitude of the Jews, and there is no good reason to go along with Alsberg when he advises us to take Tacitus's pronouncement about the Jews—"Alienarum concubitu abstinent" ["they abstain from intercourse with foreign women"]—with a grain of salt.

If we thus allow even the possibility that during this time mixed marriages influenced the Jewish racial body, this influence could hardly have been very extensive in relation to the totality of Jewry, given the brevity of time in which it occurred.[6] The religious prohibitions against marriage were lifted only for those

6. See the apt description by Jacobs, *Journal of the Anthropological Institute of Great Britain and Ireland*, vol. 15, 1886.

converts who had taken on themselves the full weight of the ceremonial law. This, however, was only a small minority compared to those who merely attached themselves in a general way to [Jewish] doctrine. On the whole, one can confidently say that over the past two thousand years, the Jews have enforced the principle of racial endogamy with great tenacity. They strengthened and consolidated thereby the [racial] inheritance that they brought with them out of Palestine. What was this inheritance?

## JEWISH RACIAL MIXING IN PALESTINE

In the history of the development of the Jewish race, surely the most significant and interesting chapter is the period of Jewish independence in Palestine, encompassing approximately thirteen centuries. The most fertile—indeed, almost the only—source for our understanding of racial mixing during this time is the Bible. The realization grows ever stronger that the Bible, despite all the criticism directed at it, has inestimable value as a source. Anthropologists as well gladly invoke it in order to substantiate this or that aspect of their hypothesis about the descent and distribution of the Semitic Völker. But when one does this, one is then also obliged to take biblical evidence into serious consideration when it proves less congenial to one's theory.

Now, what does the Bible say about the racial mixing of the Jews?

Throughout all the historical books of the Bible and the numerous speeches of the prophets, there occurs a constant repetition of the warning against mixing with neighboring peoples. Yet this fact has been evaluated in quite different ways. Many deny any value whatsoever to these [passages], claiming that this prohibition was only put into place later, after the Babylonian exile—that is, after intermixture had already taken place—in order to prevent any further amalgamation of the Jews [with other peoples]. [This is to claim that] the Jews of the pre-exilic period would have had no aversion whatsoever to intermixing. Today, however, there can be little doubt that biblical criticism, in its initial impulse, went much too far: though we are indeed presented, in the historical sections of the Bible, with many cases of a later redaction, mostly we have the use of old, often very old, sources. If we could assume that the prohibition against intermarriage was always observed with more or less that same level of faithfulness, as [we can] with those centuries after the Babylonian exile that are more amenable to historical verification, then we would have to reject almost completely the idea of an intermixture of the Jews with foreign tribes in Palestine.

Here, however, an alternative interpretation comes into play that is in many ways the opposite of the aforementioned. Alsberg[7] argues: "Were unions—both within and outside of marriage—between the children of Israel and non-Israelite, at times even non-Semitic, peoples of Palestine not a common occurrence, then those biblical passages in which the Israelites are warned against mixing with foreign peoples would be senseless." The untenability of this position has been pointed out repeatedly. In any case, it is certainly less accurate with regard to more ancient times than to more recent. In the ancient period, Jews took an active part in the prohibition against intermarriage; in the Middle Ages, they were passively subjected to it. Is such active isolation and concern about purity on the part of an ancient civilized people an exception to the rule? Or is it in fact the rule? We need only consider the Egyptians, Indians, Chinese, and Greeks. Do we have the right to assume that a "racial sensibility" (*Rassegefühl*) became powerful only after extensive intermixture had taken place, during the period of the Babylonian exile, rather than in the period of relatively greater racial purity? Gobineau[8] and Reibmayr,[9] in contrast, correctly insist that the resistance to further intermixing declines with the increasing loss of racial purity. With the sort of racial pride that the Jewish nation, on the basis of all our sources, evinces to a high degree, we should hardly wonder that measures against the influx of foreign types into the race were put in place. An analogous example can be found in the behavior of the aristocracy, who during times of minimal intermixture with "inferior" blood also evince an outlook of exclusivity.

The central question remains: Do we find positive proof in the historical sources—above all, in the Bible—of Jewish intermixture in Palestine?

### 1. *The Semitic Canaanites*

In considering the racial question, there are two categories of Jewish intermixture in Palestine, and the significance of these has to be valued quite differently. On the one hand, there are the Semitic tribes (*Völkerschaften*) in and around Palestine, most of which immigrated only shortly before the Jews did, and who, on account of their close relationship (*Verwandtschaft*) to the Jews, could

7. Idem.

8. Gobineau, *Versuch über die Ungleichheit der Menschenrassen*, Volume 1. [Joseph-Arthur, comte de Gobineau (1816–82), a French diplomat and writer, was the author of *An Essay on the Inequality of the Human Races* (1853–55), in which he set forth his theory of the superiority of the Aryan races.]

9. [Albert] Reibmayr, *Inzucht und Vermischung beim Menschen*, Leipzig and Vienna, 1897.

not alter the Jewish racial type significantly. To this group belong the Moabites, Ammonites, Midianites, Amalakites, and Edomites, all of whom more or less carry the imprint of desert-dwelling Bedouin tribes. On the other hand, we have the seemingly non-Semitic tribes, encountered by the Jews when they arrived, and whom the biblical account repeatedly identifies with the following names: Hittites, Emorites, Canaanites, Perisites, Hivvites, Jebusites, [and] Girgashites. The Bible draws a clear distinction between these two categories of peoples. In many places it deals with the first group as kinsmen [of the Jews], or in any case not as implacable enemies (with the exception of the Amalakites). "So we passed by our brothers, the sons of Edom" (Deuteronomy 2:8). The Moabites and Ammonites were also left alone by the Jews during the conquest of Palestine (Deuteronomy 9 and 19). Undoubtedly, intermixing occurred with these tribes in numerous cases. According to the biblical account, Moses's wife was a Midianite; David was a direct descendant of Ruth, a Moabite; the prophets repeatedly railed against the mixing with these peoples; [and] on his arrival in Palestine, Ezra discovered numerous cases of intermarriage with Moabites, Ammonites, Midianites, and Edomites, and took action against these. And finally, during the reign of John Hyrcanus, the Edomites were forcefully converted to Judaism and quickly dissolved into the Jewish tribe completely, for which they even provided a series of rulers, [known as] the Antipatrid dynasty. Yet all these instances of intermixture could transform the racial character of the Jews very little, since these tribes were quite closely related to them—as both the Bible and the linguistic and cultural remains of these Semitic peoples testify. It has often been claimed that these tribes themselves were already the product of myriad other elements, but we still lack any evidence for this claim. The Bedouin character displayed by these tribes makes it seem likely, judging by the behavior of the Bedouins today, that they guarded their racial uniqueness tenaciously.[10]

10. Here a rather curious misunderstanding on the part of Alsberg can be mentioned: he presents the unions of Isaac and Jacob with "Aramaean" women as racial mixing. In reality, these are extraordinary examples of a fierce protection of racial purity. According to the representation in the Bible, which agrees well with the accepted knowledge of Semitic migrations, the Abrahamites—the advanced guard of migration—chose their wives from the remnants of those tribes still living in the areas around the Euphrates. Here, in the interest of completeness, it needs to be pointed out that the Bible mentions in many places intermixture with Egyptians. Abraham, who is still treated as the personification of the nation, in terms of the national narrative (*Völkertafel*) in Genesis, took as his secondary wife (*Nebenfrau*) the Egyptian Hagar. However, this narration can hardly

Although Jewish law permitted this first category of tribes to enter the Jewish community under specific conditions and provisos, and thus permitted them to marry [Jews], the law remained all the more firmly committed to the exclusion of and hostility to the other Palestinian tribes mentioned above.[11]

[...]

## RESULTS

The above analysis of the facts regarding Jewish racial traits leads us to the following results:

> (1) Since the destruction of the Jewish state, no considerable racial mixing on the part of the Jews has occurred.
>
> (2) The Hellenistic-Roman period, which spanned the two centuries previous [to the destruction of the state] witnessed some racial mixing, but to no great extent.
>
> (3) In the period lasting from 1300 to 600 [BCE], mixing with non-Semitic Canaanites undoubtedly occurred.
>
> (4) The theory of the emergence of short-headedness among the Jews as the product of an extensive mixture with Hittites (Alsberg, Luschan) cannot be substantiated.
>
> (5) The explanation of blond hair and blue eyes among the Jews that points to intermixture with Amorites in the ancient period ought to be seriously doubted.
>
> (6) There is justification for doubts about the conventional opinion that ancient Semites must have been dolichocephalic.

---

serve [our analysis of] racial mixing, since the same Bible presents the Arabian Bedouin as the result of this union, an entity that is notably distinct from the Jewish race. Joseph also married an Egyptian. If one wishes to evaluate at all this least known and most debated period in Jewish history, when the Jews dwelled in Egypt, then one can say that such intermixing at most happened only on rare occasions and only among the upper classes. (Compare the history of Moses's adulthood). The majority of Jews, in any case, lived among Semitic tribes in the eastern Nile delta and, like the Egyptians, they were disinclined to any intermarriage.

11. [Auerbach provides an extensive discussion of the following subjects in the remainder of his article: "non-Semitic Canaanites," which include the Hittites and the Amorites; "Jewish Racial Mixing in Primordial Times"; and "Blonds and Blue Eyes among the Jews." He then summarizes the results of his research.]

(7) The lack of pigmentation among Jews ought to be considered a secondary, more recent racial heritable trait.

From our presentation it ought to be self-evident that the Jewish race offers incomparable material related to questions of general anthropology. It is a textbook example for the study of heredity and adaptation within human races, for the effects of inbreeding and mixing. The Jews are not, as one Jewish author recently exclaimed, the mixed race par excellence, but rather a relatively "pure" race, a truly inbred race.[12] Gobineau's words remind us of their particular durability, which approaches the miraculous: "I say that a Volk will never die so long as it is always constituted out of the same national components."

12. [It is important to note that the German term *Inzucht* does not carry the same connotation in this context as the everyday English term "inbred." As Auerbach and others discussing Jews and race used it, the notion of inbreeding referred to endogamy, or marrying within one's own race, religion, ethnic group, and so forth. It did not signify close marriage within a particular family, or incest.]

## 22 | The Mixed Marriage

### Arthur Ruppin

"Die Mischehe," *Zeitschrift für Demographie und Statistik der Juden* 4, no. 2 (1908): 17–23.

| For biographical information on Arthur Ruppin, see the headnote for selection 5.

Until the end of the eighteenth century, the social gulf throughout Europe between Christians and Jews was so great that a marriage between Christians and Jews would have seemed completely impossible, even if such unions had not been prohibited by religious, ecclesiastical, and civil statutes—akin to [the situation] today in the colonies of Africa ruled by the European powers, in which marriages between natives and whites are seen as abnormal and hardly occur anywhere. Certainly, one finds individual cases of Jews converting to Christianity and then marrying a Christian spouse, but such cases do not fall under the category of mixed marriage. For, in the usual sense of the term, mixed marriages are characterized by the fact that, at the wedding, one of the two marrying belongs to the Jewish and the other to the Christian religion—a characteristic missing in all cases in which one of the two individuals has already converted to the other's faith before the ceremony.[13]

For the anthropological researcher, certainly, conversion before marriage is of no significance. According to him, a marriage between a Christian and a Jew remains a mixed marriage whether there is conversion or not; that is, it constitutes a marriage between members of different races. However, this anthropological point of view cannot serve as a conceptual foundation if a valid comprehension of statistics on intermarriage is to occur; and, indeed, it is unfeasible on purely practical grounds. The racial affiliation of the individual does not fall within the purview of official statistics, at least not in Europe, and probably never will given the difficulty or impossibility of assigning European whites to specific, anthropologically uniform groups. If one thus wishes to grasp the prevalence of mixed

13. Note that it would be significant if the registrar inquired into the religious affiliation of the individuals not only at the time of the ceremony but also prior to that. But this never occurs.

marriage with the aid of statistics, one can proceed only from the religious affiliations of the individuals at the time of their entering into the marriage. Though, to the anthropologist, such results are not complete because they do not include the change of religion that occurred before the abovementioned marriage ceremony, yet they still hold meaning for him as minimum figures. Among all other Völker, religion and race have very little to do with one another; whereas among the Jews, religion is a certain indicator of racial affiliation. One should not, however, overextend the concept of race. If race is to be understood only to refer to those communities whose characteristic anthropological traits were formed in ancestral times, and which over the course of history have completely refrained from sexual commingling with other communities, then there is no racial difference whatsoever between humans of white skin color. Over the millennia they were all repeatedly thrown together and not only crossed with each other, but in a few areas also mixed with individuals of yellow and black skin color. Whether the Jews have constituted a unified race since their entrance on the historical stage and have always preserved this unified character is completely uncertain. What is certain, however, is that at the end of the eighteenth century the adherents of the Mosaic religion, on account of their centuries-long rigorous inbreeding in a relatively small and geographically curtailed region, constituted in terms of anthropological traits a community sharply distinct from that of the surrounding Christians. The totality of those individuals who are descended genealogically from this community can, lacking a better term for anthropologically unified human groups, be termed a "race"—that is, the Jewish race. In the nineteenth century many members of this race converted from the Jewish to the Christian religion; others have taken Christian spouses, and their children have been raised as Christians, so that one now finds members of the Jewish race who are adherents of the Christian religion. Contrary to this, the cases in which a Christian (that is, anthropologically speaking, a German, a Slav, and so on) converts to Judaism or, on account of entering into a sexual relationship with a Jew, becomes a follower of the Mosaic religion are so rare as to be totally negligible; and thus, one can, without fear of grave error, maintain that even today all adherents of this religion [Judaism] are also members of the Jewish race. If we term all adherents of the Mosaic religion "Israelites," and all members of the Jewish race "Jews," we can phrase the result of our contemplations in short as follows: all contemporary Israelites are Jews, but not all contemporary Jews are Israelites.

It was necessary methodologically to clarify these relations. We will now proceed to discuss the spread of intermarriage in the present.

The first impetus to the revocation of the regulations prohibiting marriages between Christians and Jews emerged out of the great French Revolution and then spread slowly from land to land—to Holland, Belgium, Denmark and Scandinavia, England, and the United States. This process was facilitated by the fact that marriage in these countries had been transposed from an ecclesiastical to a civil act. In a novel by K. E. Franzos,[14] set in Galicia at the beginning of the nineteenth century, the conflict is that of a Christian nobleman in love with a Jewess whom he cannot legally marry. The solution to this conflict is that, for the first time in a small German confederate state, a marriage between a Christian and a Jew is allowed to occur. With the law of the Reich dated February 6, 1875, which makes no mention [any longer] of difference of religion as legal grounds for prohibiting a marriage, unions between Christians and Jews became permissible in all German states, insofar as such marriages were not already permitted by law [in some particular states].

In Hungary, mixed marriages were first legally permitted in 1895; they are also allowed in the Christian Balkan states. However, mixed marriages are still forbidden in Austria, Russia, Spain, Portugal, and Islamic countries today.

The most propitious places for mixed marriages are those countries in which the Jews have been settled and prosperous for quite some time, but in which their numbers are so small that their rise into the upper classes does not anger the Christians and result in anti-Semitism. The list of such places today includes Denmark, Italy, and Australia.[15]

[...]

Summarizing all the relevant data collected thus far, one can divide those countries in which mixed marriages take place into four classes, depending on the frequency of occurrence.

Denmark, Australia, and Italy belong in the first class. In these countries, mixed marriages make up more than one-third of all of the Jewish marriages and constitute a genuine threat to the continued existence of the numerically small Jewish populations in these countries, as the children resulting from these marriages will overwhelmingly be raised as Christians. The same holds true for England, France, and the United States, at least if one considers only those Jews who have resided in these places for an extended period of time and not the

14. [Karl Emil Franzos (1848–1904) was an Austrian Jewish novelist. The novel in question is *Judith Trachtenberg* (1890).]

15. [Three pages of statistical data on mixed marriages in individual countries follow.]

immigrants who arrived in the past three decades. In addition, conditions in a number of German capitals (Berlin, Hamburg) are such that one should include them in this first category.

In the second category are Protestant Germany, Holland, Lower Austria (Vienna), and Budapest. Here mixed marriages constitute 10 to 25 percent of all Jewish marriages and show a tendency to rise steeply. This tendency does not yet, it is true, threaten the numbers of the Jewish population, though the increase is already limiting its growth.

Catholic Germany, Hungary (without Budapest), and Bohemia belong to the third category, where mixed marriages make up 2 to 10 percent of all Jewish marriages.

Finally, in the fourth category, with less than 2 percent mixed marriages, we have Galicia, Bukovina, Romania, and the recent immigrant communities in England, France, and the United States.

## 23 | Fertility in Mixed Marriages

"Die Fruchtbarkeit in Mischehen," *Zeitschrift für Demographie und Statistik der Juden* 4, no. 11 (1908): 175–76.

This brief piece appears anonymously, but the author is most likely Arthur Ruppin. A significant number of short pieces appeared without attribution in this journal. Ruppin, its editor, noted in his diary that he or his assistant, Jakob Thon, wrote all the unattributed pieces. For biographical information on Ruppin, see the headnote for selection 5.

In an article by Wieth-Knudsen ("Racial Crossing and Fertility") in the *Political-Anthropological Review* (vol. 7, no. 6), we learn that the statistics on fertility in marriages in Prussia for the years 1875–1900 yield the following picture:

Pure Marriages (*Reine Ehen*):
- Catholic marriages: 5 children
- Protestant marriages: 4 children
- Jewish marriages: 3.8 children

Mixed Marriages:
- Protestant-Catholic marriages: 3.1 children
- Christian-Jewish marriages: 1.7 children

In 1895 in Prussia, 21 percent of all Protestant-Catholic marriages were childless, and 35 percent of all Christian-Jewish marriages were childless.

Wieth-Knudsen traces, via de Lapouge (*Théorie d'infécondité par défaut d'accomodation résispropue*), the lower fertility of Christian-Jewish marriages back to racial difference, and chiefly to psychological factors connected to this difference. The author [Wieth-Knudsen] is of the opinion that in mixed marriages the psychological unity or homogeneity is lacking, and that the sense of family, the joy taken in numerous offspring, is weakened or debilitated. The lower fertility rates among Christian-Jewish married couples cannot be explained by differences in age or standards of living, since such conditions are hardly any different when it comes to Protestant-Catholic intermarriages and to pure Jewish marriages—although the latter always have the disadvantage when it comes to fertility.

# 24 | The Significance of the Mixed Marriage

Ignaz Zollschan

Excerpt from *Jewish Questions: Three Lectures*
(New York: Bloch, 1914), 20–26 and 33–42.

Ignaz Zollschan (1877–1948) was an Austrian Jewish anthropologist and physician. After practicing medicine, he turned to anthropological research, focusing on Jews and the question of race. He was also very active in Zionist politics, and a highly vocal proponent of the need for Jewish thinkers and writers to use racial and social science to further the nationalist cause. This selection comes from a collection of lectures that Zollschan delivered in the United States. See the entry in the *Encyclopedia Judaica*, 21:666.

What can we say with certainty about the purity of the Jewish race? The answer to this question is of vital importance. For if intermarriage with alien races had in former years played a great role among Jews, it is self-evident that we are not justified in speaking of a Jewish race at all. Are the Jews of today really the pure descendants of Abraham, Isaac, and Jacob?

Nobody assumes today that all the Jews are the direct descendants of three patriarchs; they are derived from the mingling of various stocks which were, however, essentially varieties of one and the same race.

When in the thirteenth century before the current era the Bedouin tribe of the Habiri, that is to say, the Hebrews, took possession of Palestine, they found there a vast native population, the Canaanites, Hetites, Getites, Amorites, and Philistines. During the period of the Judges and Kings, the Jewish tribes intermarried with all these nations. Their blood was mingled with that of the nations in whose midst they lived. This slow process of intermixture continued until after the first exile, until the time when the powerful word of Ezra severed all existing marriage connections with foreign nations, and henceforth the purity of the race became the dominant principle.

It is quite gratuitous to enter into a controversy about the exact definition and classification of such nations as the Hittites, Amorites, Philistines, and others, to which, in a broader sense, the Egyptians as well as the Babylonians, Assyrians, Phoenicians, and Jews belong. Whether we speak of Semites and Hamites in accordance with the inadequate linguistic methods, or of Semites, Hittites, Amorites, and Kushites, we regard these nations as related to one another in the racial sense. Ample anthropological evidence exists for this statement, though naturally it cannot be presented in this lecture.

Many historians are of the opinion that the appearance of Ezra did not put an end to the racial intermixture. They think that also in all subsequent centuries the Jews continued to mingle with the nations of the Diaspora, just as in the time before the Babylonian exile. They advocate the theory that the Jews of today are the descendants of the heathen proselytes during the Hellenistic period, or the offspring of mixed marriages between the Jews and their surrounding nations during the Christian centuries.

We can today assert with certainty that the extent of proselytism has been greatly exaggerated. There can indeed be no doubt that Judaism found numerous adherents among the pagan nations during the Roman and Hellenistic and early Christian periods. We have, however, sufficient reason to assume that those proselytes were only the so-called "proselytes before the gate," that is to say, converts who practiced the worship of one God, but were never admitted to circumcision or marriage. They were proselytes who later on embraced Christianity.

And in the times that followed immediately, the policy of discriminating between Jew and Gentile was inaugurated. Hadrian's laws forbidding circumcision were, it is true, revoked by his successor, Antoninus Pius, but it was expressly prohibited to make converts to Judaism. In consequence of this, the formal embracing of Judaism became a punishable crime, and it remained such until quite recent times. Even during the periods when the Jews commanded respect to some extent, the Church took good care that the religious boundary-line should be kept intact. In times of persecution and oppression, no appreciable number of adherents of other religions could have gone over to outlawed Judaism. The bars of the ghetto formed a reliable dividing wall.

But even if we grant that in some cases a few heathens became Jews in every respect prior to the Christian era, they could have been of no significance. As in the Hellenistic period there already existed millions of Jews, the admixture of foreign blood must have been infinitely small. And this foreign blood was, after all, derived from the kindred nations in Syria, Asia Minor, and Egypt.

It may be regarded as certain that proselytism almost entirely ceased since the appearance of European Jewish history. Even the invasion of the Khazars in the eighth century does not alter the fact that during the Middle Ages not much of foreign blood was added to the Jews. For already in the tenth century the empire of the Khazars was confined to a small territory, something like Crimea of today, and in the eleventh century it was entirely wiped out. A small remnant of Khazarite Jews is still living in Crimea today, and belongs to the Karaitic sect. But even if we assume that the entire nation of the Khazars embraced Judaism, and professed that religion for a long time, this admixture would still be a *quantite negligeable* [negligible quantity] and would not alter the ethnic character of the Jewish race. Moreover, it is doubtful whether this conversion was not confined to the rulers and the ruling classes of the Khazars. We would be losing sight of historical proportion, if we were to infer from the conversion of the Khazars that the Jews have any remarkable admixture of foreign blood.

As far as legal mixed marriages are concerned we know that they actually existed in the times of high material culture, namely, in Egypt during the Hellenistic period and in Spain during the twelfth and thirteenth centuries. But, as is the case now in Europe, where there is a strong leaning toward intermarriage, the offspring of those marriages preponderantly went over to Christianity. Besides this, those early periods quickly passed away owing to the changed political conditions, the reaction of orthodoxy, and the decisions of the councils of the Christian Church. Moreover, this movement at that time, in contradistinction to the general spread of intermarriage of today, was only confined to one country. Intermarriage with northern nations never took place in former years to any considerable extent.

The Jewish nation accordingly has propagated itself in an essentially pure manner from the time of Ezra until today, and for more than two thousand years represents an ethnically peculiar race, which was not diluted by foreign blood. It is self-evident that a few drops of foreign blood must have found their way among the Jews during the long time in the Diaspora. But these admixtures were too insignificant to have any essential influence upon the ethnic character of the nation. Thus the Cohanim, who were absolutely excluded from mixed marriages, are typically the same as the other Jews. The state of affairs can best be described in one sentence: a great deal of blood was exported from Jewry, but little indeed was imported from outside. And, consequently, we can assume with certainty, that the blood which flows today in the veins of the Jews is the same as that of two thousand years ago.

That Ezra's commandments, among which is also the one about purity of blood, have been kept for thousands of years is due to the fact that they claimed to be religious ordinances coming from God. It is the case with all nations that social institutions which are interwoven with, and supported by, religion are kept most tenaciously. In addition to this, Ezra's prescriptions owe their strength to the circumstance that they consisted in the practical laws of the cult, and not in theoretical doctrines; and that the Jews, after being scattered among other nations, were forced to social and economic isolation.

The true consideration of this circumstance indicates the great significance of the solution of the problem of intermarriage in our own times. Economic and social isolation and the power of religious legislation, account for the fact that up until today this people did not fall a victim to intermarriage, despite its wanderings among strange nations for the last 2,000 years.

As long as ceremonial religion was a great power in the civilized life of all nations, this influence of religion was easily explained. But nowadays, for reasons which will presently become apparent, this influence upon the great masses is confined to the Ghetto environment. As soon as the Jew leaves this Ghetto environment, and participates in the national industry of his country as a factor of [citizen with] equal rights, and adapts himself to the speech and culture of his native land, he begins to free himself from the power of ceremonial religion. A century of free activity in the world of capital, combined with a secular education, entirely estranged the Jews, in all countries where the system of capital is developed, from their former mode of life. The pressure of changed economic conditions and the scientific materialistic conception of our age sap the vitality of orthodox Judaism and undermine its foundation.

Now since ceremonial religion on the one hand and economic and social isolation on the other, together with the prohibition of church and state, were the only reasons why intermarriage with foreign nations did not take place on a larger scale, it necessarily follows that affairs today have reached a critical stage. Free legislation in countries where the system of capital is developed has done away with the economic and political isolation; rationalism has shaken ceremonial religion; and no state nowadays prohibits mixed marriages.

In countries where one or another of these important conditions is not fulfilled, as, for instance, Galicia, Russia, and the Orient, Judaism is still kept alive, though the lot of the masses residing there is by no means to be envied. But in the Occident, and in all countries where the Jews are allowed to develop themselves freely, their lot is the same as that of other nations in a similar situation.

Without exception, all the nations who were compelled to leave their native soil and who never formed a compact majority in any part of the world, but were scattered in small communities, have vanished through intermarriage. And the

Jews likewise would be swept away by the immense tide of the human race in the five continents, if all obstacles were removed. As can be easily shown, Jews have always married outside the fold whenever conditions were favorable. But never were conditions which make for the disintegration of Judaism as powerful as to-day. Nations who dwell together always mingle, unless intermarriage is made impossible by outside pressure of law or religion. The Jews nowadays come into contact with other nations, the civil law permits intermarriage, and the authority of religion is beginning to wane. The laws of love and material interests are mightier than all religious barriers, especially when the latter are weakened and enfeebled as they are today. The result of these considerations is that, today more than ever, Judaism is in danger of being dismembered.

The facts derived from statistics confirm this conclusion in all its details.

[. . .]

We may epitomize our conclusions from the processes described above as follows: When the Jews in the Diaspora became prosperous, assimilation which appears on the scene takes them away more or less from Judaism. It is mainly when they are oppressed, when they are in economically unfavorable conditions, that the Ghetto environment, in its old sense, is still retained. And although conditions today are not favorable in all countries, the beginning of this development can be recognized everywhere. Under favorable material conditions, and through the prevalence of secular education, Judaism, on account of its being scattered among nations of an alien race, is in danger of being disintegrated and destroyed, since the influence of ceremonial religion is waning.

It is not for the first time that we notice this process of disintegration. There were similar phases in all countries and throughout all ages. In accordance with the laws of historical evolution ever since the exile, this process has appeared in every country where a high culture brought about freedom from political pressure, from care for [earning] a livelihood, and from superstition. These phenomena appeared in those cases where Judaism actually imported foreign cultures, as for instance the Greek culture in the second century before the present era up until the first century of the common era, and afterward the Arab culture from the eighth until the twelfth century. Greek culture, from whose combination with Judaism, Christianity sprang, brought Judaism to the brink of ruin and deprived it of a great part of its adherents. The million of Jews who, during the first century after Christ lived in Egypt, which was then the center of Hellenistic culture, appear to have gone over to Christianity. And the intimate and friendly intercourse which prevailed later on between Jews and Mohammedans in Babylon and Spain caused the frequent recurrence of mixed marriages and conversions to Islam. The fact that in the empire of Castile, from the year 1290 until the year 1474, the number of Jews was reduced from 850,000 to 150,000 may serve as a proof for this assertion.

It is impossible to deny the resemblance of these two periods with the process of disintegration of our own times. Only nowadays, the beginning of this process exists in all countries, and it has the tendency of becoming universal. Formerly, these processes were only partial, confined to certain domains of culture. Modern culture, however, has broken all boundaries and has become a world culture.

In China, the Jews, who in former centuries were quite numerous, have almost entirely disappeared without leaving a trace, through intermarriage with the Chinese. And finally, we have to take into consideration the ten tribes who disappeared among the foreign nations, because at that time religion had not yet become ceremonial in the same sense as it existed after the Reformation of Ezra and Nehemiah. And also today it is possible that wherever religion ceases to be ceremonial, the greater part of Jewry in the Diaspora will, in the near future, become absorbed among the nations in whose midst it exists.

From all these considerations it becomes clearly manifest, how significant the problem of intermarriage is today. An inexorable process of disintegration is in progress. Although this process of breaking up Judaism is only gradual, from individual to individual, from family to family, it is of significance on account of the principle and inevitable result that it involves. The future of the Jews is seriously menaced by economic impoverishment in the East, and by baptism and mixed marriages in the west of Europe. In addition to this, there is a decrease in the birth rate of [Jews in] the latter [region].

The Jewish people which existed almost from the time when the history of the world began, which flourished in antiquity, which defied fire and sword in the Middle Ages, which is the only one of the nations that survived from the earliest times until today, whose representatives even today have brilliant achievements to their credit—it is just to this people that culture and the development of civilization have brought nothing but misfortune; they have estranged many of its best sons, and through political and economic anti-Semitism have slowly but surely taken away the ground from under the feet of the great masses.

It is therefore not impossible that Judaism may be disbanded in the near future—to be more precise, when the amelioration of the lot of the Jews will enable them to spread themselves still more [broadly]. Are we justified in hindering these historical processes, which may mean the termination of thousand-fold tribulations? Can the continued existence of a nation which is externally persecuted by fate be of any value to us? What our sentiment says is quite clear; but what answer do we get from positive science? Would it not be perhaps of great benefit to the development of civilization if the Jews were to assimilate with other races of high standing?

These are questions and problems which cannot be solved from our subjective point of view, but we must seek for an answer in sociology, history, and natural science. Which is better when considered from the general point of view, race mixture or race purity? The point of view which modern science adopts toward the important questions of race mixture and inbreeding is totally different from that which prevailed up until the last quarter of the preceding century.

Whereas it was formerly believed that in the intermarriage of two different races, the qualities of both component parts would appear in the offspring, we know now that the question of race mixture is by no means so simple. It is possible, but not certain, that only kindred elements could improve through crossing. On the other hand, the interbreeding of totally different nations produces a bastard type whose character is far below the level of either parent.

The observations made in countries which have a population of half-breeds have pointed to the unfavorable effect of crossing. In India, the progress of race crossing caused civilization to retrograde. We also know very well the wretched conditions of Central and South America, which are inhabited by half-breeds whose cultural stagnation stands in striking contrast to the rapid and ambitious development of the United States and Canada. It is certain that the conditions in Central and South America must, to some extent, be considered as the result of race crossing. It is true that also in North America the population arose from a blending of various nationalities. But here it was chiefly Englishmen, Frenchmen, Spaniards, Dutchmen and Germans; that is to say, nations which were closely related to one another, who were amalgamated; whereas in South America it was Spaniards, Indians, Negroes, and Mongolians who formed affinities.

Colonization in newly discovered countries has always succeeded in those places where, like in North America, the conquering nations have avoided crossing [with the indigenous peoples]. In Brazil, on the other hand, there rules an indescribable mixed type whose bodily, intellectual, and moral energy is exceedingly enfeebled. The natives of South Africa have a proverb: "God created the white man, God created the black man, but the devil created the mulatto."

According to the laws of Nature, the general instinctive abilities, from which depth of talent and character emanate, dwindle among half-breeds, while individual abilities often become more pronounced. Almost all observers are unanimous that through cross-breeding, bodily shapeliness [and] facility of talent could be gained, but resistibility of body and strength of character are impaired. Furthermore, the ability to achieve anything great and extraordinary, as well as nobility of mind are, as a rule, unknown to half-breeds. The latter characteristics form the constitutional ability, and the former the individual. The constitutional type becomes enfeebled through crossing, and the more distant the two races are, the more pronounced is this weakening.

[...]

These examples will suffice to prove that crossing is one of the principal causes of the destruction of nations, and that the interbreeding of widely different types leads to the reduction of fertility and vitality. The difference of race and character leads, as also animal breeders assert, to the formation of discordant, irresolute characters. It is for this reason that all half-breeds who are the offspring of widely different races have a bad reputation in respect to character.

In history there are many examples of the impossibility for half-breeds, even when their parents did not belong to races very far from each other, to reach a state capable of developing a living culture. This impossibility is also observed in cases where each nationality in itself possessed very great ability. All investigations thus point to the ennobling influences of racial purity, and to the destructive effects of racial chaos.

One calls to mind the flourishing nations of the ancient Orient: the Indians, Persians, Egyptians, and Greeks. One also compares their former creativeness and influence with those of the time when the tide of foreign nations began to overwhelm them. How brave were the old Romans, and how capable did the Germanic race that mingled with them prove to be later on; and yet how wretched was the product of this crossing! After the barbarism of the Middle Ages, it took about a millennium before men of firmly rooted greatness arose once more, and before the national character strongly and harmoniously asserted itself! How changed were the inhabitants of Greece after they absorbed the Slavonic tribes! What became of the Indians after the Arabs and Mongolians broke into their country? Each of these racial components proved itself capable of high culture, and yet the result was always a change for the worse for both parent races. That these results were not due to historical and social conditions alone can be seen from the case of smaller nations like the Armenians and Jews who have retained their racial purity, and have consequently preserved and increased their cultural ability despite their unhappy lot. One calls to mind the high cultural ability of the Moors and the Goths, and one considers the result of the mixture in Spain, when the Gothic population absorbed the former after the destruction of the Moorish rule. One also thinks of the racial medley of Germans, Slavs, and Tartars in Russia. It becomes evident from these examples—not speaking of the single individuals, but of the greater majority—what a bad effect the mixture of races has. The normal historical development does not tend toward the effacement of race, but rather toward making the racial features more pronounced, and is thus combating political influences. The quintessence of race is the hero, the genius.

From experiments on and observations of our domestic animals, we also learn that thoroughbred animals, which possess superior characteristics, become deteriorated with respect to these very characteristics, through intermixture. The same holds good of the human races. It is now regarded as certain that virtues and superior qualities are mostly to be found among races which have kept themselves pure, while mixed breeds usually develop the defects and vices of their parents, but none of their good sides.

There is thus no doubt that the power of heredity is more powerful among pure races. Potential cultural energy will always predominate in pure, untainted races. It is only among such races that ingenious creative power as well as artistic and moral genius find a favorable home.

These are, accordingly, the answers which science gives today to the above questions. Even from the cosmopolitan point of view, therefore, it would be no advantage if Judaism were to disappear through assimilation with those Slavonic nations in whose midst the bulk of the Jews reside today. Such an event would be detrimental to both sides. We have to strive after race purity, not after racial chaos. Greatness of intellect, character in the highest degree, and genius can only emanate from the rich source of instincts which are to be found in pure races. In order to get an exact idea of the power of instincts and the effect of heredity, we ought to bear in mind that every man, in twenty generations, is the product of more than a million forefathers, and in thirty generations he is the product of a thousand million forefathers. If all these forefathers descend from one race, this enormous sum of similar instinctive talent, and with it the strength of constitutional capacity, becomes manifest. For it is this constitutional type, as above indicated, which produces bodily resistance, depth of intellect, and strength of character. And this constitutional type becomes enfeebled through crossing. Accordingly, if a nation wishes to achieve something great and powerful for itself and mankind, its policy with reference to the future must have only one aim: to force its way from racial chaos to racial purity.

We have proved by our investigations that the Jews have racial purity, and that an extraordinary high racial value falls to their share. Their disappearance would not only be a national loss, but also an irretrievable loss for the general culture. But unfortunately, even at this present moment, this race is in danger of being destroyed. The conservation and further development of the distinguished possibilities that are found in this ancient race, owing to its long-standing purity, are just now being questioned. For there is not so much danger to the Jew from baptism, as is usually maintained, as there is from intermarriage. [This is so] in the first place because baptism only finds its way among Jews of ignoble character, while intermarriage is found among all classes; and secondly, because intermarriage is practiced even in countries where baptism, for one reason or another, is of rare occurrence.

In conclusion, I wish to repeat the following sentence which contains the social law appertaining to mixed marriages, and for which we have previously cited statistical proofs: tribes which live together always intermarry when such marriages are not forbidden by law or religion. Since they have been scattered all over the globe, the Jews have mingled with other nations. Civil law today permits mixed marriages, and religion has actually begun to lose its authority.

In order to preserve the Jews for Judaism, two remedies are possible: to preserve the Ghetto with its external and social influences, or to abolish the Diaspora. The first alternative can only mean a continued morbid existence.

This is the Jewish Question in a quite different sense from that in which it is usually conceived—namely, the question about the future lot of the Jewish race, which, after thousands of years of splendid development and stubborn resistance, now presents the sad picture of the body of a people which is partly perishing in misery and partly in course of decomposition.

# 25 | Intermarriage between Jews and Christians
## Maurice Fishberg

"Intermarriage between Jews and Christians," in *Eugenics in Race and State: Papers of the Second International Congress of Eugenics* (Baltimore: Williams and Wilkens, 1923), volume 2.

For biographical information on Maurice Fishberg, see the note at the beginning of selection 3.

From the standpoint of the preservation of Judaism, intermarriage has been considered a disaster, robbing as it does the Jews of its best adherents. In fact, those who have recently taken stock in Jewish affairs have arrived at the conclusion that mixed marriages rob the Jews of more adherents than persecutions [do]. The reasons are obvious when we consider that it [intermarriage] is the final result of the abjuration of nearly everything that has kept the Jews alive among the nations for centuries. Without the separative tenets of its religious practices, Judaism is inconceivable and in danger of extinction through absorption by the surrounding majority of other faiths. In fact, those who marry Christians are lost to Judaism within two or, at most, three generations.

Available statistical data show that the children born to Jews married to Christians are nearly all raised as Christians. Even the few that are raised as Jews are more apt to marry out of the faith than those born to Jews [married to other Jews]. This has been the case in Scandinavian countries, as well as in Germany, Italy, France, and so forth.

Moreover, it appears that intermarriage robs the Jews of their best racial elements. Careful observation of Jewish life during the past century reveals the following interesting fact: success for a Jew in any line of human endeavor, be it financial, industrial, scientific, literary, or artistic, means that his descendants will be lost within two or three generations through intermarriage with Christians. The result is that of nearly all great and talented Jews during the nineteenth century, hardly any have left descendants within the fold of Judaism. The few exceptions that may be mentioned prove this contention because they also have Christian relatives by marriage.

Another important harm is done by intermarriage to those who remain within the fold. The proportion of parvenus is enormous among them because those who have attained eminence in any field are lost, and their descendants, if they remained within the fold, might have created a nucleus of a Jewish aristocracy. Intermarriage deprives them of it, and they are apt to be judged by their worst, or by those who have not yet adapted themselves to the higher things in life, though they have achieved success in some field.

But the Jews are not only robbed of the exceptionally able and talented through intermarriage. Wherever it is carried very far, the Jews are more or less completely absorbed by the Christians around them. Thus, the Spanish and Portuguese Jews in England and the United States, and to a certain degree in France and Italy, have nearly all disappeared by fusion with the non-Jewish population. Many of them are now recognized as members of Christian churches in the countries in which their parents or grandparents prayed in the synagogues. It is curious that in one country in which the church and state were not in the way for three or four centuries, intermarriages have completely wiped out the Jews. This occurred in China, where about three hundred years ago large and flourishing Jewish communities existed, but at present they have all disappeared. The Jews who live there at present are recent arrivals from Europe. Of the endogenous Jews hardly a trace has been left.

The Jews disappeared in China because of intermarriage with the Mongolians among whom they lived and they were not replaced by immigration from other countries. In the United States, England, France, Italy, and other Western countries, conditions not unlike those mentioned prevail. The Jews who have lived there during the seventeenth and eighteenth centuries have almost all been fused with the Christian population; very few of their descendants have been left within the fold of Judaism. But in the Eastern European countries, in which, as was already shown, intermarriage was not permitted, the number of Jews kept on increasing during the past two or three hundred years, so that more than one-half of the total number of Jews in the world live in Russia, Poland, Austria, Rumania, and so on. These Eastern Jews have been immigrating West during the past fifty years and replaced those who were lost through intermarriage. In fact, it appears that very few of the Jewish families in Germany, England, France, and so forth can trace back their ancestry as residents of those countries for more than two or three generations. Inquiry also reveals that in most cases they had immigrated from Eastern Europe during the past fifty or seventy-five years.

However, things have changed in Eastern Europe during recent years. Since the revolution, the prohibition of intermarriage in Russia and Poland has been abrogated and the result is that marriages of this sort have already become very common, and they are bound to increase in number. Some even maintain that, for special reasons, the number of Jews who will marry Christians in those countries will exceed that observed in Western countries. It is thus clear that in the near future there will not be a surplus of Jews for migration to Western countries to replace those lost through fusion with Christians. The recent nationalist movement among the Jews is mainly the result of these conditions. They face extinction among the European and American nations because they cannot rigidly observe the separative tenets of their religion, and relaxation in this regard brings them into intimate contact with the surrounding majority of other faiths. Intermarriages are the inevitable result. The Zionists believe that only in their own home, in Palestine, will they be in a position to save the remnants of Israel.

Intermarriages of the kind spoken of in this paper have been objected to because it has been alleged that race mixtures are not desirable. Some have stated that most of the vices of both original stocks are accentuated in the offspring, while hardly any of the virtues are transmitted. It has also been stated that mixed marriages turn out unfortunate in too many cases, and sterility is rather common. Most of these contentions come from sentimentalists, Jewish as well as Christian, and do not deserve serious consideration. One thing, however, must be emphasized: the flow of so-called Jewish blood into the veins of other white peoples does not introduce any new or alien racial elements. It has been agreed by nearly all competent anthropologists that the Jews are a composite ethnic unit, a racial blend into which nearly all the types of white humanity have entered. While they [the Jews] are predominantly brunet, about 30 percent have blond traits. In Italy and France fusion results, as a rule, in a racial product which cannot be differentiated from the rest of the population. In northern countries the same is true, because the proportion of brunets is more or less high everywhere. In fact, within two or three generations, the descendants of mixed marriages are fused with the general population of any country beyond recognition.

For those who look with apprehension at "race mixture," it may be stated that the flow of Jewish blood into the veins of the European and American peoples does not infuse any new racial elements for the reasons just stated. And it is well known that the intermixture of European ethnic elements has proved to be of immense advantage to the European nations. The most progressive nations are those who can lay least claim to ideal racial purity. England, Germany, France, Italy, and especially the United States, though populated by peoples in whose veins flow the blood of nearly all ethnic elements in creation, cannot be considered backward nations. On the other hand, witness the homogeneous populations of central Asia and Africa, free from any racial admixture, but in a low stage of mental evolution.

Moreover, it appears that the offspring of mixed marriages of which we just spoke is apt to be superior. Grant Allen[16] some years ago said that the number of talented and distinguished people is rather extraordinary among those descended from Jewish-Christian married couples. Indeed, when we contemplate the number of persons of half-Jewish origin who have attained distinction and eminence in various fields of human endeavor, it appears that Grant Allen was right. To mention but few: Montaigne, the great French essayist, had a Jewish mother; Sir John Herschel, the English astronomer, had a Jewish father; [others include] Mendelejeff, the great chemist, and Metchnikoff, the biologist; Bret Harte, the novelist; Francis Turner Palgrave, the critic; W. Clifford Palgrave, the traveler; Sir Henry Drummond Wolff, the English diplomat and politician; Prevost Paradol, the journalist and author; Paul Lindau, the German critic; G. Ebers, the Egyptologist; Paul Heyse, the German novelist and poet; Edwin Booth, the actor; Mrs. Keely, the actress; Daniele Manin, the Italian revolutionist; Leon Gambetta, the French statesman; Sir John Millais, the British painter; Sir A[rthur] Sullivan, the noted English composer and conductor; Ludovic Halévy, the French composer; and many others. Among those who have achieved notable success in commercial, industrial, and financial fields, the number of half-Jews appears to be enormous.

It is for this reason that those interested in improving the human breed have no apprehension at the infusion of so-called Jewish blood into the veins of modern European and American nations.

16. [Charles Grant Allen (1848–99), a Canadian author and teacher, was known as a strong advocate of evolutionary theory.]

# VI | Politics, Polemics, and Apologetics

Texts dealing with Jews and race were unavoidably political. Thus, one might argue that every selection in this volume has some political thrust or underlying motive. The texts in this section articulate political concerns and impulses in a fairly direct and explicit way. Given the centrality of racial theories and ideas to modern antisemitism, itself an ideology with a strong political agenda, it is no surprise that one major impulse behind narratives of race produced by Jews was political in turn. Racial narratives written and disseminated by Jews about Jews were intended in part as a direct polemical response to antisemites. Jewish racial thinkers believed that the Jews could use racial science as an intellectual weapon against their enemies.

One key theme in this sort of racial defense of Jews and Judaism was the cultural value or worth of Jewry. This was a response to arguments made in the middle of the nineteenth century by antisemites such as Richard Wagner, who—like Houston Stewart Chamberlain, Werner Sombart, and others more than half a century later—insisted that the Jewish racial "spirit" or nature existed in opposition to the Germanic spirit, and that this manifested itself in the cultural as well as the economic realm. Jews, Wagner had argued, were incapable of true cultural or artistic production; at best, they could mimic true art. Jews were more often instrumental in buying and selling culture than in creating it. And this materialist approach to the spiritual, so antisemites argued, had degraded German and European culture and society in general. Jewish scholars felt it necessary to respond to such charges, and to demonstrate that Jews had indeed made significant contributions to Western civilization and culture. Jewish racial thinkers, unsurprisingly, made their arguments in the context of a racialized interpretive framework.

Jews were indeed a race, these thinkers believed, but not an inferior one. Rather, Jews were at least the equal of the Aryans or Teutons. Their past contributions to civilization could be catalogued, and on the basis of this past, the promise of future contributions from the Jewish race could be guaranteed.

Such discussions of racial worth and the value of the Jewish Volk's contribution to civilization constituted a specific instance of a more general Jewish apologetics that characterized much of Jewish scholarship at the time.

Racial history and thought could also be brought to bear in the Jewish response to a peculiar but highly important turn in theological antisemitism: the racialization of Jesus, or the insistence that Jesus was not a Jew, but an Aryan, born and raised in the northern, "Aryan" part of Palestine. The selection here by Leo Sofer demonstrates that one Jewish response to this widespread "Aryanization" of Jesus was to use racial anthropology and history to demonstrate that Jesus was, in fact, racially a Jew. Just as with the question of racial value or worth, the general terms of the debate were accepted by these Jewish thinkers—in this case, the validity of the question of Jesus's race. It was the antisemites' answer to that question, and the political and cultural consequences of this answer, that disturbed Jewish racial thinkers.

Yet racial narratives about Jews were also intended as interventions in another political or ideological struggle, that between so-called Jewish assimilationists and Jewish nationalists. Here the issue was not first and foremost the influence that the Jews had had on European society, but the effect of European culture and society on the Jews themselves. What impact did emancipation and assimilation into the modern nation-state have on the Jewish body and mind? Was assimilation a form of collective suicide, the willful disappearance of a two-thousand-year-old race and people? Or was it a necessary development in the life of this people, a sort of Darwinian process of adaptation to new environments and conditions?

# 26 | The So-Called Jewish Race

## Salomon Reinach

"La Prétendue race juive," *Actes, Revue des études juives* 48 (1903):1–14.

Salomon Reinach (1858–1932) was born in Paris and educated at the École Normale Supérieure. An archaeologist, philologist, and historian, he published widely on these topics. He was also an educator, museum director, and vice-president of the Alliance Israélite Universelle. As is evident in places, this essay began as a public lecture. See the entry in the *Encyclopedia Judaica*, 2nd edition, 17:205. Also see Ruth Harris, *Dreyfus: Politics, Emotion, and the Scandal of the Century* (New York: Metropolitan Books, 2010), chapter 9; and Aron Rodrigue, "Totems, Taboos, and Jews: Salomon Reinach and the Politics of Scholarship in Fin-de-Siècle France," *Jewish Social Studies* 10, no. 2 (2004): 1–19.

If the idea that the word "race" awakens is vague, obscure, and contested, the origin of the word itself is no more assuredly established. We want first to recognize in it the Latin *radix*, or rather *radicem*, meaning root; but *radicem* would have given to French the word *rais*[1] and would never have elicited the word *razza* in Italian. Diez had thought of a word in High German, *reiza*, meaning "line"; race would therefore be a synonym of lineage. But the "a" from the first syllable in *razza, race*, creates further difficulty. Following a second hypothesis, *razza* may have come from another Germanic word, *raki*, meaning dog, from which we get *race* and *racaille* [riffraff]. A *racaille* was, properly speaking, a family of dogs, or a pack, corresponding consequently to the word *canaille* (*canaglia*) [scoundrel, rabble], which also signified, originally, a pack of dogs. In Italian, *razza di cane* is still used as an injurious term as are *kelb ben kelb*, "dog, son of a dog," in Arabic, [and] *canaille* and *racaille* in French.

If this final etymology, which presents a certain probability—for the words *race* and *racaille* must certainly be explained in the same way—merits our preference, it is quite interesting to ascertain that the very origin of the word *race* should be strictly limited in use to a variety of domestic animals, a variety whose characteristics, constituting a [biological] type, are preserved from degradation

1. As opposed to the French word *race*.

and from mixing by artificial selection. Take terriers or greyhounds, which under human surveillance breed only with terriers or greyhounds, and give them the liberty to mate with other individuals of their species: after only a short amount of time, you will no longer have either terriers or greyhounds, but street dogs—that is, the permanent characteristics that constitute the race will have disappeared on account of mixing or crossbreeding. Every domestic race has the tendency to return to a certain more general type, which is that of the species; the only ways to combat this tendency are isolation and artificial selection. As one of the leaders of the French school of anthropology, Mr. [Paul] Topinard, wrote, "No physiological barrier can defend the races against dislocation."[2]

What is true of the races of domestic animals is equally true of the races of cultivated plants, which we improperly call species. Mr. Topinard frequently insisted upon this fact, already well known, but which it is essential to recount here: "Horticulturists say that the types that they create, in practicing artificial insemination and in attending to the conditions of the environment, degenerate and disappear the moment when they are no longer looked after. The natural tendency is not in the fixing of types, but in their disaggregation."[3]

One essential remark, owing once again to Mr. Topinard, is that the word *race* is hardly ever employed by naturalists when they speak of wild animals and plants. They prefer words like *variety*, which suspend the question of permanence, a condition sine qua non of race. On the other hand, naturalists have no scruples about using the word *race* when it is a question of domestic animals and plants—that is, in those cases where within the species, the reproduction of individuals is not left to chance.

Is it permitted, given the above, to apply the word *race* to a particular subdivision of the human species? Can we speak of a French race? A Slavic race? A Jewish race? The majority of anthropologists are not of this opinion at this time. They think that the word *race* should be reserved for general types that are determined for us through the analysis of the principal branches of humanity, and that we should renounce the word for all types of the third and fourth order that we create out of idle fancy, without basis and without scientific criterion. "Race," says Mr. Topinard plainly, "does not exist in the human species, once one moves beyond these general types."[4]

2. *L'Anthropologie*, 1898, p. 643.

3. *Congrès Anthropologique de Moscou*, p. 108.

4. *L'Anthropologie*, 1896, p. 480.

What are these general types? On this matter, everyone is in agreement: there are the white of Europe, the yellow of Asia, the red of America, and the black of Africa and Oceania. The origin of these types is completely unknown to us, but we have at one and the same time established their existence and perpetuity. A Negro from Africa resembles the Negroes represented on Egyptian monuments from four thousand years ago; a Chinese from today resembles those that Marco Polo saw in the thirteenth century. Despite individual differences and those that exist between different groups of whites, blacks, reds, and yellows, each of these four large divisions of the human species offers, in addition to color, characteristics that can be defined and rigorously ascertained. On the other hand, these are varieties or races, but not species; the human species, whatever its origin, is one. This follows from an experimental fact, the fecundity of unions between individuals from every country and of every color. For physiological reasons that are still rather obscure, infertility is like a wall that bounds species, that traces between them an impassable line of demarcation. Within each species, as we have seen, the natural tendency is toward fusion and mixing; this tendency is counterbalanced by geographical conditions, by social and religious prejudices; but it exists and has already produced appreciable results, to which the mulattos and mestizos testify.

Not only have naturalists never been able to define what it is that we commonly call the Germanic race, the Slavic race, [or] the French race, but they almost unanimously agree in condemning such associations of words. It is however, in the name of the so-called rights of the Germanic race that France was mutilated in 1871, and this absurd conception, unjustifiable in the eyes of science, was used against us by politicians, served at times by blind scholars.[5] As early as the day following the treaty of Frankfurt, the anthropologist [Abel] Hovelacque protested against this abuse of false and vague ideas, placed at the service of the spirit of conquest and oppression. "Germanic blood! May as well speak of Latin blood or Slavic blood! Never has the confusion between languages and races been pushed so far. This is a fiction almost as puerile as that of a Germanic race, a Germanic blood, just as much as that of a French race, a Spanish race, an Italian race, a Slavic race . . . This French race, is it the Gascon, the Savoyard, or the Lorrain? This Slavic race, is it the Russian, the Czech, or the Slovene? Once again, fiction, all of this!"

5. See G. Hervé, *La question d'Alsace et l'argument ethnologique,* in the *Revue de l'Ecole d'anthropologie,* 1903, pp. 285ff.

And, in the same work, Hovelacque wrote these beautiful lines: "It is not for all the evil it has done to us that we claim to condemn the theory of race: had it been more calamitous for us, we would not look on it as more detestable. But [the theory] claims to depend on a series of scientific concepts with which, quite to the contrary, it finds itself in flagrant contradiction."

These words of Hovelacque, sirs, the Israelites could repeat and use to their advantage. Yes, the false and absurd theory of race has done and continues to do us harm; it is used against us at every occasion, in interviews, in newspapers, at the theater; but even if it were a thousand times more calamitous for us, I would say that I myself would be the first to adopt it, that I would even contribute to spreading it, if it were scientifically admissible—but instead I reject it disdainfully, because it is stupid.

It is in the victorious Germany of 1871 that this theory found most of its followers, where it became almost a dogma in education; an explosion of antisemitism followed it, to which Mr. von Bismarck, a grand apostle of *furor teutonicus*, was not a stranger, and which he even encouraged because he dreaded the liberal tendencies of German Israelites. Fifteen years afterward, one found men in France, allegedly better Frenchmen than their compatriots, to dig up this grave Germanic error and turn it into a weapon against a portion of their fellow citizens. The same fraudulent theory that justified the conquest of Alsace was the inspiration for French antisemitism. I hasten to add that the anthropologists from our country, those who honor science, showed themselves to be equally impervious to the theory of race, whether it was invoked to give an appearance of entitlement to violence, or whether it had as its purpose, toward the citizens of France, to substitute a *régime d'exception* [emergency rule] for the law.

In truth, the theory of race belongs neither to anthropologists nor to naturalists, but to linguists and historians. Linguists, at first, were victims of an illusion. When it was recognized, at the beginning of the nineteenth century, that the languages of most of the civilized peoples of Europe and Asia are divided in two large groups, languages related to Sanskrit and languages related to Hebrew, it was hastily concluded that the people who spoke these languages also belong to two groups, two races, one of which was called Aryan—due to the *Aryas* of India—the other Semitic, due to the biblical legend that gives the Hebrews and other peoples of Asia the son of the Patriarch Noah, Shem, as an ancestor. For a long time, one spoke of Aryans and Semites as large families, each of which were identified with a distinct ancestor—something like the Montagues and Capulets. A little reflection is enough to recognize the sophism. A Negro who speaks

English in the United States nonetheless does not belong to the white variety of the human species; language is not a physical characteristic, but something taught and acquired; it is madness to want to conclude that the language a man speaks determines his physical descent. Max Müller[6] and [Ernest] Renan, who in their youth had shared and propagated this common error, did not hesitate, when they saw the truth, to come around. "You speak," said Max Müller, "of a Semitic vocabulary, of an Aryan syntax, or you speak to us of a group of men with kinky hair or black skin; you express clear ideas, we understand you. But if you speak of a kinky-haired vocabulary or a black syntax, we will understand you as poorly as if you speak of a Semitic race or an Aryan race."[7] This was quite right, but a bit late. Mr. Bérard told us two weeks ago that public opinion, whose education is provided by the press and novels, is in general a half-century behind the current state of science; it is therefore necessary to wait until the people of the world and the journalists cease speaking of Aryans and Semites and placing in opposition the qualities or the defects of the Semites and the Aryans.

Historians at first fell in behind the linguists. They found on their path peoples, ethnic collectivities, who were called, for example, the Hebrews, the Greeks, the Gauls. The Hebrews spoke a Semitic language related to Arabic, Assyrian, Syriac; they were designated as Semites. The Greeks and the Gauls spoke Aryan languages, related to Sanskrit, Persian, Latin; they were designated as Aryans. From there, it was but one step to climb in order to introduce to history a Gallic race, a Jewish race, a Hellenic race. The sophism, as you can see, was two-sided: on the one hand, one equated the community of a language to the community of physical descent; on the other hand, one devised anthropological groups, designated abusively by the names of races, on the model of political or religious groups. Is it necessary to point out that a political grouping does not presuppose a unity of origins? Does not history itself show us a succession of empires—those of the Egyptians, [of the] Assyrians, of Alexander, of Augustus, of Charlemagne, of the Arabs that united in one more or less stable body politic peoples that did not speak the same language and whose respective origins, from the point of view of physical descent, are absolutely unknown to us?

Today, a self-respecting scholar speaks of the Hebrews, the Greeks, [or] the

6. [Max Müller (1823–1900) was a renowned German philologist and scholar of comparative religions.]

7. This is the sense, but not the literal translation, of a famous passage from one of Max Müller's last works, *Biographies of Words and the Home of the Aryas*, London, 1888.

Gauls, but does not say the Hebraic or Jewish race, the Greek race, or the Gallic race. "To argue the notion of races," writes the Abbé Houtin, "to hold forth on their qualities of attraction or repulsion, this ordinarily serves to explain historical problems with words that correspond to no reality whatsoever."[8] Pages were filled with citations of this genre, borrowed from our best historians. Unfortunately, as I have already told you, well-informed scholars are always ahead of their time, and the public continues to live for a long time on false opinions taught by their predecessors.

Around 1860, anthropologists joined in. You know that anthropology is a very new science; if it has dispelled various errors, it has substantiated others for not having known how to defend itself at the start. Forty or fifty years ago, the sophism that confounds linguistic, political, and anthropological groups was almost universally accepted. One looked to distinguish the Aryan anthropologically from the Semite, and we must say loud and clear that it was not a success. The populations that speak Aryan languages, like those that speak Semitic languages, belong, in general, to the white race; but there are blonds and brunets, tall and short, rounded heads and elongated heads. The Arab from the Syrian desert, the Bedouin, was taken as an example of a Semite, and it was remarked that he often had an aquiline nose, an elongated head, black hair, and an attractive build. It was concluded that the Semite—and, by consequence, the Jew—was a tall, brown-haired dolichocephalic with a long and arched nose. Once verified, it was found that the type in question was not dominant, but quite rare among real Jews. We know that the Jews are divided into two large groups, the Sephardim, or Jews of the Portuguese rite, and the Ashkenazim, or Jews of the German rite. The first live for the most part in the countries neighboring the Mediterranean; the second are widespread throughout Central and Eastern Europe, notably in Poland and Russia. It was believed, quite naturally, that the true Jews were the Sephardim, nearer than the others to Palestine, especially since it was believed that the Bedouin type was recognized more frequently among them. The Ashkenazim, following this theory, would not represent the Jewish race in the least; they would be Germanic or Slavic, more or less mixed with Jewish blood. But this opinion does not withstand consideration. There are blonds with slender heads, short height, and flat noses among the Sephardim as [there are] among the Ashkenazim; in London, where both groups are well represented, one finds even more slender heads among

8. G. Houtin, *L'Americanisme*, Paris, 1903, p. 44.

the Sephardim than the others.[9] Even more serious, it was eventually acknowledged that if, following a famous saying, each country has the Jews it deserves, the Jews also contribute in large measure to the physical characteristics of the inhabitants of the diverse countries in which they reside. For instance, the Jews of England and Germany are taller;[10] the Jews of Russia often represent what is called the Slavic type; the Jews of Palestine, of Asia Minor, [and] of North Africa resemble the Bedouins to a much greater extent than their Occidental coreligionists.

These observations were summarized in 1891 by a woman with a large heart and great knowledge, Mrs. Clémence Royer, before the Society of Anthropology of Paris.[11] "It is certain," she said, "that the Jews from every country resemble one another less than they resemble the populations that surround them, and that those from the North are distinguished as clearly from those of the South as the Germanics are from the Latins. There is no pure race; that of the Jews is a bit more pure than the others because, having been persecuted everywhere and forced to live apart [from non-Jews] for long centuries, they are less mixed than the other ethnic elements among whom they lived during the entire Christian era. But previously the Jews were perhaps less identifiable than today. During the last centuries before the Christian era, they produced a large number of proselytes. Each Jewish colony was recruited from among the ambient populations. It is mostly, and perhaps only, since they have been persecuted by the Christians that their type became characterized and fixed because, as soon as this moment occurred, they no longer had alliances except among themselves."

This doctrine more or less conforms to that which Renan developed in 1883, a doctrine that was equally upheld by Hebraists like Loeb and Neubauer, and by anthropologists like Topinard and Ripley.[12]

Let's take the Hebrews at the moment when they appear in history, at the close of the legendary period, at the time of the conquest of Palestine. The Bible teaches us that this conquest was very long, that the indigenous peoples were

9. J. Jacobs and J. Speilman, in the *Journal of the Anthropological Institute,* vol. XIX (London, 1890).

10. The short height of Jews in certain centers like Warsaw is simply the effect of physiological poverty; the well-to-do classes have a greater average height than the poor classes.

11. *Bulletin de la Société d'Anthropologie,* 1891, p. 544.

12. A very abundant bibliography may be found in the book by J. M. Judt, *Die Juden als Rasse,* Berlin 1903, pp. 234–240.

not exterminated, and that the invaders married women from the region.[13] These conquerors of Palestine were united by a religious and political link; but no historian would want to believe that all of them were the descendants of Abraham. Let's admit it all the same, for the sake of argument. Just as the Frankish people were absorbed into the Celtic and Roman populations of Gaul, all the while imposing their name on the region that became France, likewise the Hebrew element, supposedly homogeneous, tended to blend with the indigenous population that became Judea. Now we do not know exactly what this indigenous population was; but we are sure that it was not homogeneous, that it was comprised notably of tribes coming from the east—that is, from Asia—and others from the west—that is, the islands of the archipelago and probably the coasts of Greece and Africa. It is possible that the Philistines were Cretans; this was the opinion of the ancients, and it should be noted that an old Cretan cult of Jupiter existed at Gaza in Philistia. On the other hand, those whom the Bible calls the Hittites had penetrated Palestine from the north and seem, according to the Egyptian monuments, to have presented certain characteristics of the Mongolian type. In a word, the Syrian coastline was populated by people of every provenance, the residue of successive invasions by land and by sea.[14] It is in the midst of this human dust that the Hebrew invaders came to establish themselves. Then even had these invaders all been descendants of the same father, the ethnic mixture resulting from the conquest could not have had anything in common with this extended family that we call a race.

One wanted at times to discover, in this tribal melting pot placed under Jewish hegemony around the year 1000, anthropological elements of contemporary Jews; it was said that the old Bedouin background was responsible for the tall, brown-haired dolichocephalics; that the blonds were the descendants of the Amorites; the flat-nosed were those of the Hittites.[15] These are unwarranted hypotheses, for we know the indigenous peoples of Palestine only by the rare and quite insufficient representations on Egyptian monuments. Who is to say that the refined Bedouin type actually existed at that time? It is even rather im-

13. See, among other passages, *Deuteronomy*, XX, 14; XXI, 11; XXIII, 8; *Judges*, III, 6; *Chron.*, II, 35.

14. "The better informed we are about the state of Syria at the time of the Egyptian conquests, the more we must observe the mixing of the races and their almost infinite dividing up" (Maspero, *Histoire ancienne des peuples de l'Orient*, vol. I, p. 148).

15. V. Jacques, in the *Revue des Études juives*, Paris, 1893, p. liv.

probable because it exists today and because, as with everything human, it is a product of evolution.

The Jewish tribes are taken into captivity; those of Israel disappear—dreamers of our day wanted to find them in England and America—those from the Kingdom of Judah returned to their homeland. Then, after Alexander the Great, the Jews began to spread throughout the Mediterranean world and gained converts everywhere; many Greeks and Asians—that is, people speaking languages other than Hebrew—became Jews and started a Jewish lineage. Then came the Roman war, the destruction of the Temple, the massacre of hundreds of thousands of Jews, the reducing of hundreds of thousands of others to slavery, a new dispersion of survivors across the world. Despite the simultaneous spread of Christianity, Judaism did not lose its expansive force; there were new converts, new marriages between Jews and non-Jews to such a point that councils concerned with this were held on several occasions to prohibit mixed marriages and conversions to Judaism. In the eighth century, in southwestern Russia, a large portion of the Turkic people of the Khazar region converted to Judaism.[16] It was alleged that these Khazars began the line of the millions of Jews who populate Russia at present; others preferred to see them only as the ancestors of the Karaites, Russian Jews who reject the Talmud and do not marry Talmudist Jews. In reality, nobody knows. We do not even know how the large present-day population of Jews in Russia was formed; if the jargon[17] they speak inclines us to believe that they came from the west—that is, from Germany—on the other hand it is certain that there were, as early as the beginning of the Christian era, Jewish communities in the south of Russia. The jargon could very well be a commercial language, developed out of necessity by relationships with Central Europe, and not the mother tongue of all Russian Jews. It remains the case that the conversion of the Khazars, and quite a lot of other less important conversions whose memory was not kept by history, must have introduced into the already confused masses of the Jewish population a whole host of heterogeneous elements that it would be absolutely impossible to untangle.

You see how legitimate is the conclusion thus formulated by Mr. Topinard: "The Jews are but a religious federation. They are neither a nation nor a race."

16. On this question, see the fine article in the *Jewish Encyclopedia*, vol. IV (New York, 1903).

17. ["Jargon" was the term employed by many Jews in Central and Western Europe to refer to Yiddish, which they considered a "bastard" language, less than legitimate.]

Nevertheless, there are two important facts that must not be neglected. The first is of a historical nature: the Jews—for a long time penned up in ghettos, subject to the same conditions of existence, almost always poverty-stricken—have, for at least a thousand years, married among themselves. Conversions to Judaism, although more numerous today than one might believe, especially in Russia, could exercise in this respect but a feeble influence; the same can be said of illegitimate or clandestine unions with non-Jews. The second fact is of an anthropological nature. The Jews, although greatly varying among themselves, nonetheless have a particular *facies* [facial aspect] that enables any person to recognize them with a little practice; he will not recognize them without some doubt, but—the experiment has been attempted in Russia—he will not make an error more than thirty times out of one hundred.

These two facts are closely related. The Jews do not present a unique type, but a number of relatively limited types, which is a natural and inevitable result of endogamy—that is, of the habit of marrying among themselves. Certain types prevail in certain countries, for example Poland or Salonica [*sic*], because, despite the present-day ease of moving around, most of the Jewish population of the great [urban] centers intermarry, and because in the struggle for life that thus establishes itself between the types, sometimes one group and sometimes another prevails.[18] In this struggle or, better yet, this selection, the conditions of the environment and the climate naturally exercise a large influence. Now the environment and the climate, in each country, are favorable to the predominance of one or of several types—from the tall, blond type in Northern Europe to the short, brown-haired type along the Mediterranean. If, therefore, so many English Jews resemble Englishmen and so many Russian Jews resemble Russians, this is not explained by legitimate or clandestine unions between Russians, Englishmen, and Jews, but simply because the English environment favors the production of the English type or types, [and] the Russian environment, Russian types. These types do not come out of the land, needless to say, but they tend to prevail following the progressive elimination of others that are, for reasons that escape us, less well adapted to the environment.

The Americans paid high prices to purchase our most beautiful stallions from

18. The same appearance of relative homogeneity due simply to endogamy was observed in certain isolated valleys in the Swiss mountains by Martin (*L'Anthropologie*, 1897, p. 91). Cf. what Mr. Mahoudeau says about Algerian Jews (*Bulletin de la Société d'Anthropologie*, 1901, p. 543).

Perche; their ambition was to have a race of large horses, for those in the New World are small. And yet after a few generations, there were no more Percherons in America; they had lost the essential characteristic of their race, which is their size. The indigenous type had prevailed.

After having cited for you the Percherons, may I, without being disrespectful, speak to you of Parisian women? What has not been said of these charming, spiritual, refined beings, who know how to dress like queens in rags and who walk in a way even queens could not? Now Parisian women are comprised of women from every provenance—even Jews—few of whom were born in Paris, perhaps none of whom can count back three generations of Parisians. When one of these exquisite Parisian women, who finds herself having learned the trade of a seamstress or milliner, decides to emigrate to the United States, the daughters she can have there with a Parisian immigrant are Yankees, not Parisians; much more than that, after ten or twelve years, perhaps even sooner, she herself will have lost her Parisian qualities, her particular grace and her inventive genius. One must not believe that this sovereign action of environments was unknown to the ancients; it is the moderns who have left it unrecognized for so long. Here, in this respect I extract a rather curious phrase from the *Agricola* by Tacitus: "Among the Britons (of Great Britain), some resemble Germanic peoples, others Iberians; those closest to Gaul resemble Gallic people, either by the persistent influence of origins, or because the island was advancing on all sides; nature alone and the climate have marked the Britons with these varied characteristics" (*position caeli corporibus habitum dedit*).[19] Tacitus hesitates between the theory of race and that of atmosphere, but one sees that he is already familiar with the second and knows that the resemblances of physical types can be explained by environmental factors.

The ghetto is also an environment, a sad environment, whose influence is transmitted by heredity. Among the emancipated Jews of our countries, sons, and sometimes grandsons of the emancipated, one sees again the short height, the fearful look, the apparent nervousness betraying a heritage of long centuries of oppression. These Jews are a living testimony to the accusation against the blasphemous regime of the gospel, whose support on certain points around the globe, at the very moment at which I am speaking to you, is one of the tragedies and shames of humanity.

Renan, in 1883, had concluded that there is not a Jewish race, that there is not

19. Tacitus, *Agricola*, cap. XI.

a Jewish type, but Jewish types.[20] This great sage was right. But we may ask ourselves if, over the centuries, Jews continue to marry among themselves, will they not give birth to a true race—that is, to a group of men possessing that which they do not yet possess, certain common and well-defined physical characteristics. In theory, this would be quite acceptable. Take, as Renan said, three hundred individuals from the boulevard, lock them away on a desert island, and let them intermarry over five generations or more; by the end of a few centuries, a dominant type will form, which will tend to dominate more and more, and you could say that you have created, on a desert island, a "boulevard race." But, in practice, it cannot be so. The tendency of present-day Judaism is to spread itself out more and more across the surface of the globe; today, the greatest conglomeration of Jews in the world is no longer in Warsaw, but New York. An increasing number of Jewish centers are therefore being formed, in the most different environments and climates, where, as I have shown you, the Jewish type that tends to prevail is necessarily the one that conforms most to the indigenous type, to the type best adapted to the climate and to other exterior conditions of life. Thus, the number of Jewish types is bound to multiply again in the future; these types will localize—naturalize, if one may use that word—and the formation of a defined type, which will constitute a race, will become more and more impossible given the different conditions of existence and environments.

My conclusion, sirs, is clear and may be formulated in but a few words: "There never was a Jewish race; there is not one now; there never will be one." Those who speak today of a Jewish race commit what Leibnitz called a psittacism, "parrot talk"—that is, they couple together words, each of which offers a meaning in isolation, but which, thus associated, have none.

*Translated by Shaina Hammerman*

20. Ernest Renan, *Le Judaisme comme race et comme religion*, Paris, 1883 (cf. Th. Reinach, *Revue des Études juives*, vol. VI, 1883, p. 141).

# 27 | The Chosenness of the Jews in the Light of Biology

## Alfred Nossig

"Die Auserwältheit der Juden im Lichte der Biologie," *Zeitschrift für Demographie und Statistik der Juden* 1, no. 3 (1905): 1–5.

Alfred Nossig (1864–1943) was born in Lemberg (Lvov), in Galicia. A writer, artist, and social scientist, he was also active in Zionist politics, first in Poland and then in Central Europe. He wrote poems, plays, and an opera libretto. He also received acclaim for his sculptures. Nossig was one of the earliest proponents and practioners of a Jewish social science. In 1902 he brought together individuals committed to the cultural wing of the Zionist movement in order to create a working group for a statistical study of the Jewish people. In 1904 this became the Bureau for Jewish Statistics in Berlin. Its journal, the *Zeitschrift für Demographie und Statistik der Juden*, became one of the main venues for the publication of articles dealing with Jews and race. See the entry in the *Encyclopedia Judaica*, 2nd edition, 15:314.

[I]

The idea of the chosenness of the Jews and of its influence on their intellectual, moral, and physical development allows for a thoroughly different interpretation than that given it by Curt Michaelis in the previous issue of this journal.[21] The subject is so comprehensive that I must confine myself to offering only highlights here.

First of all, let us review Michaelis's major points. According to the Jewish view of the world (*Weltanschauung*), on which their moral account of history rests, the history of the Jews is the product of a divine will. Even someone like Isaiah still was of this opinion, and thus barred his own Volk from taking an active role in world history. Modern historiography, influenced by the natural sciences, explains the fate of peoples as the product of their particular abilities and demands, always under the influence of heredity and adaptation. In Jewish

21. [Curt Michaelis, "Die jüdische Auserwählungsidee und ihre biologische Bedeutung," *Zeitschrift für Demographie und Statistik der Juden*, vol. 1, no. 2, 1905, pp. 1-4. Michaelis was a German anthropologist and ethnologist, and a proponent of antisemitism.]

history, however, the influence of adaptation is nonexistent. For by virtue of the idea of chosenness—which, taken to this level of bizarre caricature, is an affliction particular to the Jews—their racial character has been condemned to eternal stagnation. Thus, the history of the Jews is only tradition, not progress. The idea of chosenness stems from the racial pride of the Jews. Emboldened by this concept, the racial pride of the Jews became biogenetically fatal. It brought about isolationism, strict laws of endogamy, and contempt, cruelty, and hate for all other peoples. For its practical realization, this relied on the primitive legal principle of "an eye for an eye." Over the course of history, this principle was also applied to the one occupation open to the Jews—trade. The Jew became a haggler. This racial trait was passed on unalterably. This led to the confinement of the Jews in ghettos and is reflected in the low opinion that other nations have of the Jews.

In this succession of thoughts and deductions, there is hardly a point that does not contradict the true historical facts and relations, and that cannot easily be refuted. It is not worth going into the conclusions in detail here. They exemplify a popular, long since refuted, anti-Jewish distortion of history. Every non-Jewish child educated without prejudices today knows that the Jews did not become "hagglers" because their law commanded it, but—as Michaelis himself says—because they were locked out of every means of livelihood other than trade. They were not confined to ghettos because they hated every other nation or people. On the contrary, if they were filled with resentment toward other peoples, it was a result of being treated so barbarically—a resentment, by the way, that, immediately upon [Jewish] emancipation, was replaced by a feeling of love and a hopelessly optimistic sense of solidarity with these peoples.

But let us concern ourselves with the major points [of Michaelis's argument]. Those researchers who wish to analyze the essence and the history of Jewry from a modern, ethnographically comparative, natural scientific or materialistic standpoint often make the mistake of believing that they do not need to delve deeper into the Jewish sources. They rely on the Bible and construct analogies with histories of other cultures or Völker. Applied in this way, modern science, which ought to illuminate our understanding, clouds it.

As is known, the Bible contains only the written teachings of Judaism directed at the public; alongside this exists the oral tradition, as explanation and complement of the written. Maimonides set down this oral, esoteric teaching in his writings. By reading the Bible, alongside the commentaries we have inherited from Maimonides and other Jewish thinkers, we can convince ourselves that the capricious, personal God whom the Bible employs for pedagogical reasons against the public is nothing but the highest abstraction of being, whose will is identical with the totality of the known natural laws.

The moral concept of history that the Jews have thus coincides with that of natural science. Their history is not the product of arbitrary divine will, but of their attitude toward natural laws. They in no way exclude themselves from the course of world history; on the contrary, their worldview makes them feel that they have a particular vocation to engage with it. And this leads us to the notion of chosenness.

Just like the idea of God as the highest abstraction of being, this idea [of chosenness], too, is obviously nothing more than the product of Jewish intellectual and moral ability, a result of the mental efforts of the Jewish Volk—and this despite the fact that the Bible presents it as divine revelation. Even in the Bible we can trace very precisely the development of this idea, from its primitive expression in the case of Abraham to its more idealistic form with Moses, how it was misinterpreted by the earlier prophets, and how only the later prophets taught it in its purest form.

One is completely led astray at the outset if this enormous idea is understood merely as a particularly robust expression of a general sort of racial pride evinced by all Völker. Rather, there is something here that fundamentally distinguishes the Jewish Volk and its history from others: the notion not to allow this Volk to be an unconscious plaything of its own desires and of historical events; the notion that it should be led consciously and on the basis of the higher insight or worldview it has gained toward a great developmental goal, which it will not be able to reach for millennia, or in any foreseeable future. Thereby a powerful ideological factor was introduced into the history of the Jews, one that makes those who construe the destiny of the Jews only through the one-sided prism of materialism appear to be thoroughly mistaken. We will be able to demonstrate, however, that this factor has in no way had a stagnating effect on Jewry, but on the contrary has inspired constant progressive development.

## II

Of what does the chosenness of the Jews consist? Let us investigate this idea in its most definitive expression, which was given to it by Moses.

Moses makes Israel renew its covenant with God, to which the patriarchs had committed themselves. This was to reprise, out of a clear consciousness and strong will, the resolve to live an exemplary life. Yet he [Moses] expanded and perfected the great mission that for the Hebrews arises out of this "covenant with God." He impressed on the descendants of his Volk that they were duty bound to strive to be above average in the pursuit of learning, justice, and purity; and to transmit an understanding of the highest human ideals to other nations, to lead them to strive for the same elevated ideals. This double mission of Israel's—the ideal of self-perfection and the perfection of others—was articulated in these words given at Sinai: "You shall be for me a kingdom of priests and a holy people" (Exodus 19:6). Thus history bequeaths to the Hebrews the task of a great worldly existence: this is the meaning of their chosenness.

What Mosaism promises to the Hebrews as a certain result of this striving after holiness is the eternal continuity of their tribe (*Stamm*). It is a reward, but at the same time a duty—that of eternally testifying to the wisdom of God's commandments, of being the eternal instructors of other nations: "The law shall go forth from Zion and the word of the Lord from Jerusalem" [Isaiah 2:3]. Thus, the chosenness of Israel, which was originally based merely on one specific school of thought and on the careful preservation of redemptive teachings, became an active mission encompassing the entire realm of mankind and all of world history.

Chosenness thus was not conceived of in the sense of material power and military expansion. This is articulated clearly in the fifth book of Moses: "It is not because you are the most numerous of peoples that the Lord set His heart on you and chose you—indeed, you are the smallest of peoples" (Deuteronomy 7:7). The Bible warns Israel constantly about seeking to become "like other Völker"; it prohibits "imperialism," the pomp or glory of royalty, the policies of revanchism and expansion.

Nevertheless, the Mosaic law also encompasses all aspects of practical life and promises its followers, through adherence to its decrees, that they will blossom healthily within the unshakeable confines of a small community.

This notion of chosenness to which Moses had refined the Abrahamic conceptualization, making it the sole authoritative and binding interpretation for Israel, admittedly was not grasped at all times in its entirety by the Volk; indeed, even the prophets did not do justice to it in each and every era.

In the age of the sovereign existence of a Hebrew state, in particular during its early development and its heyday, an interpretation of the idea of chosenness along national lines prevailed, as it had among the Abrahamites. The interpretation [of the concept of chosenness] was often a materialistic one, even a militaristic one. Now and then, Moses's intellectual and ethical genius, which was ahead of the developments of its time, was edged out by the primitive and brutal instincts of national politics.

The prophets, even with their chauvinism, never neglected to associate the triumph of Israel with its vocation—to promulgate the true faith. The Volk, however, completely disregarded the spiritually austere character of what had been imposed on it; it forgot its priestly mission while, at the same time, being nonetheless intoxicated by the idea of its own chosenness.

It was precisely then that Israel was most alienated from its true chosenness, shorn of any justification for having a special position within humanity. Inherited from generation to generation, passed along in flesh and blood, this national arrogance would undoubtedly become national misfortune; it, too, deserves blame for the downfall of the Hebrew state.

However, gradually the understanding of the true character of Israel's chosenness emerged. "Second Isaiah appreciates the blessing of being called by God (*Jahweh*) but recognizes as well the obligations that are imposed. It is a highly elevated status to which He assigns His Volk. But the responsibility that this brings is in complete accordance with this elevated status. Israel is favored above other nations, yet also therefore destined to make them [the Jews] partake in what is best and has been received from Jahweh."[22]

Arrogance, pride, and vanity stand, then, in direct opposition to Israel's genuine calling, and to its spiritual and moral character as it was exemplified by the leaders as an ideal to the nation. Thus, the teachers of Judaism sought in later epochs to implant insight and modesty into the hearts and minds of the *Volk*.

## III

Even though this educational work should in no way be thought of as finished and successful, even though the racial pride of the Jews blossoms forth until today out of some mistaken understanding of the responsibilities of chosenness, the idea of chosenness in the Mosaic sense of the word nevertheless has had an unmistakably positive influence on the history and organization of the Jewish people (*Stamm*).

The first and most striking biological result of this idea is the fact of the

22. A. Kuenen, *Volksreligion und Weltreligion*, German edition, Berlin, 1883. [The page number is unreadable in the original.]

continuing survival of the Jews, and their exceptional vitality and reproductive power. The Mosaic concept of "an eternal people" appears to have been realized. This alone already demonstrates that the chosenness of the Jews is something other and deeper than the ordinary racial pride that could not prevent the decline of other, far more powerful peoples. It brought about the eternal existence of the Jewish Volk through the biological effects of its intellectual ideals and its moral law.

The obligation to live a pure and holy life yielded, in the physiological sense, a healthy and long-lasting life. As is well-known, Mosaism went to great lengths to take the necessary measures for this to happen, by enacting strict laws concerning diet and marriage—thus regulating in an exemplary way the two chief physiological functions of ingestion and reproduction. The same care has been applied to organizing the spiritual education of the Volk, as the Mosaic doctrine obliges all its adherents to study the Law. This, at the same time, nurtured the moral sense: for the study of the Law not only implants the commandments of familial and neighborly love within broad sections of society, but also produces a conscious awareness of Israel's unique moral mission. And there is no doubt that, during the thousands of years of the Jewish Volk's existence, despite periods of decline, this idea has exerted the highest degree of educational influence.

Numerous generations of thinkers and communal leaders have bred [*gezüchtet*] a [Jewish] Volk characterized by pure blood, not poisoned by venereal disease or alcohol; a Volk that has a marked sense of family, a deeply rooted habituation to the virtuous life, an unusual intellectual dexterity, and an ideal spirituality. Therefore, it was self-evidently necessary to establish strict guidelines to protect these foremost ethical treasures from annihilation through intermixture with less carefully bred races. The prohibition on intermarriage ensured that the primary component in racial formation, heredity, could operate at the height of its potential and power; not only did the positive qualities referred to above get passed on undiminished from generation to generation, but—thanks to endogamy, or inbreeding—they were constantly increased. That is what it took for the Volk that Ibsen called "the nobility of mankind" to emerge.

In no way, however, has the second factor—adaptation—been retarded through the complete actualization of heredity, nor was evolution (*Entwicklung*) prevented. The intended goal of the idea of chosenness—constant improvement [moving] toward perfection—involves evolution. Related and relevant to this above all else was Jewish teaching. This has been the foremost instrument of racial identity formation, so significant from the outset that any stagnation [in its interpretation] was guarded against, and its unending reinterpretation or reform to meet contemporary demands was put in place instead. It is the task of the spiritual leaders of each era to concern themselves with this endeavor (Deuteronomy 17:9–11).

On the other hand, the struggle for perpetual existence, which was a commandment of chosenness as well, engendered a selective breeding that is almost unequaled in human history. In the struggle for existence of the [Jewish] nation—convulsed as it has been to its core by fire and sword, by the severest economic and moral pressures, and by the constant allurement of desertion—only those individuals who were intellectually and spiritually the strongest and physically fittest survived and reproduced; those who, to the greatest degree, did not place the existence of the Jewish people in danger, but who possessed the art or skill of adaptation. And thus, up until today, the Jewish Volk is taken to be the most skilled at adaptation.

A brief glance at the history of the Jews is sufficient to convince us of their uninterrupted development by adapting to the succession of human cultures. Think of Babylonian and Alexandrian Jewry, Spanish and German Jewry. Consider the Jews of Eastern Europe and their reformation under the influences of American culture.

Without surrendering their essence, their carefully guarded inheritance from previous generations, the Jews have walked hand in hand with other peoples, in a constant advance toward the greatest goals of mankind. That they have done this with complete awareness, that they have not allowed themselves to be driven from history, but have sought to influence it—therein is the culmination of the idea of their chosenness, and it is from this point of view that the biological effects of this idea must be understood.

# 28 | To Which Race Did Jesus Belong?
## Leo Sofer

"Welcher Rasse gehörte Jesus an?" *Zeitschrift für Demographie und Statistik der Juden* 5, no. 6 (1909): 81–87.

Leo Sofer was a physician and anthropologist working in Vienna. He published extensively on the Jews and race, particularly Jews and pathology.

It cannot be my task here to enter into the debate over whether or not Jesus existed. A succession of theologians, from Bruno Bauer to Kalthoff,[23] have advanced and contested the existence of Jesus; the silence or the indeterminacy of the contemporary Jewish sources plays a not insignificant role in this. I also would not want to decide this question simply by reference to the tradition of the New Testament, according to which Jesus descended from the House of David. I will merely remark parenthetically that even those who believe in the divine origins of Jesus nonetheless must still give credence to his descent from the Davidic line, since, according to the Gospels, his mother Mary came from the House of David. I allude to this, since H. St. Chamberlain[24] in his chauvinism goes so far as to write, to give an example from his foreword to the fourth edition of *Grundlagen des 19. Jahrhunderts*, 1903: ". . . and whoever disavows the historical approach, and takes the genealogical account in Matthew and Luke as authentic, gains nothing, as this refers him back to Joseph, who, for the faithful, was not the father of Christ." However, [the fact] that the faithful believed that Mary, whose motherhood of Christ is not contested by them, descends from the priestly line of Nathan and the House of Solomon, this Chamberlain conceals in his usual manner. I also do not resort to the dialectic of Adolf Harnack,[25] who responded

23. [Bruno Bauer (1809–1882) was a German theologian and philosopher who wrote on the Jewish Question and the early history of Christianity. In his writings, he was highly unsympathetic to the Jews and Judaism. Albert Kalthoff (1850–1906) was a German theologian and philosopher.]

24. [Houston Stewart Chamberlain (1855–1927) was a British author whose works on European history and culture advocated the idea of Nordic or Aryan supremacy, and the danger and degeneracy of the Jews.]

25. [Adolf Harnack (1851–1930) was a German theologian and historian of Christianity.]

to a question along these lines by saying: Were Jesus not a Jew, his Jewish opponents would undoubtedly not have identified him as such [literally, would not have bestowed this reproach upon him].

I say rather: Supposing Jesus did exist, and that he did on the whole play the role the Gospels assign to him, then to which racial origins [of Jesus] does the historical and ethnographic evidence most likely point, given that a decisive answer is not possible because of the lack of absolutely reliable sources? Even the Church Fathers possessed no definite conception of Christ's external appearance. Thus, Origen wrote the following (circa 200 years after Christ's death) contra Celsus: "We cannot deny that the writings about Jesus tell us that he was ugly in appearance (*hässlich von Gestalt*); however, that he had a low or ignoble form, as Celsus maintains, of this there is no proof. Even less can one argue that he was of a diminutive stature. I will set forth the words of the prophet Isaiah (53:1–3), in which it is foretold that Jesus would not appear in the world with any particular beauty or impressive figure."[26]

Syria is called, in Assyrian inscriptions as well as in the biblical book of Joshua, the land of the Hittites. This Volk, whose participation in the first flowerings of human culture is becoming increasingly evident thanks to recent excavations, made its original home on the coastal gulf of Antioch, at the foot of the Taurus Mountains. From there they migrated north and west, toward Asia Minor, and to the south, to Syria and Palestine.[27]

Among the ruins of the city of Chuen-Aten (in Upper Egypt), called today Tel-el-Amarna, a letter in cuneiform was discovered in 1888, written by the Egyptian administrator of the Palestinian possessions, sent from Lachis to the Pharaoh Amenophis III (1500–1450 [BCE]). In this letter he related how the Hittites pressed upon Palestine from the north, and how the Habiri (the Hebrews) did so from the east.

From this letter we can form a picture of the cultural and anthropological structure of Palestine at the time of the migration of the Jews into the land. In the north and in the middle of the country, including Jerusalem, the Hittites were a heavy presence. They constructed a series of loosely connected semiprincipali-

26. Origen, *Contra Celsus*, Book 6, Section 75. [Sofer edits Origen's remarks here, summarizing and in the process somewhat changing the meaning of the quote from Isaiah. Origen reproduces the verse from Isaiah, and then quotes Psalm 45, which refers to "comeliness" and "beauty," and which Origen suggests refers to Christ.]

27. See also: Dr. L. Sofer, "Armenier und Juden," *Zeitschrift für Demographie und Statistik der Juden*, v. 5, 1907.

ties that exhibited a relatively highly developed culture. Yet politically they were so weak that they were conquered first by the Egyptians, under Tutmosis (Thotmes III, 1504–1449), and then by the Hebrews. Anthropologically, the Hittites were brachycephalic, belonging to the Alpine race; the Hebrews, on the other hand, were dolichocephalic, and Semites. However, there is no reason to assume that the Hebrews themselves were a pure race in the anthropological sense. On the Euphrates, where we have to assume the Hebrews originated, there dwelt a number of brachycephalic nations (Hittites, Elamites, Akkado-Sumerians); as a part of this same race we must also consider the Chaldeans, who came from western Asia Minor, from Lydia, and who were exiled from their land by the Thracian invaders. The Assyrians, on the other hand, exhibit the Semitic type more strongly. The Hebrews had already absorbed brachycephalic elements during their wanderings from their homeland, before they settled in Palestine; this makes it clearer why, in the end, the brachycephalic type showed itself to be the dominant one among the Jews, and the Semitic elements became more and more displaced.

Southern Palestine was occupied by a Volk, the Canaanites, who anthropologically belonged within the Semitic realm. The influx of neighboring Egyptians did not alter this, since we assume today that the ancient Egyptians also belonged to the Mediterranean race, of which the Semites constituted a part. Culturally, three groups were living in proximity to one another in southern Palestine: the Babylonians, the Egyptians, and the Hittites.

In this part of Palestine, the excavations done by Professor Sellin[28] (from Rostock) in Lachis and Jericho have been pathbreaking. The Canaanites were already carrying on a thriving trade with the Phoenicians and the inhabitants of the Greek islands 2,500 years before Christ. This is demonstrated by the ceramic objects excavated by Sellin, which have been found with the identical designs in Palestine, Phoenicia, and Cyprus. As regards culture, the Babylonian influence predominated. This is made clear by the numerous excavated clay tablets, which are inscribed with Babylonian cuneiform. On the other hand, the powerful Cyclopian walls of Jericho are reminiscent of the Hittite structures of Boghazköi, the capital city of the land of the Hittites.

Among these [Canaanites] lived the Amorites, who are believed to have be-

28. [Ernst Sellin (1867–1946) was a German theologian who had a strong interest in archaeology. He excavated in Palestine, most famously in Jericho, and is celebrated for having integrated archaeological evidence into biblical criticism.]

longed to the blond race; their settlement, however, did not stretch further north than Jerusalem.

Last but not least, we must remark upon the Aramaeans. The Aramaeans were a Semitic tribe (*Völkerstamm*), distinct from the Babylonian and Canaanite Semites, that beginning in the middle of the second millennia migrated out of Arabia into the lands of Asia Minor. We are told about the Aramaeans in fourteenth- and thirteenth-century cuneiform; around 1100 they must have already been settled in Damascus, in Hauran, and in the eastern regions of Jordon, from the Sea of Tiberius to the Hermon. The Bible, along with Babylonian and Assyrian sources, has much to say about the powerful Aramaean state, with its capital in Damascus, during the reign of Solomon, and at the time of the dissolution of the Davidic Kingdom; this state of affairs lasted until Tiglat-Pileser of Assyria conquered Damascus in 732 and around 710 made the Syrian-Aramaean state an Assyrian province. There also took place an Aramaean immigration to Assyria and Bablyonia, which, however, did not result in any significant autonomous nation building. The Aramaeans in these areas were gradually assimilated into the Babylonian culture. However, in one realm the defeated Aramaeans proved triumphant: in Assyria, since the eighth century, Aramaic had been the conversational language; we know this from evidence from monuments. Aramaic displaced Babylonian; it made its way to Palestine and conquered Hebrew, which assuredly was still the written and spoken language of the educated. The Jews of later times came completely under the influence of the Aramaic language, which ruled over the entire Near Eastern cultural world of the period. The later literature of the Jews is written in the western or Palestinian and eastern or Babylonian dialects of this language: hence, the Aramaic portions of the Old Testament, the Talmud, Targum, Midrash, and Apocrypha.

Let us review. When we draw a straight line from the southernmost point of the Caspian Sea toward Jerusalem, ending at the Mediterranean, we almost separate two races from each other [with this line]: the broad-headed Alpine race and the long-headed Mediterranean race. From the first one derive the Hittites, the Elamites, and the Chaldeans; from the second, the Babylonians (Assyrians), Canaanites, and Aramaeans. However, political events in this part of the world led to members of one race infiltrating, either peacefully or militarily, the region of the other race, and the two races mixed with one another. This intermixture left its anthropological traces—however, not enough of the sort that could have produced a total amalgamation of the races.

In comparison to a collective of such sharp anthropological distinctness and to such an original culture, about which we have learned so much from excavations,[29] the attempts of those who, for the greater glory of the founder of the Christian religion, desperately want to transform the Galilee, and all of northern Palestine, into an "Aryan" milieu, appear rather artificial.

When we enter into a discussion such as this, we must first and foremost clearly define what we understand by the word "Aryan." Aryan refers to an affinity of languages; it has nothing to do with racial affinities or similarities. Aryan languages are spoken by Völker of the Nordic race, but also by Völker of the Alpine and Mediterranean races, and by Völker of brown or black skin, such as in India. The adherents of Aryan chauvinism, however, propagate the following deception. On the one hand, they understand Aryan to refer to the traits (blond, blue-eyed) of the Nordic race. On the other hand, however, since a number of geniuses and cultural nations do not fall into this category—for example, the Near Eastern cultures—they avail themselves of the opportunity to use the word "Aryan" in its philological sense. In this sense of the term, however, one component, the Hittites, would fall into this category; for the Hittite language, according to Jensen, must be placed in the Alarodic family, related to Armenian. It is not feasible, however, to posit language as a criterion for racial membership. Völker take up a number of different languages in the course of their history. But they preserve their race with great tenacity. Therefore, we must designate the Hittites as well as the Hebrews as members of the Alpine race, as opposed to calling the former Aryans and the latter Semites. We say this even though both groups at different times and in different places have mixed—on the one hand, very strongly with the Mediterranean races, and on the other hand, less strongly with the Nordic—however without suffering a loss of type.

The chauvinists for Aryanism mainly raise two points. Solomon bestowed a part of the northern district on King Hiram of Tyre; thereby, naturally, a closer connection developed between the Jews in the Galilee and the inhabitants of Tyre. On account of this, however, some Mediterranean (Phoenician-Semitic) blood would merely have been added. Moreover, Sargon and Tiglat-Pileser relocated the native people to some extent, and settled colonists in their place. Yet, as the names of their native towns and their deities demonstrate, these colonists were Semites and Hittites (2 Kings 17, 24–30; cf., Hertz, *Moderne Rassentheorien*).

29. Among which also belong the excavations done by Morgan in Susa and those of E. J. Banks in Bismya. I do not have the space here to discuss these.

From this, therefore, can come no support for the idea of a racial influence in the "Aryan-Nordic" sense.

This sort of distortion of history misunderstands, in the first place, the ethnographic map of the Near East, which, setting aside the Amorites, knows nothing of the Aryans as a race; moreover, it misunderstands the inertia of the race in its homeland. Luschan has maintained that during the thousand-year history of the territory in question, those with broad heads have dominated, and it is so even today. Reciprocally, we can conclude from this [that is, from what Luschan observed] that the racial character of this stretch of land has not been disturbed in any decisive way by military or political events.

It is just as false to speak of "Hellenization" on account of Alexander and the Seleucids. It is, above all else, an arbitrary choice to designate the ancient Greeks simply as Aryans, racially speaking. The latest research has just verified, on the one hand, the Hittite character of Asia Minor, which extended to the Greek islands (Crete!); this research has also proven, on the other hand, the existence of an Illyric-Mediterranean race in Peloponnesia. (Compare William Ridgeway, "Who Were the Dorians?," *Anthropological Essays Presented to Edward Burnett Tylor*, London: Henry Trowde, 1907). The Achaeans, making up the third component, are seen as sons of the Nordics. As you can see, it is more than audacious to simply equate Greeks with Aryans. And suppose the Greeks would have been racially pure Aryans: a Hellenization of language, manners, and morals—and this extended, naturally, only to the most tenuous, superficial level—meant as little an Aryanization of the race as the ensuing Aramaeanization over time meant a Semiticization of the race. Thus, for instance, when at present in Hungary thousands of Germans are Magyarized linguistically, this signifies a national transformation, not a physical, racial one.

Furthermore, according to tradition, Jesus came from a tiny village in the hills, namely Nazareth; and it is particularly in such isolated villages that the ancient race is preserved in a most unadulterated state . . .

As has already been mentioned, during the time of Christ, Aramaic was the language generally spoken. True, the Sabbath reading was conducted in Hebrew, but the average populace by now understood little of that, and it soon became necessary to bring forth an interpreter who would render the chapters of the Torah into Aramaic—that is, into the particular Chaldaic dialect with which the Jews were most familiar. Around the time of Christ it was even deemed necessary to write down this oral Chaldaic tradition, and Jonathan ben Ussiel, the teacher of Hillel, sought to meet this need.

Jesus also spoke Aramaean-Chaldean. Nikolaus Heim, a Catholic theologian, writes: "Modern 'researchers,' however, have ventured to cast into doubt this fact that has been long confirmed by all sides, and sought to support their argument in the main with the notion that at some point Greek was widespread and widely understood within Palestine. This claim may very well be correct when it comes to Jerusalem, Caesarea, Gaza, Tiberias, and all the other significant cities within Palestine, where, by the way, one could, during the time of Christ, hear most of the universal languages in use spoken—Roman (*Römisch*), Arabic, and so forth. Greek would certainly have been well understood, particularly among merchants and the well-educated. Nevertheless, the Babylonian and even more so the Palestinian Jews were the bearers and defenders of their ancestral traditions and of the rules of the Hebrew—that is, the new Hebrew language; in other words, it is not only that Hebrew was common to them, but that they took a particular pride at all times in the fact that they would converse only in this language of their forebears. We must understand the reports of the Gospel in this sense, when it says (Luke 9)[30]: "And he came to Nazareth, where he had been brought up; and, as was his custom, he went to the synagogue on the Sabbath day, and stood up to read (the Torah in ancient Hebrew) . . . he then rolled up the scroll, gave it to the assistant, and sat down. He then began to speak to them (in Syro-Chaldaean)." And in another place we find: "And then they sang (in Hebrew) a hymn (Matthew 26:30)" and a few other similar reports. Even later, when Paul (whose native land was Tarsus, in the midst of the land of the Hittites) came to Jerusalem at the conclusion of his third missionary trip, he witnessed the angriest of the Jews calmed when he spoke Hebrew—that is, Syro-Chaldaean. With the provincial officials he spoke Greek. Whenever the Evangelists want to present to us individual words of Christ in an authentic fashion, they give them in new Hebrew, that is Syro-Chaldean. *Talitha kumi* (Maiden, stand up!), *Eloi, Eloi lama sabachtani* (My God, my God, why have you forsaken me?). Jesus was always addressed by his apostles and disciples, as well as by others such as Mary Magdalene, as rabbi (John 1:38; Mark 10:51; John 20:16; Matthew 27:46). The discussions between Jesus and Pilate were almost certainly carried out not in Aramaic or Latin, but in Greek; and Mary Magdalene also most likely spoke to Jesus in Greek when she took him for a gardener. Once she recognized him, she reverted to the more familiar Aramaic, in which she called him 'Rabbuni.'"

Jesus also proved himself to be a genuine Palestinian in that he almost never

30. [The reference here is incorrect. The quote is actually from Luke 4:16.]

spoke without employing similes, and happily and frequently spoke in parables. He also had a preference for proverbs. This preference, to state one's opinion in a simile, was congenital to the Jewish Volk, as was the joy taken in proverbs—an entire biblical book, with thirty-one chapters, is filled with them.

I can, naturally, only really consider the anthropological evidence when it comes to answering the question about Jesus's racial affiliation. These philological and psychological points, however, may serve as a supporting argument for the view that Jesus, presupposing the correctness of the tradition, sprang from the Hittite race. In all likelihood, a Mediterranean (Semitic) influence is indicated; a Nordic (Amoraic, but not Greek) influence is possible, though unlikely. Now if we accept, following the current prevailing theory, that these three components—in descending levels of strength of influence—are indeed components of the Jewish race, then we cannot but identify Jesus with the greatest probability as a member of the Jewish race. As I have already mentioned in the introduction, we can speak only in terms of probability here rather than certainty, under these circumstances.

# 29 | Foreword and Introduction from *The Racial Problem, with Particular Attention Paid to the Theoretical Foundations of the Jewish Racial Question*

## Ignaz Zollschan

*Das Rassenproblem unter besonderer Berücksichtigung der theoretischen Grundlagen der jüdischen Rassenfrage*
(1909; 5th ed., Vienna: W. Braumuller, 1925).

For biographical information on Ignaz Zollschan, see the note at the beginning of selection 24. Zollschan's major work was *Das Rassenproblem*, which first appeared in 1909 and went through five editions.

### FOREWORD TO THE FIRST EDITION, 1909

We understand the "racial problem" as the question of the way in which the racial factor is significant for historical and cultural development.

The actual point of departure for the treatment of this theme was the Jewish Question. However, it soon turned out that the Jewish racial problem, in which the Jewish Question culminates, is inseparable from the vast problem of race in general. This fact, as well as the profound significance of the racial question for the worldview of our age and for how we live our lives—a significance that is probably surpassed only by the social question—made it seem justified to dig deeper, and to examine the foundation of the current perspectives on raciality and its importance for the course of history.

For we can only arrive at a judgment concerning the decisive factors related to the Jewish Question if we subject to an exact analysis those arguments that have been decisive for European racial politics as a whole. When it comes to the racial politics within Europe, we are dealing in essence with a struggle of Germans versus *Romanen* [that is, the French, Italians, and Spanish] as well as the struggle of Germans against Slavs, and the struggle of all the above against the Jews. This latter opposition, between Aryans and non-Aryans, manifests itself in the sphere of European foreign affairs as a political opposition against the "black" and "yellow" dangers outside [of the continent]. For Europe the classic representatives of the Aryan and non-Aryan indeed are the Teutons and the Jews. Nonetheless, we must, when we speak in what follows about the Jewish Question—which captures most of our interest—still frequently leave the realm of this question and broaden our discussion to [include] matters of the philosophy of history, racial divisions, the issue of heredity, of ancient history, and so on; the argument will, then, actually end up being a genuine engagement with the general foundations of racial theory. Discussing the specific cultural worth of the Jewish and German races will only serve as examples in this regard.

Antisemitism accounts for its political goal of stripping Jews of their rights by pointing to the inferior morals and—in regard to more noble intellectual activity—the inferior capabilities of the Jews. Regarding the first point, the moral opinions of the Jews: they are a product of the social situation (*Milieuverhältnisse*) and the doctrinal religious literature. Responding to such attacks aimed at the principles of Jewish ethics is mostly a matter for Jewish studies (*Judaistik*)—that is, the science of Jewish literature. This subject has been more than adequately treated, and should not fall within the purview of this work.

The claims concerned with the idea of an intellectual or spiritual inferiority, however—which derive their foundation from the works of Renan, Dühring, Richard Wagner, [and] Chamberlain[31]—are treading on the grounds of cultural history and of natural science. They presuppose that everything that German industry, British energy, Roman power, Greek art, [and] Indian philosophy have so magnificently accomplished must be an emanation of the Aryan spirit common to these cultures, and they [the above-named authors] compare these demonstrations of "Indo-Germanic" racial talents to the cultural accomplishments of "Semites." Since they assert the "natural-scientifically established" immutability of racial traits, as well as the dependence of the congenital on the consanguineous, it is our task, in responding to such claims, and in the furtherance of correcting historical fact, to investigate the question of consanguineous relations and of the heritability of racial characteristics.

Furthermore, if we wish to know something about the cultural worth of any particular race, we must first of all establish if and in what way the cultural value

31. [Renan and Chamberlain have been identified in previous notes. Eugen Karl Dühring (1833–1901) was a German political economist and philosopher, and an open advocate of racial antisemitism. Richard Wagner (1813–83) was a German composer and the author of the antisemitic essay "Das Judentum in der Musik" (Jewry in music), published in 1850.]

of a social community is dependent on racialness; that is, we must first arrive at a determined perspective on the racial problem itself. There are no recognized or accepted scientific theories regarding this matter, only hypotheses; we thus face the major task of, first of all, erecting a solid foundation so that we can then move to a discussion of the special racial worth of the Jews.

Thus, in a large part of this book, we examine the racial problem in only the most general of ways, and return to the Jewish race only now and again.

In concluding this foreword, I would like to introduce a purely formal matter. The stated purpose for the writing of this book was to offer the most objective illumination possible of these materials, and to gather together materials on a generally unknown theme that lie hidden away from the public in journals and brochures. For this reason, and to prevent my conclusions from appearing merely as subjective opinion, I have preferred, whenever possible, to let other authors speak [that is, to quote from other authors].

The goal of this book is not to offer the literary confessions of its author; rather, the goal is an impersonal presentation of the material, for reasons relating to the intended scientific and political effect of this presentation, which can provide a clearer understanding and judgment in this difficult area.[32]

## INTRODUCTION TO THE FIFTH EDITION

Insofar as one cannot escape from the general interest taken in the Jewish Question, the issue ought to be considered by posing the following queries:

(1) Are the Jews economically and culturally harmful, insignificant, or useful to the countries in which they reside?

(2) Is there a homogeneous Jewish race, and, if so, does it possess distinct traits that determine its historical trajectory for all eternity?

The work at hand deals with these problems by isolating from them its core aspect, the problem of racial worth.

An investigation into the racial worth of the Jews would have to deal with two groups of factual material. Its procedures would have to be deductive, advanc-

32. [One of the mainstays of the anti-Semitic argument was that Jewish scholars, precisely because they were Jews, were incapable of maintaining an objective or neutral position on the scientific question of the Jews. Zollschan, like many others at the time, thus felt it necessary to stress his desire and ability to remain as objective as possible.]

ing from the results derived from anthropological research into the brain, and inductive, relying on historical materials.

However, the analysis of results obtained through anthropological studies does not offer sufficient data, as a result of the still-primitive state of this science; thus, almost all of the authors who have taken a position on this question have relied on historical evidence, and we too in large part are obliged to do the same. At least the progress in the realm of the theory of heredity affords us, happily, the possibility of supporting the reasoning behind our approach using natural science.

In addition, this investigation pursues higher goals, which transcend contemporary political aims.

At present a process of dissolution of the Jewish race is at work. It is possible and at the disposal of today's society either to retard or advance this process through political intervention. The type of intervention will, however, depend on a judgment regarding the cultural worth of the Jews. Thus, the Jewish Question appears to be, from the much more elevated standpoint of large-scale historical evolution, the question of whether or not the Jewish Volk should continue to exist.

Is it to be hoped that the Jewish Volk shall be maintained, or should it be dissolved and completely absorbed into the surrounding populations? Above all, who or what possesses the decisive competence with regard to the decision about the question [whether or not the Jews ought to survive]? It is not hollow phrases and not sentimentality; it is only science.

But, one will interject, has the proof been furnished yet that we indeed face the alternative, that of disappearance? Official Jewish nationalism justifies itself precisely on the assumption that the Jewish nation cannot die; that is, that it cannot completely assimilate itself. As we shall see, this chain of thought rests on unjustified presuppositions. Provisionally, let us accept as a given that which we shall later demonstrate: the correctness of the alternative [that the Jews in fact can disappear through assimilation]. And let us for now pay strict attention, then, to the question of whether the continued existence of the Jewish nation is desirable.

There exists of course a large antisemitic literature that has already answered this question according to its own criteria.

According to Dühring, who is the most scientifically significant of the antisemitic authors, "the Jewish race has developed its characteristics in the most marked opposition to that of general humanity. The injection of these Jewish racial traits into other nations or Völker would constitute the greatest danger for these others' character. The actual reason, however, for the profound disdain and contempt for the Jewish race, [and] its cause and motivation is [the Jews'] absolute inferiority with regard to all higher intellectual aptitude. They lack all scientific proclivity, they are inadequately equipped for philosophy, they are incapable of creativity in mathematics, and incapable in the other sciences: they are able only to reclaim insignificant things from memory, and the inaptitude of the Jews for the realms of art and music is easily recognizable. The Jews have never produced anything in the realm of the sciences over the course of their long history. When they have involved themselves in the sciences, this was due only to economic interest. Loyalty, respect for the magnificent and all that is noble in general, is foreign to the Jew. The whole Jewish race therefore is depraved and inferior."

That is indeed the tenet of the general ruling opinion about the Jews. Together with a swarm of middling men of letters, there are also authoritative writers such as Renan, Chamberlain, and Weininger[33] who embrace this negative response to the question of the cultural value of the Jewish race. One should not, on account of the aggressiveness and vehemence of Dühring's and Chamberlain's notions, be led astray into placing their work on the same level as the shriekings or scribblings of those who made antisemitism their profession.

Are the hypotheses that originate with Dühring, Chamberlain, Wagner, and others correct? The fact is that they are receiving ever-increasing public legitimacy. Can it appear desirable then, that a Volk of this sort [the Jews] should continue to exist?

Conversely, a first, impartial view of conditions in which Jewish and Christian achievements are equitably compared will always have the impression of a superiority of the Jewish spirit, and the faith in the intellectual superiority of the Jews is a common subjective conviction.

The notion of a possible Jewish racial superiority, even in the form of a mere mention, will be seen as audacious to the highest degree, and would certainly be understood by both sides as an exaggerated assertion and as a characteristic example of arrogant racial claims. However, if it ought merely to be granted that

33. [Otto Weininger (1880–1903), an Austrian Jewish scholar, was trained in psychology and the natural sciences. His best-known work, *Geschlecht und Character* (Sex and character) appeared in 1903, and set forth his ideas about the inferiority and danger of women and Jews.]

this part of humanity is equal to the "better" [elements] of humanity, that they are not wretched or inferior, then it is a categorical imperative to call attention to this fact. Nothing, however, justifies a reaction to the aforementioned attacks more than the fact that the Jews themselves, who of course are also influenced by general opinion, have today started to believe what their opponents put forth about their character and ethnic traits.

Now there is no doubt that the Jew in his present condition has his share of bad habits, that he possesses actual negative traits in abundance.

However, scientifically it is not a question of whether the Jews possess or possessed faults, but whether, when they actually do possess these traits for which they are reproached, these are innate, inalienable traits. It is a question of the principle of "inheritance," of "immutability" of "specific racial traits." It is a question of whether or not there even exist specific racial traits. Entering here into the realm of modern racial problems, we already leave the narrower realm of the Jewish Question far behind us.

In order to arrive at a clarification of these matters, it becomes a question of which of these possible deficiencies are ephemeral and which a product of the immutability of race, inherited in the blood, and inseparable from the blood. This is a question of immense significance. If it were to emerge that Jewish racial blood is inferior, then the disappearance of the race would be desirable.

Now let us, conversely, accept provisionally the hypothesis of Jewish racial superiority. From this fact, and from the additional consideration that, generally, it would have to be the common pursuit of all to reach the highest possible level of culture for the sake of the totality of human civilization, it would follow that it would be deemed valuable to retain the integrity of the [Jewish] race.

Evidence of the validity of this thesis of a Jewish racial equality is to be derived from an exact and intensive ethnological and historical, as well as rational, examination of the traits, and of the national and racial typologies of the Jews in comparison with the traits and typologies of the other outstanding races.

If we wish to determine the racial worth of the Jews, then we must have some standard against which to measure it. Now in the eyes of all theorists of race it is the Aryan race, and in particular the Germanic branch or family, that is deemed to be culturally the most valuable. It is this object of comparison that is thus the most suitable.

It is a matter, therefore, of determining whether or not the Jews and their racial makeup are inferior to the Indo-Germans.

In this task it is necessary, first of all, to establish through historical and anthropological investigations the cultural worth of the Jews in relation to the great general race around them; and second, to arrive by the same sort of investigation at a correction of a possible overestimation of the cultural worth of the Aryan—that is, of the Germans.

[...]

The dominant racial theory is thus an Aryan-Germanic racial theory. As a foundation of this theory, its creators use the following equation: Ur-Aryans equal *homo Europaeus flavus*[34] equal the German, and this school of thought then literally claims that everything in the present and the past, reaching back into the grayest mists of primordial time—everything that is of cultural value, without exception, was produced either totally by, or through the intervention of, a wave of blond-haired Germanic peoples.

[...]

34. [A term that refers to members of the so-called Nordic race, coined by the German racial theorist Ludwig Woltmann. See Ritchie Robertson, *The "Jewish Question" in German Literature, 1749–1939* (Oxford: Oxford University Press, 1999), 164.]

# 30 | "There Is No Jewish Race!" The Testimony of the American Jewish Committee and Union of American Hebrew Congregations before the United States Immigration Committee

"There Is No Jewish Race!" *Maccabaean* 18, no. 1 (1910): 16–29.

The United States Immigration Commission, informally known as the Dillingham Commission, met between 1907 and 1911 to investigate the purported negative effects of immigration, principally that from Southern and Eastern Europe, on the United States. It was headed by Senator William Paul Dillingham of Vermont and included Senator Henry Cabot Lodge of Massachusetts; Senator Asbury Latimer, South Carolina; Representative Benjamin Howell, New Jersey; Representative William Bennet, New York; Charles Neill, US Commissioner of Labor; Jeremiah Jenks, a professor at Cornell University; and William Wheeler, Commissioner of Immigration for California. In 1911 the commission published its findings in forty-one volumes, concluding that immigration from Southern and Eastern Europe posed a significant threat to American society, and calling for restrictions on immigration. These restrictions were instituted in the 1920s.

Simon Wolf (1836–1923) was a US lawyer and Jewish communal leader. Julian Mack (1866–1943) was a judge, Jewish leader, and one of the founders of the American Jewish Committee. Eventually, under the influence of Louis Brandeis, Mack became an ardent supporter of Zionism.

*The Maccabaean*, which started in 1901, was the first English-language Zionist newspaper in the United States.

We give at length the testimony offered by the Hon. Simon Wolf, representing the Union of American Hebrew Congregations, and by Judge Mack, representing the American Jewish Committee, before the United States Congressional Commission now investigating alien immigration.

These two gentlemen have translated into legal testimony the ideal of Jewish assimilationists, and have attempted to have their interpretation of the facts of Jewish history fastened upon the entire Jewish citizenship of this country not for personal reasons, but in order to retard the growing anti-Jewish feeling which, they declare, will result in immigration restriction should the American people become aware of the numbers of Jews who come to this country.

Though their motives are prompted by interest in the welfare of the Jewish people, we cannot permit them to utilize arguments, and to misinterpret facts, in a manner to bring the Jewish people of this country into contempt with the legislators who are now considering the immigration situation.

Without entering into the merits of [the] argument, which was advanced by them not as matters of conviction, but primarily as matters of policy, we desire to dissociate ourselves from their point of view, from their logic, and from their policy.

As Zionists, as Jews, and as American citizens, we, who are charged with being unpatriotic, declare that we have more faith in the fairness of the American people than they, who constantly reiterate and affirm their American patriotism. We think that the American people will not be prodded into anti-Semitism by the mere disclosure of the number of Jews who come to this country; and we believe that if anything could stimulate prejudice against the Jews it would be the shifting, unmanly, and undignified pretense of representatives of a people who, against fact and history, and against their own private convictions, disown their racial and national birthright.

When men speak in the name of a people, the duty is imposed upon them to be more careful of their utterances than if they spoke in their own interests. It is incumbent upon every one who comes forward to serve the Jewish people to be certain that what he speaks in their name will have their approval. The honor of an entire people ought not to be sullied for the sake of any alleged temporary advantage which may accrue to some of the individuals composing that people. By asserting boldly a theory that there is no Jewish race, but only a conglomeration of people professing the Jewish religion, Judge Mack and Mr. Wolf, and the organizations they represented, uttered a statement, which, if true, would exclude from among our ranks many who are devoted to the welfare of the Jewish people but who are not religionists in the accepted meaning of the term.

We believe we speak in the name of the entire Jewish people when we say that the Jewish people, native-born and naturalized in this country, are not ashamed to have themselves or their brethren classified as racial Jews; that if it serves the purposes of the United States government to know the quality of the alien immigration coming into these ports, we welcome a classification which will enable the Jewish people to prove that they [are] physically, morally, and spiritually good material for the United States.

As American citizens, we believe it is our duty to assist our government in arriving at correct conclusions as to desirable immigration. If our people are undesirable, we are aiding in the perpetration of fraud upon this government if we oppose a fair investigation of the facts, and the classification of Jews as such is merely a necessary step in the direction of ascertaining the facts.

The Jewish immigrant, we assert, is not an undesirable. The United States needs immigration of all sorts, and more especially it needs the immigration of a people who bring with them religious, industrial, and moral values, who are industrious, ambitious, and eager for democratic liberty. A scientific classification of alien immigration will prove that assertion. An evasion of the test will foment distrust and create an impression of unknown dangers which is just the meat the anti-restrictionist feeds upon.

The Jewish people cannot afford to adopt a policy that smacks of Jesuitism; it is bound therefore, to repudiate any policy that is in essence based upon the theory that the end justifies the means; that is the ground upon which Judge Mack and Mr. Wolf stand, and the American Jewish Committee and the Union of American Hebrew Congregations are responsible for the utterances of their agents.

For the length of the testimony, *The Maccabaean* must offer an apology to its readers. As a matter of record, however, it deserves to be published in full in this magazine [*sic*]. It becomes all the more urgent to publish it in full, owing to the disinclination of the American Jewish Committee, for reasons best known to itself, to publish it on its own account.

## THE HON. SIMON WOLF AND JUDGE JULIAN MACK TESTIFY BEFORE CONGRESSIONAL COMMISSION ON IMMIGRATION

Washington, D.C., December 4, 1909. The Commission met at 10:00 o'clock a.m. Present: Senators Dillingham (chairman), and Lodge; Representatives Howell and Bennet; Messrs. Jenks, Neill, and Wheeler.

### *Statement of Simon Wolf*

*The Chairman.* Mr. Simon Wolf, who is present, has asked for an opportunity to present certain views, and I have asked him to be present this morning. Mr. Wolf, we are now ready to hear you.

*Mr. Wolf.* Chairman and gentlemen, I do not know on exactly what lines you wish me to speak, but it may be you desire to ask me certain questions, and, if so, I shall be very glad to answer them as best I can.

*The Chairman.* You wrote me a letter saying you desired to be heard on certain questions.

*Mr. Wolf.* Yes.

*The Chairman.* It is for the reasons stated in your letter that we have appointed the meeting for this morning.

*Mr. Wolf.* One of the questions I wish to bring to the attention of the Commission is the classification of immigrants by faith. That is what it amounts to, as far as the Jewish immigration is concerned. Some years ago that question arose in the Immigration Bureau, when Mr. Powderly was Commissioner General, and I was invited to New York. We argued the matter there at length, and the Bureau finally came to the conclusion to eliminate the word "Jew" from the immigration list, and I supposed that the subject had ended then and there. But it has been revived, and the word is now being used, I believe, not only by the authorities, but its use is also contemplated in the report of your honorable Commission, as I have been informed. The point we make is this: A Jew coming from Russia is a Russian; from Rumania, a Rumanian; from France, a Frenchman; from England, an Englishman; and from Germany, a German; that Hebrew or Jewish is simply a religion.

*Senator Lodge.* What is he if he comes from Poland?

*Mr. Wolf.* I suppose he is a Pole, if he belongs to—

*Senator Lodge.* "Poland" is a geographical expression.

*Mr. Wolf.* That is all. It is not for me to inform intelligent gentlemen like yourselves that Poland has been divided among different states of Europe.

*Senator Lodge.* Do you think that Poles ought to be classified as Prussians, Austrians, Russians, depending upon which part of Poland they come from?

*Mr. Wolf.* I do.

*Senator Lodge.* And the Irish as British?

*Mr. Wolf.* Yes, sir. I wish to state right here, for the purpose of avoiding any conflict or misunderstanding, that a certain portion of the Jewish people claim that the Jews are a race, especially the Zionists, who cling to the idea of returning to Palestine and founding a Jewish state; and I am not speaking for that portion of the Jewish people.

*Senator Lodge.* No; I understand that there is a difference.

*Mr. Wolf.* The Reform element in the United States and throughout the world, that class which has not been living in Russia and Rumania under medieval conditions, is decidedly on the lines I have indicated; that is, that we are citizens of the country in which we reside, and we have been fighting in every possible way against the idea of founding a Jewish state. It is under all circumstances the only course for the government of the United States to pursue, to ignore the action taken by Russia and Rumania, who recognize the Jew racially, and who confer no rights or privileges upon him as a citizen; in short, they do not recognize him. Therefore, the tabulating of the Jew as such, especially coming from these countries, is simply strengthening the hands of the people who have oppressed him in other countries, and the same unfortunate condition is [has] caused the incoming immigrant who has never been a citizen to claim that the Jewish people are a race, never having been recognized as citizens of their respective countries, although in their condition of noncitizenship, as well as that of full-fledged citizenship, they are equal to the best and worthy of the highest recommendation. In this connection, it might be stated that great stress has been laid upon the fact that the Jew refuses to intermarry, claiming superiority or racial objections. That has been fully discussed time and again, and even recently at the Rabbinical Conference in the City of New York. The question is not of race, or of differences in blood, but purely religious; that the natural conditions arising between different faiths create domestic disturbances and lead to acrimonious results, injurious to the peace and harmony of the home, and to the permanent injury of the children, who are made shuttlecocks between the separate faiths of husband and wife. The Russian government recognizes the religion and not the race, from the very fact that when a Russian of Jewish faith becomes a convert to the Greek Catholic religion he is recognized as a citizen, thus confirming all our contention that it is not racial, but religious.

*Senator Lodge.* Do I understand you to deny that the Jews are a race?

*Mr. Wolf.* How?

*Senator Lodge.* Do you deny that the word "Jew" is used to express a race?

*Mr. Wolf.* As the representative of the Union of American Hebrew Congregations—which I have been for nearly thirty years—when the question whether the Jews were a race arose some years ago, I took up the matter and propounded a series of interrogatories to some of the leading Jews of the United States, among others the Hon. Mayer Sulzberger, who is president of the American Jewish Committee; Dr. Cyrus Adler, who was librarian of the Smithsonian Institute and is now president of Dropsie College in Philadelphia; Dr. Emil G. Hirsch, a noted rabbi in Chicago; Dr. K. Kohler, president of the Hebrew Union College in Cincinnati; and Doctor M. Jastrow, who was one of our most noted Jewish scholars; and each and every one of them (and their views are to be found in this little pamphlet which I will leave with you) states that the Jews are not a race.

*Senator Lodge.* That, I think, is an important point. I have always supposed they were. I find in the preface of the *Jewish Encyclopedia*, which is signed by Cyrus Adler, among others, this statement:

> An even more delicate problem that presented itself at the very outset was the attitude to be observed by the encyclopedia in regard to those Jews who, while born within the Jewish community, have, for one reason or another, abandoned it. As the present work deals with Jews as a race, it was found impossible to exclude those who were of that race, whatever their religious affiliations may have been.

In the same encyclopedia is a statement by Joseph Jacobs, BA, formerly president of the Jewish Historical Society of England: "Anthropologically considered, the Jews are a race of markedly uniform type, due either to unity of race or to similarity of environment."

Do you mean to deny—I want to understand your position—that the word "Jew" is a racial term?

*Mr. Wolf.* I have made my statement, and my opinion is in this pamphlet.

*Senator Lodge.* Let me get at it. How would you classify Benjamin D'Israeli?[35] Was he a Jew?

*Mr. Wolf.* He was born a Jew.

*Senator Lodge.* No, he was not born a Jew, for he was baptized in a Christian church.

*Mr. Wolf.* He was born of Jewish parents, and subsequently, at a certain age, was baptized.

*Senator Lodge.* He was baptized as a Christian. He then ceased to be a Jew.

*Mr. Wolf.* Yes; religiously he ceased to be a Jew.

*Senator Lodge.* Ah! Religiously. He was very proud of the fact that he was a Jew and always spoke of himself in that way. Did the fact that he changed his religion alter his race?

*Mr. Wolf.* It did not change the fact that he was born a Jew; not at all; and I know the Jewish people throughout the world have claimed him, [Heinrich] Heine, [Ludwig] Börne, and others, who were born of their blood as being Jews,

35. [Benjamin Disraeli (1804–81) was a noted British politician and novelist. He served as prime minister of England twice in the second half of the nineteenth century.]

when they speak of persons who have accomplished something wonderful in the world. But they ceased to be Jews from the standpoint of religion.

*Senator Lodge.* Undoubtedly. What I want to get at is whether the word "Jew" or "Hebrew" is not a correct racial term.

*Mr. Wolf.* You will pardon me, you will find a letter from Dr. Cyrus Adler right at the close of the pamphlet, which, perhaps, you might read for the benefit of the committee.

*Senator Lodge. (After reading letter referred to.)* I do not think that answers anything.

*Mr. Wolf.* You can keep this pamphlet if you desire, and look it over. There are a number of other opinions there.

*Mr. Wheeler.* It treats of the entire subject?

*Mr. Wolf.* Yes, and kindred subjects. It is the report of the Board for the year ended January 1904.

*The Chairman.* You may proceed, Mr. Wolf.

*Senator Lodge.* Excuse me for interrupting you. I merely wanted to find out what your position is.

*Mr. Wolf.* The position we have broadly taken is that in the classification of immigrants the word "Jew" is entirely uncalled for; that those persons come from the respective countries of their birth and arrive here as other immigrants [do], and therefore ought not to be classified as Jews unless you classify every immigrant by faith—a Russian of Jewish faith, a Russian of Greek faith, and so on and so forth. If you make no discrimination, we have no objection at all, but if you are going to discriminate and mark the Jew distinctively, we do object.

*The Chairman.* Do you make any distinction between the terms "Jew" and "Hebrew"? The word "Hebrew" is the one used by the Department and the government generally in its classification.

*Mr. Wolf.* I am not prepared to answer that question intelligently, as I am not a scholar to the extent of defining those words.

*The Chairman.* I was merely asking because of the fact that the government invariably uses the word "Hebrew."

*Mr. Wolf.* I know.

*Senator Lodge.* Not in any religious sense, but in a racial sense.

*Mr. Wolf.* Personally I have always used the word "Jew," and I have never shirked responsibility therefore, nor do I regard it, as it seems to have been taken by some, as a term of reproach, and who use the word "Hebrew" simply to soften the aspersion. I have never considered it in that way and I do not think the best of our people do.

*The Chairman.* With you the words would be synonymous?

*Mr. Wolf.* Yes.

*Representative Bennet.* The words "Hebrew" and "Jew" describe the same people?

*Mr. Wolf.* Oh, yes.

*Rep. Bennet.* The only difference being that they would apply at different times in the history of the same people. Is that not correct?

*Mr. Wolf.* Yes, sir, that is correct.

*Mr. Wheeler.* "Hebrew" is equally objectionable, from your standpoint, in regard to the matter in question here.

*Mr. Wolf.* Equally so. These people simply come as citizens of the respective countries in which they were born, and from which they have emigrated, and we here in this country claim that we are citizens of our common country and that what our faith is concerns no one but ourselves. Here is a pamphlet from the Jewish Historical Society, taken from the book I published—*The American Jew as a Soldier, Patriot and Citizen*—which gives a résumé of what citizens of Jewish faith in the United States have accomplished since the days of the [American] Revolution up to the present. We were not enlisted as Jews, but as citizens.

*Senator Lodge.* Are there not a great many Jews who are not of the Jewish faith or the Israelitish [*sic*] religion? I have been told that there are many Jews in this country at the present moment who are not of the Jewish faith.

*Mr. Wolf.* A man is either a Jew in faith or he is not. He may be of the Orthodox or the ultra-Orthodox or the Reform. There are agnostics among the Jews, of course, as there are in Christian churches.

*Senator Lodge.* Certainly. But I was told by the police commissioners in New York some years ago that there are a considerable number of Jews, people who were classified as such on entering as immigrants, who are not adherents of the ancestral faith.

*Mr. Wolf.* Very likely. I have no doubt [that] there are 500,000 Jews in the City of New York [who], if you asked them whether I was a Jew, would say "No," because I do not cling to the old traditions and liturgy to which they religiously and faithfully adhere.

*Senator Lodge.* But those people—certainly some, I do not know how many—who are Jews, but who for one reason or another, have abandoned their faith, as people in all religions frequently do, would be classified as Jews.

*Mr. Wolf.* Classified by whom?

*Senator Lodge.* In the returns of the immigration officers.

*Mr. Wolf.* That may be.

*Senator Lodge.* I have never supposed for one moment, and I do not now suppose, that the Jews who are put down in the immigration returns as such are classified according to religion.

*Mr. Wolf.* You classify them, under the supposition, as I understand—

*Senator Lodge.* On the supposition that it is a race.

*Mr. Wolf.* That the Jewish people constitute a race as the English are a race, as the Germans are a race, and so forth.

*Senator Lodge.* Yes; as the Poles are a race, though they have no country and no nationality; as the Irish are a race, [although] they have no nationality and no country.

*Mr. Wolf.* I understand, but how much there is in that information I do not know, that the opposition to classifying these people as immigrants from Russia is owing to the protest made by the Russian authorities, we do not wish it understood that so many Russian subjects are emigrating to the United States.

*Senator Lodge.* I never heard of that.

*The Chairman.* Nor have I.

*Mr. Wolf.* That has been stated.

*Senator Lodge.* I do not imagine that has anything to do with it. It never occurred to me until I heard you were coming here that the classification as made by the immigration authorities had anything to do with religion. I supposed it was a race classification. It is important, very important, to get the race classification as nearly [correct] as we can.

*Mr. Wolf.* Yes.

*Senator Lodge.* As you all know there are what are called scientific races; that is, the races which are defined by physical peculiarities; the great divisions, like the Mongol, the Negro, the North American Indian, the Aryan, the Semitic. Those are what are called the scientific races, where the difference in the skulls and so on has all been retained. Of course, in Europe there has been a great mixture of races and the scientific divisions have largely disappeared. But there are peoples which have been formed gradually, as the English, the German [have], in which there is a great mixture of blood, but which are historically racial, just as the Poles are historically a race. They may not be scientifically a race, because there is a considerable admixture of blood. But the classification made by the Immigration Bureau is on the basis of historic races in contradistinction to the broad scientific divisions which would be of no value whatever in making returns. I have always supposed that this classification was made exactly as they classify the Irish and the Pole, as the Syrian and the Armenian. It would be an absurdity to classify the Syrians and the Armenians as Turks. They are subjects of the sultan of Turkey, of course; they are Turks politically.

*Mr. Wolf.* You are aware that the Census Bureau some time ago attempted to classify in the same manner, and it was prohibited from doing so.

*Senator Lodge.* The word "race" was stricken out of the census report. I think it was a great mistake. It makes the returns almost valueless.

*Mr. Wolf.* I can simply repeat what I have said, that I am voicing the opinions of those whom I represent—the Union of American Hebrew Congregations and the Order B'nai B'rith. They are opposed to the classification as made in the last few years and as contemplated, so far as I am informed, in the report of the Commission. Of course, no one can foreshadow what the report will be. There are other questions that I desire to bring to the attention of the Commission, if you desire to hear me.

[...]

*Senator Lodge.* Is no man a Jew unless he is of the Jewish faith?

*Mr. Wolf.* As a matter of glorification and an illustration of the genius inherent in the Jew as such, when born as such, as I stated at the inception, a great many claim D'Israeli, Heine, Börne, [Felix] Mendelssohn, Barthold, and other great celebrities in all the walks of literature, arts, and sciences as Jews, but they became Christians.

*Mr. Julian W. Mack.* Permit me to say a word. If D'Israeli had come to this country, after he had attained his fame, he certainly would have said, in answer to the question asked him at the port, that he was an Englishman.

*Senator Lodge.* He would have been classed racially as a Jew.

*Mr. Mack.* Would some officer of the port have that power?

*Senator Lodge.* It is not a question as to where a man happens to live or what his allegiance is. If we were to classify men according to their allegiance, we would classify them in a manner which would be useless.

*Mr. Wolf.* You claim if a man is once a Jew, he is always a Jew.

*Mr. Lodge.* Yes; if he is of the Jewish race.

*Mr. Mack.* If one parent is a Jew and the other is not—

*Senator Lodge.* There you mix the blood.

*Mr. Mack.* Where would you put D'Israeli's children, if he had any? Where would you put Felix Mendelssohn's children, if he had any? Mendelssohn became a Christian. I do not know where you would put his children. He considered himself a German, and the Germans, in large part, except the anti-Semitic element, consider him a German.

*Senator Lodge.* Your proposition is that the classification is according to religion. That is certainly not the fact.

*Mr. Mack.* Then of what value is your classification?

*Senator Lodge.* The Jews are classified according to their race and not their religion.

*Mr. Mack.* What is its value?

*Senator Lodge.* All classifications must be more or less inexact.

*Mr. Mack.* Take the Jews who come from Germany, whose ancestors have lived in Germany three or four hundred years, ever since Spain drove them out of that country, who have become thoroughly identified in every way with their German neighbors, and are deemed by all to be Germans, except by the anti-Semitic element; of what possible value is it to anybody to classify them as Jews simply because they adhere to the Jewish religion?

*Senator Lodge.* Because there is a general belief that the Jews are a strongly defined race.

*Mr. Mack.* I think they are strongly defined.

*Senator Lodge.* I mean they have maintained their racial status in a very extraordinary way.

*Mr. Mack.* I am not ethnologist enough to say. I think they have kept their blood purer, perhaps, than many other nations. But intermarriage has been common.

*Senator Lodge.* There is a general belief, I think widely accepted, that they are a race. There are, I know, bodies of Jews who are not racially Jewish at all. Doctor Adler refers to one tribe in Abyssinia. If we had here an immigration of Abyssinians they would never be classified as Jews, no matter what their faith might be. There are Christian Abyssinians, and it is a curious form of Christianity. There is also there a tribe of Jews called Falashas. But if there was any immigration to this country from that country, they would be classified as Abyssinians—all of them, whether Christians or Jews. They would not be classified as Jews on account of their religion.

*Mr. Mack.* Take a Jewish immigrant from this country into England. Of what possible value would it be to England for England to classify him, not as an American, but as a Jew? Of what possible value would it be for England to classify you as an American and me as a Jew? I do not know you could claim to be any more of an American than I am because your ancestors have been here probably ten generations and mine only three generations, although I know of plenty of Jews who have been here for eight generations.

*Mr. Wheeler.* You would not be classified other than as an American.

*Mr. Mack.* I would not?

*Mr. Wheeler.* Under the present system.

*Mr. Mack.* Now Senator Lodge just said that he would classify Beaconsfield [Disraeli] as a Jew and not as an Englishman.

*Senator Lodge.* Racially.

*Mr. Wolf.* That is the same case.

*Senator Lodge.* I am not now speaking of political classifications. I am speaking of racial classification, and this is used by the immigration authorities solely as a race classification. For the allegation that it is used as a religious classification, I have seen no warrant [evidence] whatever.

*Mr. Mack.* I can understand a racial classification from a country which does not classify its people racially, in which the race is recognized as a unit. Take it under the old Turkish rule; not as today.

*Senator Lodge.* Would you classify any Jew coming from Palestine as a Jew?

*Mr. Mack.* That would depend. There is a Jew from Palestine sitting next to me here who would be glad to be classified as a Jew, who would insist upon it. (He pointed to Mr. A. Aronson, the agricultural expert and Zionist, who was present.) But a great many would not, and there are a great many Jews in America who, if they go to Palestine, would insist upon being classified as Americans.

*Senator Lodge.* There is no discrimination whatever, as I understand. I should be the last man to favor any discrimination whatever.

*Mr. Mack.* I cannot understand that when it comes to classifying Jews from Germany or England or many other countries as Jews. I can understand the proposition that there is no discrimination meant and no desire to get at religious differences, when you classify people of Austria as Croatians, Galicians, and so on, and possibly even as Jews, although Austria does not recognize the Jews as a nation in the sense that it does the Bohemians, or the Croatians or the Galicians. I can understand it in Russia, where they recognize different races; and so in Turkey under the old regime, where the Jews had certain national rights as Jews; jurisdiction over their own bodies, among themselves, legally. But I cannot understand it from the standpoint of Germany, of France or England or any of those countries in which there is no difference, in which, just as in America, they are all deemed for every purpose, to be English or German or French.

*Rep. Bennet.* As 76 percent of those classified as Hebrews come from Rumania and Russia, as to which you admit a justification for the classification—

*Mr. Mack.* I do not admit the value. I am not prepared to discuss that. But I can understand reasons for a classification along the lines that the country itself classifies its people—not with respect to religion.

*Mr. Wolf.* I can easily understand that, from the standpoint of ethnology, you would be trying, from a scientific standpoint, to get at this subject.

*Senator Lodge.* That is the precise point. This is purely an attempt to get at the ethnology of it. It must be approximate. All ethnology is approximate.

*Mr. Mack.* I am afraid ethnology is not in a position at the present date to form the best basis. Ethnology has not advanced that far.

*Senator Lodge.* You can go approximately that far.

*Mr. Mack.* You can divide the world into five races.

# 31 | Assimilation versus Zionism

## Maurice Fishberg

Excerpt from *Jews, Race, and Environment* (1911; New Brunswick, N.J.: Transaction, 2006), 470–81.

For biographical information on Maurice Fishberg, see the note at the beginning of selection 3.

[...]

To the Zionists, the Jews are a distinct, non-European race which has preserved itself in its original purity in spite of the Jews' wanderings all over the globe. They [the Zionists] hold that the Jews can never merge with the European races and are bound to remain distinct from their Christian or Mohammedan neighbors. The Jewish problem can therefore not be solved by emancipation, as is evident in Western Europe, where they still have troubles after one hundred years of freedom and political equality. Nor will emigration solve the problem of the Jews in countries where they suffer from political oppression. "Like previous migration of Jews, it has produced fresh trouble," say the Zionists in an "Official Statement to the Christian World." "These large numbers of poor Jews are, at best, not welcome in the places to which they migrate. Their immigration is not that merely of an alien people who, whatever temporary inconvenience may be caused by their arrival, will soon merge in the general population of their new home. The immigration of Jews is different. They form or augment a body differentiated from the general population."[36] They object to assimilation. "With whom is the Jew of Eastern Europe to assimilate if he is to assimilate at all? Clearly not with the Russian muzhik or the Galician or Polish peasant. But this is a proposal that a superior race shall become absorbed by a greatly inferior, a stronger by a weaker, a sober by a particularly unsober one, and is altogether contrary to the course of race absorption. The Jew has no mean opinion of the status of his race in the world. Purer than most, it is one of the oldest; its preser-

36. *Zionism: a Jewish Statement to the Christian World*, p. 4; published by the Federation of American Zionists, New York, 1907.

vation is part, a great part, of his religious belief. He does not readily yield it even to advance civilization."[37]

To the Zionists the Jews are not only bound together by a common religion, differing from others only in creed; they are not only a race having a common origin; but a nation with a distinct history, traditions, aspirations, ideals, and so forth. "The hypothesis upon which political Zionism is based is that there is a Jewish nation," says Nordau,[38] and "whoever maintains and believes that the Jews are not a nation cannot in truth be a Zionist." Says another Zionist, in reply to a question whether the Jews cannot completely identify themselves with the English nation: "They (the Zionists) feel that as Jews this is not possible. They cannot be as entirely English in thought as the man who is born of English parents and descended from ancestors who have mingled their blood with [that of] other Englishmen for generations. Jews must always have a feeling of sympathy and brotherhood with the Jewish people in all other parts of the world, and must always, in some degree, remain socially separate if they are to continue loyal to their religion. There is no use disguising this fact. To me it seems impossible to separate religion from nationality in Judaism without destroying both. The Jewish religion is and must for ever remain national, and Jewish nationalism is and must ever be religious . . . The fundamental cleavage between Judaism and Christianity was that the Christian community rejected the national law, while the Jews felt it to be essential."[39] Amplifying this statement, after being taken to task by eminent British Jews, the same writer says: "'Englishman' is a word used in two senses: it means either a person who is a citizen of the British nation—and in this sense a Jew may, of course, be fully an Englishman and born of English parents—or a person who is a member of the Anglo-Saxon people as distinguished from a Welshman, a Scotchman, or an Irishman. Try as he may, a Jew cannot become fully English in this sense unless by intermarriage he 'mingles his blood'; and then he ceases to belong to Jewry. Not only is the Jew different from other members of the nation in blood, but he has a history, a literature, a culture, and traditions of his own—these are among the chief

37. *Ibid.*, p. 7.

38. Max Nordau, *Zionism: Its History and Its Aims*, p. 10, London, 1905. [Max Nordau (1849–1923) was a renowned author and polemicist, whose best-known work is *Entartung* (Degeneration, 1892). He became a fierce adherent of Theodor Herzl's brand of political Zionism and Herzl's closest associate.]

39. Norman Bentwich, in *Jewish Chronicle*, p. 22; London, March 26, 1909.

elements of nationality which he does not share with other Englishmen; and he can only disown this splendid heritage at the price of disloyalty to his people and the certain disintegration of his religion."[40]

This fear of the disintegration of Judaism which is at the bottom of Zionism had already been indicated by Spinoza, who stated that the emancipation of the Jews must inevitably lead to the extinction of Judaism wherever the process is extended beyond the political to the social sphere, and throughout it has been evident that such is the case with the modern Jews. Moreover, the Zionists see no relief in emancipation. "The attempt to make the Jews of France and Germany entirely French and German in thought, and to identify them entirely with the French and German nations, has been tried in the last one hundred years. It has succeeded in detaching many of them from Judaism, but it has failed to avert anti-Semitism. The attempt to make young English Jews entirely English in thought and to identify them entirely with the English people has already succeeded in weakening English Judaism; by cutting at the root of Jewish idealism and impairing the hold of the religion, with all that it means for the strengthening of moral character and the suppression of material aims, it may even foster anti-Semitism in this country."[41]

It is thus evident that the Zionists' raison d'être is not only their sympathy with their suffering coreligionists in Eastern Europe, where they are being discriminated against politically, but is a sense of fear, of apprehension for the future of Judaism. In other words, although they maintain that the modern Jews are a race quite distinct from the other racial elements in Europe and America; although they claim that they are a separate nation, with tendencies, hopes, and aspirations differing greatly from the tendencies and aspirations of the non-Jews around them; and although they state a Jew can never become entirely a German, Frenchman, Englishman, or Italian in feeling and thought, they also

40. N. Bentwich, "Zionism at the Universities," *Jewish Chronicle*, p. 13; April 16, 1909.

41. *Ibid.*, p. 14. The Jewish nationalists cannot conceive of a country in Europe without anti-Semitism. Wherever it is not yet evident, they foresee its imminence as soon as Jews shall settle there in substantial numbers. (Cf. T. Herzl, *Der Judenstaat*, p. 47.) [Israel] Zangwill (*Jewish Chronicle*, August 7th, 1908) maintains that although the ratio of Jews in Great Britain and Ireland is only one to every two hundred non-Jews, he already sees that England feels unable to digest this alien mass and is beginning to complain of her suffering from indigestion. "We may be sure," he concludes, "that if the number in this country reached only 5 percent of the Jews in the world—that is, under half a million, we should have violent anti-Semitism."

confess that the most important fear they entertain is that the Jews are becoming estranged from the religion of their forefathers, discarding their traditions, ideals, and aspirations as soon as they come in intimate social contact with the Christians. It is to preserve Judaism and to prevent the impending assimilation and perhaps fusion with the non-Jews that the Zionists are aiming most of their energies, indicating thereby their recognition that the assimilation of the Jews is not only possible, but has been going on since they have been emancipated in Western Europe.

[. . .]

It is evident from what has just been stated that the Jews of today cannot be considered a nation. The national traits of the Jews were distinct during the Middle Ages, when they lived in Christian theocratic countries; some of these traits have been lingering in Russia, because the government is there to a high degree a Greek Orthodox theocracy, but during the last thirty years the national characteristics of the Jews have even there been on the wane. And when we consider the Jews of the world, scattered as they have been all over the face of the globe, we find that they are not at all a nation. The only thing they have in common is their religion. It is the consensus of opinion of all modern statesmen as well as ethnographers that religion alone cannot be considered a basis of a modern nationality. It is true that "in the beginning religion was essential to the very existence of the social group. The social group was an extension of the family. Religious rites were family rites. The Athenian religion was the cult of Athens itself, of its mythical founders, of its laws and customs. It implies no dogmatic theology. This religion was in every sense of the term a state religion. If anyone refused to practice it, he was no longer an Athenian, . . . to refuse to participate in such a worship was like a refusal of military service in our modern societies. It was a declaration that one was not an Athenian."[42] But in modern nations we find that "no longer are there masses of people professing a uniform belief. Everyone believes and practices after his own fashion, what he can, as he pleases. The state religion is a thing of the past. One can be a Frenchman, an Englishman, or a German, and at the same time be a Catholic, a Protestant, or a Jew, or else be of no creed at all." Moreover, in the case of the Jews there is another point which militates strongly against religion as a test of nationality. While an Englishman adopting the Catholic or Buddhist religion still remains nationally an Englishman, and a German converted to Mohammedanism

42. E. Renan, *What Is a Nation?* English translation, pp. 77–78.

[Islam] does not forfeit his national allegiance, the Jewish nationalists look at their nation differently. They agree that a Jew who abandons his faith in favor of Christianity or Mohammedanism loses his claim to allegiance to the Jewish nation. This conception of nationality is not in agreement with the modern view as to what constitutes a nation.

[...]

There are thus seen two tendencies among the modern Jews. One class, represented by the various factions of nationalists, is aiming at the segregation of their coreligionists in Palestine, or in some other territory, where they may live under an autonomous government. Meanwhile they strive to reawaken the national consciousness of the Jews, keep them together in the cities in which they live, and thus prevent assimilation with its concomitant dangers of disintegration of Judaism, fusion with their non-Jewish neighbors, and ultimate absorption by the other elements in the "melting pot" of modern society. Against this tendency are to be seen arrayed all the assimilated Jews, those who have adopted the culture, habits, and customs of the[ir] non-Jewish neighbors, and who consider themselves citizens of the countries in which they live. They have given up most of their separative rites and practices in order to facilitate adaptation to their environment and to be fit for the intimate social contact with their neighbors. They do their best to disperse their coreligionists who cannot or will not remain in their native lands in Eastern Europe and are compelled to migrate westward. Considering that this class is represented by the vast majority of the Jewish elite society, the money powers, the students, litterateurs, professional men, and merchants, and that they in addition control the millions left by the Baron de Hirsch[43] for the purpose of alleviating the lot of his coreligionists, it is evident that they are more effective in their work. If in addition it is considered that history shows conclusively that as soon as the Jew is emancipated and given human rights, he always discards his separative practices and does his best to assimilate, and that reactions, such as were witnessed in Spain and in other countries during medieval ages, are at present unlikely, it is not difficult to foresee which tendency will prevail among the Jews in the near future.

43. [Baron Maurice de Hirsch (1831–96) was a German Jewish banker and philanthropist. He was involved in aid efforts aimed at Jews in the Ottoman and Russian empires. In 1891 he founded the Jewish Colonization Association, with the aim of training Jews in the Russian Empire for new occupations and preparing them for resettlement in South America and elsewhere.]

# 32 | The Racial Identity of the Jews

"Die Rassenzugehörigkeit der Juden," unsigned editorial, *Die Welt* 16, no. 44 (1912): 1356.

*Die Welt*, started by Theodor Herzl in 1897, was the first official journal or newspaper of the Zionist movement.

BERLIN

At a gathering of the Central Organization of German Citizens of the Jewish Faith[44] Tuesday evening, the Berlin anthropologist Dr. [Felix] v[on] Luschan gave a talk on this theme [of the racial identity of the Jews] in the *Oberlichtsaal* [skylit hall] of the Philharmonia, which was so overcrowded it had eventually to be closed off. His starting point was the question of the relationship of the Jews to the Semites, and how the latter then relate to other races; at the same time, he emphasized that the concept of race remains very unclear, and that it is generally questionable whether a pure race actually exists. One speaks therefore with greater certainty about human groups, which are constituted through a common language, religious and political unity, and specific physical traits. The ethnology of Near Eastern peoples has now been completely determined. In certain isolated high mountain valleys, one finds tribes that are thoroughly similar somatically, and whose appearance has remained unchanged for many thousands of years. Among Semitic-speaking groups from antiquity, we recognize the Babylonians, Assyrians, and the large groups of Hebrews, Phoenicians, and Aramaeans, who 1,000 years before Christ invented alphabetic writing.

The types, however, branch off one from another. One can certainly differentiate the actual Bedouins, who are small-nosed and long-headed, from the Syrians, with their short, high skulls and their large noses. They are not related to one another. Only the Bedouins are racially pure, having come to Syria long before Mohammad, to impose their culture upon the indigenous, pre-Semitic population, remnants of which can still be traced today. He [von

44. [The *Centralverein deutscher Staatsbürger jüdischen Glaubens* (or CV) was founded in 1893 in Berlin. The CV was the most prominent liberal organization of German Jewry, dedicated to representing and defending the interests of German Jews.]

Luschan] mentioned a specific inscription from a collection of ancient inscriptions in which the Hittites are designated as farmers who had been subjugated by a Semitic dynasty. On a relief displaying the king of this dynasty, he is shown to have had the same side locks still worn by Orthodox Jews today. Regarding the crania of the Jews, measurements mainly done on the living have indicated the existence of two types—one that is high and short, the other long and low; and one finds that with regard to mixed marriages, one type of these two will usually recur in a pure way in the children. A comparison of the shapes of the skulls of Jews, Greeks, and Turks shows these types to have almost parallel shapes. One can therefore not speak of a Jewish type, but merely of an Oriental type.

Concluding, the speaker discussed the future of the Jews, which in his opinion will proceed along parallel lines with that of urban European civilization. Just as tuberculosis, alcoholism, and syphilis decimate city dwellers, and only the influx of new blood from rural areas meliorates this, so it shall be with the Jews. The greater their distance from the ghetto, the more they lose their social, anthropological, and racial-hygienic particularities. To the extent that they give up their exemplary family life in the ghetto, they will be destroyed by the same infectious diseases [as affect non-Jews]. In addition to this, the Jews have adopted the two-child system just as have the Christians. For the Jews, the uncultured East represents what the rural countryside does for the big city. He [von Luschan] declared Zionism, which he indicated to have barely understood at first, to be the same sort of fanatical arrogance that characterizes the antisemites.

Christians and Jews have common interests; they are both fighting against what is damaging [their] culture. The Jews are heirs to an ancient and venerable culture; they are our co-workers and brothers in arms in a struggle for the highest goods of mankind, progress, and freedom of the mind.

[. . .]

We will set aside the scientific side of the Jewish racial problem and address ourselves only to Professor Luschan's Judeo-political views. We have no doubt that he provided the members of the *Centralverein* with extraordinary delight when he offered tuberculosis, alcoholism, and syphilis as the future of Jewry. So, do the members of the *Centralverein* not desire the continuance of the ghettos, which the professor posits as the Jewish reservoir of power—comparable to the rural plains? The prattle about the common struggle of Jews and Christians against the harms within the culture cannot erase the fact that Professor

v. Luschan foresees the decline of the Jews through these very harms. We will bear with equanimity, therefore, the reproach of fanaticism, since this fanaticism consists of believing that we will not permit the Jewish Volk to perish through tuberculosis, alcoholism, and syphilis, but desire their regeneration on the land of their fathers.

# 33 | On the Jewish Racial Question

"Zur jüdischen Rassenfrage," unsigned editorial, *Die Welt* 16, no. 5 (1912): 141–42.

Like the previous selection, this item expresses the views of the Zionist newspaper *Die Welt*.

The number of distinguished scholars who are engaged with the Jewish racial problem and who have on account of this been won over to the Zionist cause is increasing.

The Amsterdam chapter of the Netherlands Organization of Zionist Students held a well-attended meeting on Wednesday evening, at which Herr Professor Dr. S. R. Steinmetz, professor of ethnology at Amsterdam University, appeared as a speaker.

The chairman, Mr. B. P. Gompertz, welcomed those present and pointed out that, given his academic subject, Professor Steinmetz is in a position to speak about the Jewish problem, too. His chosen topic is surely one that must demand the interest of all intellectual circles, (particularly) as so many new works on the topic [the Jewish Question] have appeared in recent times.

Herr Professor Steinmetz said that before he accepted the invitation of the executive board to speak about the cultural worth and the future of the Jews, he asked himself whether there still was good reason to address this question in the twentieth century, a century after all of cosmopolitanism and general brotherhood. He said that he had to conclude, however, that the Jewish Question unfortunately remains an issue of current interest, and that there could hardly be a place better suited to addressing it objectively than Holland. For, on the one hand, it can certainly not be claimed that this should be a burning issue here, while the fact that there are nonetheless many thousands of Jews to be found in the country allows for an accurate assessment.

After a number of statements of a general sort, the speaker turned to the actual theme of the lecture. What, then, is the Jewish race? We must confess that our science, in dealing with the problem, has not yet arrived at any definitive conclusions. There is as yet not even any unified notion about the criteria for racial classifications. It has been proposed to view the Jews as a mixture of Hittites, Semites, and, to a lesser degree, Amorites; there are also those who would claim that the Jews are actually not Semites at all. Furthermore it has been claimed that, due to the Diaspora, the Jews have been so intermingled with others that one should actually no longer speak of a Jewish race at all. And finally, there are those who wish to demonstrate that the two main groups of European Jews have nothing in common racially.

The Jewish race, whose relative purity and persistence the speaker believes it is necessary to maintain, constitutes a particular group within the Near Eastern race; they are closely related to the Völker of Arabia and North Africa and, somewhat less closely, to the Völker of Southern and Southeastern Europe. Together with the Jews, the ancient Babylonians, Phoenicians, Arabs, and perhaps also the Egyptians must be reckoned as belonging to the Near Eastern races.

This sort of classification of the Jewish race is necessary in order to understand in which environment and under what types of influence, of nature, and of neighboring peoples the Jewish Volk developed during those periods that history sheds no light upon; and to know as well, with which peoples with similar innate traits to compare the Jews.

[Ignaz] Zollschan, then, correctly enters into elaborate detail about the truly imposing culture of the ancient Babylonians and Assyrians; Weber[45] testifies to the fact that ancient Arabic culture, before Islam, had already inseminated the noblest of minds. The Phoenicians and Carthaginians did indeed perish, but what power emanated from them despite their small numbers! Eduard Meyer,[46] who judged the Jews severely, asserted nonetheless that they constituted an extraordinarily gifted racial Volk, with enormous achievements for the history of mankind. And truthfully, Islam, which brought countless primitive peoples to a higher level, must be seen as a powerful cultural achievement. And how much has the Arabic golden age done for the preservation and development of Greco-Roman culture! A race that brought forth ancient Babylon, Egypt, Phoenicia, Carthage, and the great Arabic era certainly cannot be said to be incapable of high culture.

As for the overall central features of the Jewish psyche—if we may be allowed to judge it by drawing an analogy with those of the peoples to whom the Jews are related—there is certainly no justification for judging it inferior. The Arabs no more lacked courage and bravery than did the Maccabees or the defenders of

45. [Max Weber (1864–1920) was the preeminent German sociologist of the early twentieth century.]

46. [Eduard Meyer (1855–1930) was a German historian of the ancient world.]

Jerusalem against Titus. The overall inherited ability of the race must without doubt be judged to be very high. In order to evaluate Jewish intellectual achievements correctly, we must always bear in mind that this Volk was never numerous, and that more than half of it lives under conditions that excludes them from access to higher education. And still, for how many of the highest achievements of mankind do we have to thank this numerically tiny people!

The general ability of the Jews, therefore, must, on the one hand, be assessed in terms of hereditary racial traits; on the other, it must be evaluated in light of what this [numerically] small Jewish Volk has achieved. If only half of all that Sombart credits to the Jews is true, then their economic power must be positively miraculous! And this implies the possession of very important psychological qualities that, if directed elsewhere, could achieve other things.

Psychologists have always argued for the hereditary nature of certain psychological traits; recently this has been substantiated to a certain degree. If we assume tentatively this hereditability of psychological traits, this in no way means that the influence of specific environmental factors can be denied. On the contrary!

This [environmental] factor is indeed of outstanding significance for the Jews. Many of those traits that are held against the Jews as genetic, national, or racial traits are most likely only transitional, wholly the consequence of particular living conditions.

Werner Sombart seeks to demonstrate that the Jews possess an inherited predisposition to capitalism. However, how can he label this a deeply rooted racial trait? The religion and ethics of the Jews sanction the traits that, according to Sombart, constitute the particularity of the Jewish national or racial character, namely: greater intelligence, diminished emotionality, the tendency always to focus in on a sharply defined goal, and a great flexibility of intellect or spirit. From these basic traits, Sombart infers their [the Jews'] agility and their great ability to assimilate. All of these attributes should make Jews born entrepreneurs and capitalists, and even more traders, stockbrokers, and financiers. The renowned historian Eduard Meyer for the most part takes the same position when he talks about the traits of the Jews.

The speaker [Steinmetz] now wishes that we consider as the most characteristic psychological traits of the Jews the following: a sharp, clear intelligence; an agile spirit; a sense of the practical; a probably lower level of emotionality than that evinced by other European peoples; but on the other hand a greater energy. Some other traits—the sense for trade, lack of idealism, sobriety—could better be considered the result of particular external conditions that acted upon the above-mentioned fundamental traits. The Jews, indeed, were locked out of the highest professions for centuries; they existed outside of the national life and did not take part in the ideals of their hosts! No wonder, then, that they become sober realists, and that, having been injured too often, their sensitivity caused them to withdraw. With their enormous abilities, they were forced to devote themselves to trade, and so they became—more out of necessity than out of some inner disposition—the most salient representatives of a type of trade and finance.

We find an analogue for the Jews of Western Europe in the Parsees of India, especially in Bombay.

We should not, as Sombart seeks to do, trace the chief characteristics of the Jews back to the desert and to a nomad existence, since other nomadic peoples do not possess these same traits. Rather, such traits are to be explained by the centuries-long difficult struggle for existence, together with the intimate cohesion of their original or primary living space. The Diaspora, in contrast, stimulated their mental agility and the other acknowledged Jewish traits. The great artists and scholars produced by the Jewish Volk over the past centuries demonstrate, however, that the Jews are not exclusively predisposed to trade and finance.

The negative traits for which the Jews are so often reproached must without doubt be accounted for by reference to the impoverished conditions in which they found themselves for so long. Even today, the Jews in Western Europe are not fully recognized as equal. No wonder that this still exerts a negative influence on them.

Even as we gladly acknowledge the high cultural worth of the Jewish Volk, we must also unfortunately allow that the prognosis for their future is not favorable. The emancipation of the Jews, as the facts provided by Dr. Ruppin prove, inevitably brings with it their assimilation.

It is, therefore, highly desirable and in the interest of culture that the Jews be able to construct an independent community in accordance with the ideals of Zionism. Whether or not this oft-tested Volk are up to the mighty task that is required, concluded the speaker, only the future will tell.

# 34 | Concerning Racial Theory

## Robert Weltsch

"Gelegentlich einer Rassentheorie," *Die Welt* 17, no. 12 (1913): 365–67.

Robert Weltsch (1891–1982) was a Zionist writer and editor. He was born in Prague, which was then part of the Austro-Hungarian Empire. In 1920 he was appointed editor of *Die jüdische Rundschau*, the official organ of the Zionist Federation of Germany. He remained in that position until 1938, when he emigrated to Palestine. See the entry in the *Encyclopedia Judaica*, 2nd edition, 21:9–10.

Zionism rests on the fact that all Jews around the world feel some sense of belonging together as Jews. This feeling of unity, which is rooted in the historical origins of contemporary conditions, generates not only a historical but also a living connection, which one might designate as nation, Volk, tribe, race, or whatever one likes. Someone can always come along and say, for instance: "I understand the word 'nation' to refer only to those groups that share a common language; thus, the Jews are not a nation." The fool! He assumes he has contributed something vital, while he has only ventured into a question of terminology. May whoever has the time and inclination enter such a discussion. However, those who are interested in getting to the essence of things will not pay much attention to words. When it comes to the unity of the Jews, there is one irrefutable proof: the consciousness of this unity, which is an inner experience that every individual Jew possesses.

I have an insurmountable mistrust of any attempt to trace back an intellectual or spiritual disposition to material causes; the same holds true for all racial theories, which derive consciousness from anthropological facts and thereby seek to ground consciousness in natural science. As if such a spiritual fact requires a "natural scientific" foundation, as if its very existence were not in itself the most powerful proof! It was one of the most pathetic errors of an age, worshiping natural science as its false god, to seek to explain the wonder of the human spirit by means of zoology. It is also true that in the past half-century, not a year has passed without some racial theory being overturned and a new one put in its place; yet human consciousness remains unstirred by such things. If, on occasion, a particular racial theory, such as Chamberlain's, found its way into public opinion [literally, into the thinking of the Volk], this was not a consequence of its (nonexistent) scientific nature; rather, it was a consequence of the fact that it corresponded with the instincts of the Volk, out of which it may even have been derived.

I recently got hold of a book [called] *The Racial Traits of the Jews*, by Dr. Maurice Fishberg.[47] The author says in the introduction: "For the scientific anthropologist race is a biological concept, which means in general the same thing it does for the zoologist and the botanist: a group of animals or plants connected by common descent. The primary or most important indicator of race is type—similarity or uniformity." He then warns against the confusion of race with "ethnic unity" and goes on to say: "That I will encounter opposition in circles that take a common or shared religion to be a mark of racial identity is as irrelevant to me as is the opposition I anticipate from certain European racial thinkers who see race not merely as a zoological category, but also as a historical and ethnic one." Considering these programmatic statements, I would have expected to have agreed with the author: for isn't he very insightful, sticking with what he knows best, zoology? The fact that the Jews ought not to be conceived of as an independent "race," but only as "a genealogical unity, which can no longer be accounted for anthropologically but merely historically" had, of course, been already established by Zollschan. And yet [Fishberg's] entire book again offers proof of the nonexistence of the Jews as a race, and ends with the following stupefying sentence: "Judaism was and remains a religion—it was never a race." Quite a zoological conclusion indeed!

The book offers an abundance of extremely interesting material. It deals in specific chapters with a number of alleged racial traits, and demonstrates through a comparison of different Jewish types that one would not be able to speak of any homogeneity. Anthropological traits such as skin color, cranial size, body shape; physiological characteristics such as somatological development and fertility; pathological traits such as particular diseases, alcoholism, nervous disorders, idiocy, suicide—all these undergo examination. The author then arrives at the unobjectionable position that "race" proves attractive as an explanation for a phenomenon when other hypotheses, such as the influence of milieu, have been rejected. The section on "Jewish anthropological types" is very interesting; the types are illustrated through a large number of very successful artistic representations. Whether or not the enormous amount of statistical material is truly

47. *Die Rassenmerkmale der Juden*, Munich: Ernst Reinhardt, 1913.

exhaustive, I cannot judge. I doubt, in fact, that such compilations can ever really be complete and reliable. But I will take Dr. Fishberg's representation on blind trust. He demonstrates, not only in regard to the myriad different anthropological types but also historically, that there occurred an infusion of foreign blood into Jewry. Thereby, in the author's view, the racial pride of those Jews, who thought of themselves as part of a 4,000-year-old tradition, is destroyed. "At the same time, this also makes the firm ground beneath antisemitism vanish, since its basic assumption is that Jewish blood cannot mix with the blood of others, and that the Jews remain an undesired 'foreign' element in Western countries."

Is this not a tilting at windmills? That Jewish blood can, speaking in strictly zoological terms, mix with the blood of non-Jews our own Dr. Ruppin has already demonstrated in his work; and we have gratefully received this wisdom. But Dr. Fishberg overlooks something entirely: indeed, the physical possibility of such intermixing is there, but not the will. Fishberg mentions Zionism in only one place (the original English version, which I unfortunately do not have at my disposal, is supposed to contain a more extended discussion of Zionism); there [in that one place] it is said with regard to intermarriage (p. 75): "It has been demonstrated statistically that after three or four generations of this sort of intermarriage, one rarely finds an adherent of the Jewish religion among the descendants. Thus, on account of this, those Jews who desire the continuity of their faith protest against intermarriage; and the colonization idea propounded by Zionism appears in no small measure to rest on the belief that, as things now stand, intermarriage cannot be hindered or prevented. Therefore, we see the desire to isolate the Jews through colonization. One may allow oneself to have a healthy skepticism, however, about whether Judaism can be 'saved' in this way."

In any case, one "may." Not a soul can prevent our Don Quixote from doubting, and maintaining with satisfaction, the unrecoverability of Jewry. We nonetheless believe that world history is made not by zoologists, but by ideas. In his thick book, Dr. Fishberg proves that the Jews can and must disappear; indeed, he proves that Jews do not even really exist. I'm afraid that the entire theory will make very little impression; we do not want to disappear, and we in fact do exist, however much one might try to talk us away. *Quod (non) est in actis, non est in mundo* [what is not in the documents does not exist].

However, the author does impose limitations. If there is no zoological type of Jew, one must nonetheless still explain the fact that a differentiation is made between Jews and non-Jews. "What is it, then, that marks one as a Jew and another as a non-Jew? It is not the body, but the soul. In other words, a type is not defined anthropologically or physically, but socially and psychologically." In a somewhat unusual use of the term, the author labels this characteristic "religion," offering a *pars pro toto* [a part for the whole]. He will have little understanding of the fact that it is not zoology that is important to us, but this "spiritual" type; that we do not feel a sense of unity on account of our cheekbones, but because of a feeling of unity that is deeply rooted in our nature. Moreover, we know that one should not falsely generalize and declare this or that to be "Jewish" per se, as the antisemites do when they ascribe certain things they have noticed about one Jew or a group of Jews to the collective. We know that within the Jewish Volk, alongside the prophets, the heroes, and the martyrs, there can also be found hagglers, cowards, and traitors. Even Dr. Fishberg shows, albeit unintentionally, just how different from each other the Jews are. Some dedicate their entire lives to the rebirth and renewal of their downtrodden nation, taking on themselves the task—both immensely difficult and burdened with responsibility—of the reconstruction of a new Jewry. Others write books in which they offer proof to the antisemites that there really are no Jews, and that their blood is in fact "capable" of mixing with that of others. Dr. Fishberg could have presented this possibility far more blatantly: Go forth, get baptized, and "disappear" as quickly as you can. It is well known that there were periods of Jewish history when great masses of Jews deserted; the fundamental stock remains. The fundamental stock will remain this time as well.

There is today a vitality within Jewry that has not been seen in many decades. Anyone who is not partaking of this vitality may imagine that Jewry is dead. Whoever possesses this powerful, warm, and throbbing feeling of life will chuckle at such scholarship [that posits the death of Jewry] and not even get upset about it. I live: this reality requires no authentication. Jewry is not a mineral, it is an organism; with organic beings it is not matter but the "vital force" (*Lebensschwungkraft*) that counts.

Zionism is not something that can be explained "scientifically." We know that Judaism lives in us; this knowledge is the most powerful proof of Judaism's hold. We seek to build a new, purer house for this [vital] Judaism; this will is the only reason we need to give for our action. [. . .] Zionism is not a science, it is a way of life; it does not require knowledge, but spirit; it is above all not about cogitation, but about will. [. . .] The great works of mankind have all been the product of spirit, not the result of materialist developments. In the realization of such great works, such as the renewal of Jewry, one requires the powerful force of an idea. [. . .] Zionism is the faith in the spirit that exists in us. Zionism is enthusiasm.

# 35 | The Jewish Racial Problem

## Moritz Goldstein

"Das jüdische Rassenproblem," *Die Welt* 17, no. 48 (1913): 1625–26.

Moritz Goldstein (1880–1977) was a writer and Zionist activist. Born in Berlin, he studied German language and literature (*Germanistik*) at universities in Berlin and Munich. He wrote numerous plays, stories, and novels, only some of which were published. He is best known for his essay "The German-Jewish Parnassas" (1912), which spurred a public debate over the role of Jews in German culture. In 1933 he fled Germany to Italy, and in 1938 he migrated to the United States. He lived in New York City until his death in 1977. See the entry in the *Encyclopedia Judaica*, 2nd edition, 7:731. Also see Elisabeth Albanis, "A 'West-östlicher Divan' from the Front: Moritz Goldstein beyond the *Kunstwart* Debate," in *Towards Normality: Acculturation and Modern German Jewry*, edited by Rainer Liedtke and David Rechter (London: Mohr Siebeck, 2003), 217–35.

The blond type of man can be found among the Egyptians, the Chinese, the Incas, and the inhabitants of the South Sea Islands. Obviously, two conclusions can be drawn from this logically: either the ancient Germans undertook expeditions to Africa, East Asia, America, and the South Seas long before the era of trade, or blondness and all that that entails is not a proof of German ancestry. One might think that the latter explanation would be considered the more likely, whereas commonsense would have to be in revolt against the former. Nonetheless, the unbelievable occurs: science has decided in favor of that which reason contradicts. Suddenly German blood is discerned everywhere around the earth, and everywhere and always it is supposed to be this special liquid or juice that brought forth and continues to bring forth all the cultural achievements of humanity. That such a hypothesis flatters the self-regard of the researcher doesn't seem to concern a single one of them. This doctrine of the superior Teutonic man is being shouted from the rooftops and taken up by people who have a use for this sort of thing; it transcends the professional circles of anthropologists and becomes common knowledge among the educated and cultivated. No wonder, then, that in his latest book so cultivated a Jew as

Walter Rathenau[48] deplores with such noble objectivity the de-Germanization of Europe!

Meanwhile, the theory of Teutonism—surely one of the most remarkable examples of human error—teaches us just what a dangerous science anthropology is. Undergirding it is an extrascientific interest that stirs all the positive and negative passions. It concerns itself with the worth of human types, and thus with the worth of you and me; and the world would have to have changed in a strange way if the researcher were not always to discover that just the race or group to which he belongs is superior. This was equally the case at a time when we were still quarreling about the hierarchy of religions. Despite all our dearest objectivity, it has never occurred—as far as I know—that someone finished his studies with the result that it was not his but someone else's religion that would have to be deemed genuine and true. Lessing had to come along first and offer his parable of the three rings to the hotheaded fighters.[49]

It is about time that the Germano-maniacs and like-minded chauvinists are brought to their senses with this sort of parable [of the rings]. Until that happens, however, we will have to seek refuge in just that science and scholarship that wanted to deny us Jews—and not only Jews—any worth or honor.

We, too, have an extrascientific interest when we approach this research. We leave that fine nonpartisan attitude—which Germanic theory so readily claims for itself, while publicly bemoaning de-Germanization—to those Jews whose motives, conscious or unconscious, are all too apparent, if not comically apparent to us. We others know, before any and all science: a theory that would render us Jews as being naturally and once and for all second-rate human beings must be wrong. Each and every one of us lives in protest to this every single day and hour.

It is obviously out of this experience, and out of the conviction that his studies must result in a refutation of all theories disgracing the Jews, that [Ignaz] Zollschan has approached the racial problem.[50] His book is already in its third

48. [Walter Rathenau (1867–1922) was a German Jewish industrialist, statesman, and author who strongly advocated for Jewish assimilation and against Jewish nationalism.]

49. [The reference is to the German playwright Gotthold Ephraim Lessing (1729–1781) and his well-known play *Nathan der Weise* (Nathan the wise). The play, published in 1779, was an important Enlightenment articulation of religious tolerance.]

50. *Das Rassenproblem*, Dr. Ignaz Zollschan, 3rd edition, expanded and revised. Wien und Leipzig. Wilhelm Braumüller, 1912.

edition—testifying to just how urgent the desire is to be informed about questions of race value—and so we may ask today, what do we gain from this work?

We have here the scientific justification of all that we, as modern Jews, believe and must believe if we wish to retain our self-esteem in the face of those who despise us, and if we are supposed to have trust in the future of our Volk. An unendingly rich amount of material has been compiled here from his own and other people's research; this material has been processed and judged from his own point of view, while being delivered to us with an almost ascetic concern for objectivity and fairness. This author permits himself no emotional expressions, no mysticism, and no hypotheticals, though one might sense a passionate temperament and an enthusiastic partiality pulsating beneath that cool façade. This author does not want to dazzle (or hoodwink) like Chamberlain or Sombart; he accumulates material and with a calm gaze evaluates every for and against, to then draw his conclusions with a powerful logic.

Thus, through his work we find our national Jewish convictions completely justified. We learn why the Jews are a "race"—that is, a unity tied by blood (*Blutseinheit*) that, though having originally emerged from a myriad component elements, maintained its purity over thousands of years. Furthermore, we learn that our descent or lineage does not place us—as it does the Mongol or the Negro—in opposition to Western culture, but rather that we indeed belong to it; moreover, if there is still a degree of separation between us and the Germanic peoples, we must nonetheless be counted among those who—albeit not recently, but generally—have contributed the most to Western culture.

These remarks about our relationship with the world in which we live feel particularly liberating to me. For the need, under the given conditions, to constantly emphasize our national Jewish unity and individuality will foster a feeling of foreignness, isolation, and solitude that makes those who, next to the desire to be honest, possess a certain sensibility, experience their relation to their surroundings as one continuous anxiety. This book demonstrates—even to the chauvinists within our own camp—where unity surpasses diversity, and it demonstrates that if the struggle between the European peoples and the Jews has become embittered, it is a bitterness between brothers who basically still have the same task and the same goal.

We are a race, but what is there to this race? Is it worth maintaining it? Here, too, Zollschan offers us a rich and, for those fainthearted among us, uplifting source of material. It becomes evident what actually ought to be understood by the notion of racial talent (*Rassenbegabung*): namely, not an inborn, eternally immutable trait, but an inherited disposition to cultural achievement that emerges through either an extended or a brief cultural process. And it does not appear open to question that we belong, from this point of view, to those peoples that are eminently well suited for culture.

At the same time, it remains without doubt that this cultural capability is being neutralized by our situation. The author [Zollschan] has emphatically proclaimed that what is known and disrespected as the Jewish type is in fact a false type of Jew, a type that had to arise under these despicable conditions, as it was the only one that could arise. Whereas the silent types among us—the deep ones, the dreamers, the ones who among the Germans, for instance, contribute most to the glory of their people—all these remain in the dark and lead a futile existence as schlemiels.

Finally, it [Zollschan's book] shows how this Volk, whose decline and disappearance (*Untergang*) would represent a terrible loss for humanity, is nevertheless heading toward its decline. Once again, and maybe more strikingly than ever before, the enormous danger of our condition becomes apparent in Zollschan's book, the crisis in which the Jewish Volk finds itself: it appears that the choice is between being pressed to waste away by others or losing ourselves to dissipation from the inside.

And this is how strictly scientific logic leads to and, indeed, cannot help but lead to Zionism. However, the question as to whether or not the national goals and plans will be realized is not being answered here, and the author—who will not permit himself to utter hopes or fantasies about the future—leaves us with the possibility that his rescue of the Jewish Volk's honor really only has the merit of being a eulogy.

This book, with the merits of the abundance of its material, its many-faceted research question, and the matter-of-factness of its answers, has in the end only one fault—if I may be permitted to set forth the paradox: its value depends on its content's being correct. This might seem like the most reasonable of all demands. Yet there are books whose significance resides in something other than their correctness, and perhaps these are the ones actually deserving to be called books in a higher and authentic sense. I am referring to those books that exercise the highest human right, the right to establish values. What does it detract from the works of Schopenhauer or Nietzsche if one demonstrates their mistakes? Zollschan is quite certainly correct when, in the foreword to the third edition of his book, he subjects Sombart's theories about the origin and type of all that is

Jewish (*das Jüdische*) to a devastating critique; still, I fear that the imaginative formula of that poetically gifted national economist, "forest and desert," will prove more powerful than Zollschan's proof to the contrary. Chamberlain's disastrous book [*The Foundations of the Nineteenth Century*] likewise is easily refuted, and yet the energy with which he thereby proclaims and "establishes" the value of the Germanic people cannot be made to disappear from the world. What would be essential here would be to reply to those value judgments so hostile to us with our own counterjudgments. Zollschan refuses to do any such thing; he apparently considers it a particular virtue of his work that it has not articulated notions of value or worth, has not passed judgments, but has offered the facts. For this we are very grateful; nevertheless, we eagerly anticipate whoever it is who will accomplish the former. Whoever seeks material with which to achieve this will find it in Zollschan's book. However, whether his information is correct, whether ongoing research will have to correct it, and whether his conclusions will hold water—this will have to be judged by anthropologists, historians, and sociologists. As the author tells us, no fundamental objections had been raised by the publication of the third edition. In any case, we hope for his benefit and for ours that his book is correct and that it continues to be seen as correct.

# 36 | Jews and Jewishness
## Chaim Zhitlowsky

"Yidn un Yiddishkeit," in *Yidn un Yiddishkeit* (New York: Dr. Chaim Zhitlovsky Verlag-Komite, 1939).

Chaim Zhitlowsky (1865–1943) was a socialist and Jewish writer, and one of the chief advocates of Diaspora nationalism and Yiddishism. Born in Vitebsk, Russia, Zhitlowsky lived in St. Petersburg before moving to Berlin and Zurich, where he was active in socialist and Jewish politics. In 1908 he moved to New York, where he continued his work as a writer, editor, and political activist. This article was first published in the Yiddish newspaper *Der Tog* (New York), May 31, 1927. See the entry in the *Encyclopedia Judaica*, 16:1009–11.

Who and what is a Jew? What is Jewishness (*Yiddishkeit*)?

The Jew and Judaism have existed on this planet for a long while; nonetheless, it appears that when it comes to these questions one can't do without disagreement and controversy... Georg Brandes[51] dies, and already comes the question, can we include him in the category of "Jewishness," and can we say that he, Brandes, the great writer, was also a great "Jew"?

It appears to me that the lack of clarity here derives from the fact that with the words "Jew" and "Jewishness" we are actually designating two very different things that are everywhere and quite commonly bound together. Yet they are not so closely tied to one another that the one should not be able to exist without the other. Often we identify only one type of Jewishness and take that as the genuine article (*etz toch fun dem inyan*), negating all other versions and placing ourselves in contradiction to real life and to every natural classification, which it—life, I mean—expresses.

It is therefore absolutely imperative that we have a clear conception of the very real variations of Jewishness, so that we might arrive at the correct standard by which we are able to evaluate this or that Jewish essence or nature (*mahut*).

The simplest and clearest sort of Jewishness is the religious. This is a discrete collection of beliefs and opinions that are known around the world as either

51. [Georg Brandes (1842–1927) was a Danish writer and critic.]

"Jewishness" (*Judentum*) or "Judaism." A Jew is someone who believes in the ways of Judaism today. He may do that like the Vilna Gaon or like the New York Rabbi Stephen Wise[52] [. . .] Moreover, one does not have to be a Jew from birth. The [members of the] Russian sect that called itself Gerim are kosher Jews according to Jewish law (*ke-din u ke-dat*). According to its internal aspirations, the Jewish faith ought to be a religion not only for the Jewish Volk but for all peoples and races, for humankind in general. That is its ideal, its greatest hope, because like its children—Christianity and Islam—Judaism too is a universal faith, for all mankind. "And He shall make everyone into one community (*Agudah*)," this we don't cease to ask of God.

A former Jew, from a strictly religious standpoint, is anyone who renounces Judaism. This could be someone who formally converts to another faith, or someone who liberates himself from the formalities of religious confession.

In earlier times, when every Jew was a religious Jew, one understood that religious Jewishness alone was the meaning of Jewishness, and thus no other form of Jewishness was possible. In recent times, we've begun to think differently about this subject. There have emerged "Jews" who have absolutely nothing to do with the Jewish religion. In the first place there are the national Jews—or, more correctly, nationalist Jews. Furthermore, this type of Jewishness is bound up with a particular manner of thinking, a certain conscious striving, and also often with emotions that flow from such thoughts and strivings. But our Jewish consciousness insists on a solidarity with the national destiny of the Jewish people, and in the explicit desire for a national destiny that is more beautiful and more significant. Dr. Herzl and Dr. Nordau can serve as splendid examples of just such a type of nationalistic Jewishness.[53] It is clear that religious considerations play absolutely no role for them. Let's set Herzl aside; but with regard to Nordau, there is clearly no doubt that he never had and never could have had the slightest truck with "Jewish theology."

Most people are accustomed now to looking on such figures as heretics (*apikorsim*), even if also as exalted national (or nationalist) Jews. However, one

52. [Rabbi Eliyahu of Vilna (1720–97) was the leading Jewish scholar of his age and a fierce advocate of traditional Judaism, an opponent of both Hasidism and the Enlightenment. Stephen S. Wise (1874–49) was a Hungarian-born American rabbi and educator, one of the leaders of the American Reform movement.]

53. [Theodor Herzl (1860–1904) was a journalist and writer, the author of *Der Judenstaat* (The Jewish state, 1896), and the creator of the organized mass movement of political Zionism.]

is not always consistent in this regard. For many, it is still quite difficult to take that final necessary step and regard as valid the idea that one can be a highly exalted "national" Jew and also disavow or deny religious Jewishness, or likewise that one can remain at the level of a high exalted national Jew even when such a person takes on another faith, either officially or not—and this, even if this faith be Eastern Orthodox or Catholicism. Dr. Herzl's son, who became a Catholic, insists that by means of this "conversion" or "baptism" (*shmad*), his "national" Jewishness has not been diminished at all. And we would like to believe him. And no individual in the world has the right to exclude him. In the Land of Israel, where Jewish national life is gradually becoming normalized, it is already coming to pass, as genuine Christians are manifesting solidarity with the Jewish national fate. One such individual, who has only recently passed away, announced before his death that he wanted to be buried in a Jewish cemetery. The rabbis have not permitted this. This is a genuine barbarity. For the time being, the barbarians have power only over the dead. Their grip, thank God, does not extend to the living. In the realm of the living, Jewish national identity (*yiddishe nationalität*) is increasingly liberating itself from the religious sensibility and is becoming open to all beliefs and opinions.

The two types of Jewishness that we invoked above, the religious and the national, both depend on a certain sort of subjective point or position (*moment*). There is a certain type of consciousness that makes religious Jews religious, and nationalist Jews nationalist. Life, however, offers up two other types of Jewishness, which do not depend on subjective consciousness but only on factual, objective being.

One type of Jewishness (the third in our account) is what one might call racial Jewishness, if one understands by the word "race" not what the anthropologists study when they speak about the Caucasian, the Malaysian, [and] the Mongolian races, the way humanity is divided into categories. Rather, I mean by this what the sociologists, psychologists, and cultural researchers have in mind when they speak about the role of "race" in the history of culture and in the creation of humanity's cultural treasures. Moses Hess, Gobineau, Duhring, [Eduard von] Hartmann, Chamberlain, [Ludwig] Gumplowicz (with his sociological theory of "racial war"), Hippolyte Taine, Georg Brandes—to name just the best-known figures—have collected an enormous amount of material and brought forth numerous contradictory and extravagant theories on the topic of "race" in its specific sense.

It is understood that each Volk is endowed with certain characteristic traits, some bodily, some mental. Such traits are transmitted hereditarily from generation to generation, and determine how in fact a people receives the phenomena of the external world and how it reacts to these phenomena. On such traits depend the particular and specific national customs or manners (*ofen*), insofar as the blessed children of a people, the most gifted by nature, bring forth human cultural treasures.

Are there, in fact, such objective characteristic traits among peoples? I shall leave the other peoples aside for the moment. I only wish to mention here the plain fact that no reputable researcher has denied such traits: this is evident from the fact that specific inherited traits are passed on through "flesh and blood" and automatically implanted in the inheritance from generation to generation; this from every learned man who stands within the tradition of Weismann[54] and who denies completely that acquired characteristics can possibly be transmitted through natural inheritance to offspring. Now, indeed, the Weismannian noisemakers, out of necessity, retain and cherish a belief in the purity of the racial Volk (*Volksrasse*), if it is of a "higher type."

Furthermore, I must add that all authorities completely recognize that such racial traits cannot be thoroughly investigated with the help of natural science alone, with a microscope or with chemical reagents. Other, more complex methods and forms of analysis are required.

Does the Jewish Volk in fact have such racial traits—that is, unambiguously identifiable physical and mental features, which are to be found exclusively among the Jews, or with greater frequency and more intensively [there] than among others, or in an alternative, purely "Jewish" combination?

The day-to-day experience and the theoretical and scientific observation of the Jewish essence, the Jewish nature, the Jewish character offer a unanimously positive response to the question. Allow me to bring a few facts and examples to illustrate this idea.

Even in the distant Jewish past, the fact was known that "*malkay beit Yisrael . . . malkay hesed hamah.*"[55] At that time, tribes organized around religious consciousness or identity did not exist, since religious people in this period—even the Jews—were still permeated with a savage hatred of foreigners, particularly

54. [August Weismann (1834–1914) was a German evolutionary biologist whose theory of the germ plasm was a highly influential explanation of how heredity works. His theory was understood to have undermined the Lamarckian theory of acquired characteristics.]

55. [1 Kings 20:30: "The kings of Israel . . . are magnanimous kings" (Jewish Publication Society translation).]

during those times of war. At the same time, tribes were not organized around nationalist consciousness, because even though they did have national interests according to the notions of the time, the same sort of savage hatred of foreigners was required, particularly during times of war; and certain ancient prophets had become highly dissatisfied with the measure of righteousness of the Jewish kings (Samuel with Saul; Elisha with Joash, the king of Israel). This measure of righteousness came not from a Jewish consciousness, but rather from a deeper, hidden or concealed Jewish being (*sein*). This is the same quality that the sages of the Talmud later captured in the words "Israel is merciful, the children of mercy are they"; Jews possess this manner of mercy "in the blood," as an inheritance from their ancestors. This is the same manner that we perceive daily, and because of which we—a thoroughly peaceful Volk—suffer to such an astounding degree living among other peoples of a completely different, warlike, being; ours is a manner of character that can be summed up in the words "a Jewish heart" (*a yiddishe hartz*).

The same everyday experience also testifies to the characteristic qualities of the Jewish mind or intellect, and is expressed in the phrase "a Jewish head" (*a yiddisher kop*). We are still not able to describe what these natural intellectual traits consist of; indeed, it will require a great deal more research in order to clarify this fully. At present, we have, for example, Professor Möbius's[56] discovery, made while studying the conditions that play a role in mathematical ability. Among the conditions identified, he claims one is "race." He demonstrates that German and French geniuses in mathematics express their creativity in two totally different ways: the Germans in a "geometric" or "synthetic" way; the French in an "algebraic" or "analytical" way. Jewish geniuses, who were educated within the sphere of influence of German mathematics, nonetheless do not in their work demonstrate the influence of the German type, but rather the French (the results of my own investigations into the field of Jewish theoretical research must be left aside for the moment).

Furthermore, when we speak of a "Jewish" facial feature (the "Jewish nose," "Jewish eyes"), we mean by this something akin to or having to do with a Jewish corporeal "being" and not with a Jewish "consciousness." And it is indeed true that it is difficult to pinpoint in which anatomical features such traits reside. But anyone who at any time has seen them, knows them and understands them

56. [Paul Julius Möbius (1853–1907), German neurologist, author of *Über die Anlage zur Mathematik* (On the talent for mathematics), Leipzig: Barth, 1900.]

to be Jewish. And what is significant in this is that the same exact features that we find on the monuments from the ancient world have become identifiable with the Semitic people in general, and with the Jews in particular (Babylonia, Egypt, Rome.)

Modern medicine has also found that certain diseases such as tuberculosis (consumption), for example, affect the Jewish body in a different way than they do non-Jewish bodies.

"Racial Jewishness"—or, better: Jewishness by descent, psycho-physical Jewishness—is what Brandes had in mind when he made explicit certain Jewish character traits in his work on Lassalle and Disraeli-Beaconsfield.[57] As an aside, allow me a moment here to offer up a saying by Lassalle: "At present there are two types of individuals that I hate more than any others: journalists and Jews. And I am both of these." I know that this was meant as a joke. But it is even more certain that Lassalle, as a Jew, considers his "Jewishness" to reside not in certain subjective opinions and desires, from which at some point he might free himself, but rather in particular objective physical and mental traits that are inherent in his "Jewish blood." And this is of course how the rest of the world looks on him. And this is of course how the rest of the world—and rightly so—looks on all eminent Jews.

Jewishness by descent, or "racial Jewishness," must be of tremendous interest for us for two specific reasons. In the first place, [it is important] in order "to know thyself" and understand the unique Jewish nature. Second, however—and this is significant not only for us but for the entire civilized world—it is important for the history of culture to discover what each nationalist race has achieved and produced among the cultural treasures of humanity. This is necessary in order to clarify the fundamental role of biology in human progress. Here the history of culture must be considered together with racial descent in thinking about the creator of culture, and it is not a superfluous or meaningless thing to take [the biological] into account—for instance, to recall that Karl Marx descended from a long line of Jewish rabbis and scholars. Indeed, cultural history—and we, too, all of us—must consider the Brandeses, the Karl Marxes, the Lassalles and Beaconfields not only as great men but also as great Jews.

All right, enough at present about Jewishness by descent, a category to which

57. [Ferdinand Lassalle (1825–1864) was a German Jewish socialist leader. Benjamin Disraeli, mentioned in an earlier note, took the title Earl of Beaconsfield when Queen Victoria made him a peer.]

every Jew belongs by birth. We still have to identify, if briefly, a type of objective Jewishness, which exists, so to speak, in-between the purely objective Jewish psycho-physical creative powers—from which no one [no Jew] can conceivably escape, except by dying—and the purely subjective religious and nationalistic opinions, which each and every person can contest. This is linguistic-cultural Jewishness. And this is, like racial Jewishness, absolutely independent of religion and nationalism, and in terms of identity may even be contrary to "Jewry" (*Judentum*) and to Jewish nationalist strivings.

Take the entire Jewish socialist and anarchist movement within the entire period of assimilation, along with the most important Jewish literature that this movement brought forth, with the richly colorful and talented gallery of leaders on display, and the thousands of high-minded workers and intellectuals that they gathered around them. No one of any intelligence would be able to deny that all of these were Jewish phenomena, and that they must automatically be associated with a certain *yiddishkeit*, even if they struggled fiercely against the Jewish religion and against Jewish nationalism. Now the new Jewishness, the linguistic-cultural Jewishness, arises and awakens from within itself, gaining more and more significance within our life and our historical fate.

We have, it is said, not one type of Jewishness but, on the contrary, a total of four. Each type can have its great Jews. Each type has its own criteria according to which one ceases to be a Jew. It is no great trick to pluck out one or two types from among the four and assert that only in these lie "the essence and the basic substance of the thing itself," then to argue that this negates the other [types] as negligible[58] and contradicts the proper meaning of the terms "Jews" and "*yiddishkeit*." The objective historian must keep all four of the types in mind and undertake some very particular considerations, in order not to falsify the judgment by the world of our Jewish self and our Jewish achievement within the world.

58. [*Klipat ha-shum*—literally, garlic skin.]

# Suggestions for Further Reading


PRIMARY SOURCE MATERIAL

Fishberg, Maurice. *Jews, Race, and Environment.* 1911. New Brunswick, N.J.: Transaction, 2006.

Jacobs, Joseph. "Are Jews Jews?" *Popular Science Monthly* 55 (1899): 502–11.

———. *Jewish Statistics: Social, Vital and Anthropometric.* London: D. Nutt, 1891.

Ruppin, Arthur. *The Jewish Fate and Future.* Translated by E. W. Dickes. London: Macmillan, 1940.

———. *The Jews of Today.* Translated by Margery Bentwich. New York: Holt, 1913.

Salaman, Redcliffe N. "Racial Origins of Jewish Types." *Transactions of the Jewish Historical Society of England* 9 (1920): 163–91.

Zollschan, Ignaz. "The Jewish Race Problem." *Jewish Review* 2, no. 11 (1912): 391–408.

SECONDARY SOURCE MATERIAL

Abu El-Haj, Nadia. "The Genetic Reinscription of Race." *Annual Review of Anthropology* 36 (2007): 283–300.

Anidjar, Gil. *Semites: Race, Religion, Literature.* Stanford: Stanford University Press, 2008.

Arkush, Allan, ed. "The Jewish Race?" Special issue, *AJS Perspectives,* Fall 2007.

Avrutin, Eugene M. "Racial Categories and the Politics of (Jewish) Difference in Late Imperial Russia." *Kritika* 8, no. 1 (2007): 13–40.

Efron, John. *Defenders of the Race: Jewish Doctors and Race Science in Fin-de-Siècle Europe.* New Haven: Yale University Press, 1994.

———. "The 'Kaftanjude' and the 'Kaffehausjude.' Two Models of Jewish Identity: A Discussion of Causes and Cures among German-Jewish Psychiatrists." *Leo Baeck Institute Yearbook* 37 (1992): 169–88.

Endelman, Todd. "Anglo-Jewish Scientists and the Science of Race." *Jewish Social Studies* 11, no. 1 (2004): 52–92.

Falk, Raphael. "Three Zionist Men of Science: Between Nature and Nurture." In *Jews and the Sciences in German Contexts,* edited by Ulrich Charpa and Ute Deichmann, 129–54. Tübingen, Germany: Mohr Siebeck, 2007.

———. "Zionism, Race, and Eugenics." In *Jewish Tradition and the Challenge of Darwinism,* edited by Geoffrey Cantor and Marc Swetlitz, 137–62. Chicago: University of Chicago Press, 2006.

Gatrall, Jefferson J. A. "The Color of His Hair: Nineteenth-Century Literary Portraits of the Historical Jesus." *Novel* 42, no. 1 (2009): 109–30.

Gilman, Sander. *The Case of Sigmund Freud: Medicine and Identity at the Fin de Siècle.* Baltimore: Johns Hopkins University Press, 1993.

———. *Jewish Self-Hatred: Antisemitism and the Hidden Language of the Jews.* Baltimore: Johns Hopkins University Press, 1986.

———. *The Jew's Body*. New York: Routledge, 1991.
———. *Smart Jews: The Construction of the Image of Jewish Superior Intelligence*. Lincoln: University of Nebraska Press, 1996.
Goldstein, Eric. *The Price of Whiteness: Jews, Race, and American Identity*. Princeton: Princeton University Press, 2006.
Hart, Mitchell B. *The Healthy Jew: The Symbiosis of Judaism and Modern Medicine*. New York: Cambridge University Press, 2007.
———. *Social Science and the Politics of Modern Jewish Identity*. Stanford: Stanford University Press, 2000.
Heschel, Susannah. *Abraham Geiger and the Jewish Jesus*. Chicago: University of Chicago Press, 1998.
———. *The Aryan Jesus: Christian Theologians and the Bible in Nazi Germany*. Princeton: Princeton University Press, 1998.
Hirsch, Dafna. "Zionist Eugenics, Mixed Marriage, and the Creation of a 'New Jewish Type.'" *Journal of the Royal Anthropological Institute* 15, no. 3 (2009): 592–609.
Hoffman, Matthew. "From Pinetele Yid to Racenjude: Chaim Zhitlovsky and Racial Conceptions of Jewishness." *Jewish History* 19, no. 1 (2005): 65–78.
Leff, Lisa, and Nadia Malinovich, eds. "Jewish Racial Self-Fashioning in Comparative Perspective." Special issue, *Jewish History* 19, no. 1 (2005).
Morris-Reich, Amos. "Arthur Ruppin's Concept of Race." *Israel Studies* 11, no. 3 (2006): 1–30.
———. *The Quest for Jewish Assimilation in Modern Social Science*. New York: Routledge, 2008.
Mosse, George L. "The Influence of the Völkish Idea on German Jewry." In *Studies of the Leo Baeck Institute*, edited by Max Kreutzberger, 1:81–114. New York: Fredrick Ungar, 1967.
Penslar, Derek. *Shylock's Children: Economics and Jewish Identity in Modern Europe*. Berkeley: University of California Press, 2001.
Presner, Todd Samuel. *Muscular Judaism: The Jewish Body and the Politics of Regeneration*. London: Routledge, 2007.
Schorsch, Jonathan. *Jews and Blacks in the Early Modern World*. Cambridge: Cambridge University Press, 2004.
———. *Swimming the Christian Atlantic*. Leiden, the Netherlands: Brill, 2009.
Slavet, Eliza. *Racial Fever: Freud and the Jewish Question*. New York: Fordham University Press, 2009.
Stepan, Nancy Leys, and Sander Gilman. "Appropriating the Idioms of Science: The Rejection of Scientific Racism." In *The Racial Economy of Science*, edited by Sandra Harding, 170–93. Bloomington: Indiana University Press, 1993.
Tuchman, Arleen Marcia. "Diabetes and Race: A Historical Perspective." *American Journal of Public Health* 101 (2011): 24–33.
Weindling, Paul. "The Evolution of Jewish Identity: Ignaz Zollschan between Jewish and Aryan Race Theories, 1910–45." In *Jewish Tradition and the Challenge of Darwinism*, edited by Geoffrey Cantor and Marc Swetlitz, 116–36. Chicago: University of Chicago Press, 2006.

# Index

Page numbers in italics refer to tables.